PAYING ATTENTION
TO PEOPLE

PAYING ATTENTION TO PEOPLE

An Essay on Individualism and Christian Belief

Vernon White

First published in Great Britain 1996
Society for Promoting Christian Knowledge
Holy Trinity Church
Marylebone Road
London NW1 4DU

British Library Cataloguing-in-Publication Data

A catalogue record for this book is available
from the British Library

ISBN 0-281-04988-2

Typeset by Pioneer Associates, Perthshire
Printed in Great Britain by
The Cromwell Press, Melksham, Wiltshire

Contents

For Charlie Moule,
whose constant care for individuals
has been inspirational

Preface

This essay muses on the matter of particularity. It is the third book I have offered on the theme. The first pondered the possibility of any particular divine action in the events of this world. The second had to do with the particularity of the Christ event and how it might be effective for salvation. This book now is concerned with the particularity of people.

All these essays reflect on some of the paradoxes posed by particularity: the relationship of one particular with another; above all, the relationship of particular things, actions and people, to God. In one way or another they attempt a theological view of particularity, relationship and universality.

They do so without any pretence to cover all the issues. They are essays, not systematic surveys. They scan a wide field, but with only one or two specific questions in view. They run with a few ideas to see what others will gather around them, but cannot deal adequately with all that do. This present essay is no exception. It pursues the specific question of individualism – but in doing so raises a huge range of other issues in its wake, like clods of earth behind a plough, turned over, waiting for further attention. So it is partial and provisional, offered just as one part of a continuing conversation.

But if it does offer anything worthwhile, however small, then this certainly owes as much to others as to my own thinking. The stimulus for it began a long time ago amongst teachers and students in Theology and Philosophy at both Oxford and Exeter Universities. Latterly I have benefited much from the Theology department at Nottingham University. I am also grateful to St George's House, Windsor which provided useful impetus *en route*; and to Alex Wright, my Editor, for his valuable guidance.

Perhaps there is an even greater debt, however indirect, to the more immediate *sitz-im-leben* of my writing: two small parishes in the Surrey hills, then Lincoln Cathedral. Whether these very particular places have restricted my vision or enhanced it I must leave others to decide. But I shall always appreciate their generous hospitality.

Most of all I thank Joy. Her constant support, keen interest and encouragement, have been vital. They have been a foundation for all these books, the help which has mattered most.

Introduction

Attention must be paid – even to a salesman. This is the memorable plea of Arthur Miller's powerful post-war play, *The Death of a Salesman.* It makes the straightforward moral point that the life of an ordinary person *matters.* The so-called ordinary person has potential for meaning (and tragedy) just as much as the story of a Shakespearian prince and nobleman. It represents a generally recognized ethical perspective of modernity. A sense of equality in the value of all individuals is commonly acknowledged, at least in principle. It is widely accepted as one of the significant contributions of Christian faith to social ethics and attitudes (particularly in the Reformation period). It has also become common currency in modern culture beyond the bounds of explicit Christian allegiance. People matter equally, regardless of social status or other differentiating factors. This is as much an agreed moral axiom as most in our morally plural world – however poorly lived out in actual social practice or individual attitude.

But while there may be some consensus behind the plea to pay as much attention to the 'ordinary' individual as to the privileged, we no longer settle so easily into consensus about the moral meaning and status of the individual *per se.* Here the moral map is shifting. In Miller's post-war period the Enlightenment and Reformation legacy had not yet peaked in the unfettered individualism of the last few decades. But now this extreme form of individualism has provoked a critique of gathering momentum, calling into question some of the assumptions about the individual which have undergirded it. It is an understandable reaction, when the perceived triumph of the culture of individualism has produced neither social nor (paradoxically) individual fulfilment.

The reaction is further fuelled by continuing philosophical scepticism about the very concept of enduring personal identity, and by the growing fascination with eastern philosophies of pantheism and the self's absorption into other realities. So the pendulum is swinging

1

back fast, and sometimes furiously, pushed hard by a multitude of media commentators, political, sociological and theological sources. The movement is not so much a return to hierarchy of value amongst individuals, although that could re-emerge as a consequence. It is more a redefinition of the meaning and value of individuals *per se*, in relation to community and the rest of reality (so less a swing of the pendulum and more like the new curve of a spiral; a genuinely post-modern movement, therefore, if we use current terms). A good deal of this reaction shelters under the broad title of 'communitarianism' – which is itself a fluid notion, spawning its own counter-movements.[1]

Of course, this brief comment is already an over-simplified account of developing ideas. If we follow some pathways in the history of ideas there is plenty of serious and sustained criticism of Enlightenment individualism long before these last decades, and this has a complex relationship with more recent critiques. This is because ideological or theological seeds of change often take long to germinate. And even when they do grow into a visible crop of changed social attitudes and practice, there is not always a straightforward dateable pattern of birth and death. They grow, mutate, wither or re-seed in different fields altogether (cross-fertilization was one of the better metaphors of recent decades). It all makes any attempt at a history of ideas notoriously difficult.[2]

Nonetheless, however complex and arguable the historical process behind our current situation, there is less doubt about its effect. Our contemporary culture conveys little sense of stability for the individual. The status of the individual is, or is becoming, insecure. This is an inevitable consequence of a reactive situation, which produces a climate fraught with destabilizing rhetoric. The infamous and polemical claim that 'there is no such thing as society' is all too easily replaced with an equal and opposite nightmare that there is no such thing as the individual. One sign of this polemical insecurity is the evident ten-dency to false packaging. Most obviously this happens when the Enlightenment is conceived (then rejected) as a spurious whole. Both the babies of individuality and the bathwater of individualism are unceremoniously thrown out together. *Mattering* then becomes prob-lematic in relation to *anyone*, whether 'ordinary' or privileged. This is nowhere more evident than in the fevered quest of the modern media to search out 'personalities'. Individuals are sought out and paraded for their heroic exploits in sport, entertainment or even crime. But they are passing shadows, shallow, and one-dimensional. Their mattering relates only to some focal achievement. And they quickly fade from the screen. They are not presented with any depth or breadth to their personhood, no enduring substance in the wider narrative of their lives, except in so far as it relates to that transient focal point which has launched them temporarily into the spotlight. We may yearn for lasting significance in individuality, but it seems to elude us.

Such a sense of instability will clearly matter to theologians concerned with Christian anthropology and social ethics. But it is also a matter of much wider concern. Whatever status and meaning of the individual we give (or withhold) is going to be a pivotal presupposition in the organization of all our social, personal and spiritual affairs. Without some sort of stability in our understanding of the individual and the relationships in which the individual subsists we are bound to experience serious social and personal malaise. A reaction to unfettered individualism may indeed be necessary and inevitable, but the absence of any alternative (and positive) understanding about individuals will leave the reaction dangerously undirected. It will almost certainly mean that the cement of society cracks further, and the flux of experience becomes still more fatally fragmented.

Of course, we must quickly acknowledge that a sense of insecurity about these issues is not new. There has always been something of a dialogue and dialectic between individual and community, at various levels of discourse, for as long as intellectual and religious traditions and social practices have been recorded. There has been both a 'monodic quest', and its collectivist or corporate counterpart.[3] In that sense the present situation is not necessarily more unstable than in some times past. To some extent it may be recapitulating past eras. On the other hand it may also contain some ingredients which can only be understood fully within the culture of post-modernity. The present curve of the spiral will not exactly replicate the past, even if it bears some echoes of it. Thus it remains important to address our particular, present situation as best we can.

In fact this situation has already attracted considerable attention. In that sense this is nothing like a pioneering essay. A good deal of recent literature has already engaged with the issues, within theology, political philosophy, moral philosophy and social anthropology.[4] What follows in this short book is therefore offered only as another sentence or two, primarily from a theological perspective, in a long and necessarily continuing debate. But what (I hope) justifies this attempt to offer a few more words is the conviction that Christian insights are particularly pertinent. They can offer a well-grounded, constructive and sometimes distinctive contribution in the present climate of uncertainty. And while these may already be heard and mostly accepted within the Christian community, they have not always been marshalled in a systematic way, specifically in relation to the phenomenon of individualism, and in relation to the wider debate in society at large. A reactive situation makes this a particularly urgent task now (though it is not the first time it has been attempted in the twentieth century).[5]

These insights of Christian theology include doctrines about the nature of God as Trinity, and humankind created in his image. A good deal certainly has been recently written on this, and some of it with wider social issues in mind.[6] I shall be reviewing some of this briefly and appreciatively (though with some qualifications). But I also wish to suggest that other doctrines to do with the incarnation, redemption, life after death, and more general Christian insights into the nature of love and providence, need more attention – specifically in relation to the phenomenon of individualism and the reaction against it.

This sets an agenda in which I shall be discussing doctrine chiefly according to its credibility in our wider social situation and its particular malaise. For those who do not think theological language connects easily (if at all) with a world beyond our religious communities I suppose this is bound to be greeted with some scepticism. But I believe it is both possible and necessary to make the attempt. If God so loved the world then theological language can and must bear on the matters of this world in some way. Such an assertion rides on the back of some large theological and philosophical assumptions – but I believe they are sustainable.[7]

This essay therefore offers an explicitly Christian evaluation of individualism, but always in conversation with wider social analysis. That is its chief end. And just because it is trying to engage with a phenomenon which belongs to a wider world of different discourses, it cannot begin with theology alone. There must also be a prior quest to understand that wider intellectual and social world which we inhabit. So this determines the structure of what follows. The main concern of the first part of the book offers a general analysis and evaluation of the phenomenon of individualism, without specific appeal to theological criteria. This will also require some discussion of the diverse definitions of the self, personhood and personal identity which underly it. It is a survey which will suggest some general moral and intellectual resources around which the western mind might still rally, with at least some degree of consensus (and without any specific allegiance to

Christian faith). Equally, it will attempt to pinpoint those areas of moral and intellectual confusion which remain unresolved – and which contribute to our present precariousness. Only then will the second part of the book attempt to engage with the same issues from a specifically Christian perspective; in particular an account of how Christian doctrine can both accommodate – and illuminate – some of the problems at issue.

All this is a huge terrain to cover, and I shall only be able to suggest signposts at many points, rather than detailed discussion. So it is also important to make clear at the outset the limits of what the essay attempts.

Crucially, it is limited by its theoretical approach. That is, it is chiefly an exercise in charting the interrelation of moral, intellectual and religious ideas, *qua* ideas, rather than offering detailed evaluation of their embodiment in social practice. This holds throughout the book, but is particularly apparent in the second half, where consideration is given primarily to Judaeo-Christian belief *in principle*, as distinct from its practice either within the institution of the Church or in the Church's actual relations with wider society.

One implication of such a theoretical approach is that there is not a great deal of direct engagement with socio-political accounts of individualism which begin specifically from an historical and empirical analysis of power: that is, how the quest for power determines the shape of society and its beliefs. Feminist critiques, amongst others, would certainly wish to offer such accounts. They demonstrate how the exercise of power produces profound resistance to, and distortion of, moral ideas when these are embodied in actual social practice. They also show how, in actual practice, concern for power stifles and skews the very perception of moral ideas at a theoretical level.[8] And I have no doubt that such accounts are crucial, in both a corrective and complementary sense, compared to the more abstract methodology of this essay.

To take one obvious example, purely theoretical talk about ideas of 'community' as an antidote to extreme individualism badly needs a feminist focus to help unravel the actual practice of certain communities. This reveals that the structures of particular families, neighbourhoods and national organizations have often oppressed, depersonalized and excluded women (and other groups), rather than fulfilled them.[9]

So I fully acknowledge the restricted and potentially distorting nature of a theoretical emphasis. And I have tried, as a consequence, to include at least some reference to the way in which ideas have been incorporated in actual historical and social practice.

Nonetheless, the main emphasis remains theoretical and abstract in some degree. This is because the emphasis offers its own advantages, as well as limitations. One advantage will emerge as the discussion progresses. It will help clarify the potential for some of the core ideas of individualism to transcend any one particular historical or social context.[10] The emphasis also offers a critical methodology in itself, to offer in relation to the limitations of other perspectives. For the feminist filter, as with the perspective of any social group, is itself partial, and will benefit from the critique of other methodologies. So although this more abstract approach of the western academic tradition is both limited in scope and partial in perspective, I am still content to offer it. It is intended simply as one tool alongside others in the wider task which this essay does not attempt: namely, a fully applied social theology and practical ecclesiology.

One other consideration also drives this essay. It is not offered just because our current social malaise cries out for more Christian confidence at the intellectual level of ideas. Nor just because the intellectual issues involved are intrinsically interesting. It also has to do with a certain personal, existential, pressure. It matters personally. This is the ancient and pervasive question of all human existence. Do 'I' really have any permanent, enduring, identity, meaning or value? To what extent is my sense of an individual self just an illusory and transient (even pernicious) product of other causes? Do I (does anyone) really matter at all? Is the very question merely an unhelpful product of a western philosophical and theological error?

For the most part I find such questions lurk safely behind the scenes, suppressed by the ordinary business of daily living and surviving. But they are always poised to strike, sometimes unaccountably, often with great poignancy. Indeed, it is hardly surprising if the current climate is particularly wont to provoke them in existential as well as intellectual form. For if we have become wary about the social consequences of our Enlightenment legacies of individualism; if we are constantly bombarded with reductionist analyses of the human self from biology or with philosophical scepticism about enduring personal identity; or by the burgeoning appeal of Buddhist theories of the (non) self; or by non-realist rejection of *anything* 'out there'; if all this is the cumulative climate of scepticism about the individual which we inhabit, *then pangs of personal anxiety about our existence become virtually inevitable.* They are bound to be flushed out of us all at some stage, even from the most humdrum of lives.

In short, if this book addresses the existential pang, as well as the wider social and intellectual issues, I should be well pleased. Attention must be paid to the salesman *himself*, as well as to the intellectual trends and social forces which may be threatening to marginalize and de-value him.

PART ONE

1

Analysing Individualism (1):
General Ideas and
Historical Perspectives

As indicated in the Introduction, generalized judgements about chronology and causes in the history of ideas are notoriously hard to make. The problem is partly one of scale. The canvas of 'modernity' or 'western'/'northern civilization' is too vast to paint except with a very broad sweep of the brush. The same will necessarily be true of any attempt just to concentrate on the current situation. Even if it were possible to understand the present without recourse to its origins, contemporary culture proves too huge, complex and unwieldy a phenomenon to be confidently characterized as a whole. And in any case, its meaning is so permeated with the past that it *cannot* be abstracted for consideration purely as a present phenomenon. Synchronic and diachronic perspectives interpenetrate inextricably. The task of providing a portrait of the present is always going to be difficult, provisional and partial.

In other words, the brief snapshot of the present situation offered in the Introduction is certainly going to need further explanation, justification and qualification. It is easy enough to offer a general diagnosis that we are in a state of reaction (be it spiral or swing of the pendulum) against the excesses of individualism, and that we lack consensus about the status and meaning of the individual. But if these are not merely to be the blandest of generalizations then more must be offered by way of conceptual analysis, and at least some historical understanding.

This will demand some scrutiny of the term 'individualism' itself, and its variety of meanings. For although often used as if it were a simple, self-evident (and pejorative) notion, it is actually a complex notion under which a great variety of moral values and concepts take

11

shelter. To offer one example immediately, here is just a flavour of Alasdair MacIntyre's influential, penetrating and very bleak analysis of contemporary society, in which he identifies a specific form of modern individualism which he describes as 'bureaucratic':

> . . . there are only two alternative models of social life open to us, one in which the free and arbitrary choices of individuals are sovereign and one in which the bureaucracy is sovereign, precisely so that it may limit the free and arbitrary choices of individuals . . . Modern societies oscillate between a freedom which is nothing but a lack of regulation of individual behaviour and forms of collectivist control designed only to limit the anarchy of self-interest . . . Thus the society in which we live is one in which bureaucracy and individualism are partners as well as antagonists.[1]

MacIntyre's analysis also suggests *why* modern individuals can call on no agreed public criteria, apart from the bureaucratic, to justify their choices. It is the result of a profound and progressive failure to achieve consensus on any common rational or moral tradition, effectively since medieval times. So if the individual wishes to protect his or her autonomy, there is (paradoxically) little else to draw on apart from these modes of behaviour which normally belong to collectivist or bureaucratic practice. Thus, for example, we will advance our own field of responsibilities at work by sidelining a colleague, 'justifying' it with reference to the overall efficiency of the company. It locks us inevitably into manipulative forms of behaviour. It also exposes the incoherence and contradictions at the heart of our situation:

> Seeking to protect the autonomy that we have learned to prize, we aspire ourselves *not* to be manipulated by others; seeking to incarnate our own principles and standpoint in the world of practice, we find no way open to us to do so except by directing towards others those very manipulative modes of relationship which each of us aspires to resist in our own case. This incoherence of our attitudes and our experience arises from the incoherent conceptual scheme which we have inherited.[2]

This is only a foretaste of MacIntyre's powerful critique of contemporary society, to which we shall return. But it is just sufficient to indicate not only how pervasive and pernicious he sees this particular sense of individualism to be, but also how complex its relationship with other forms of social order. It alerts us to the need to establish how far moral and conceptual incoherence belong together. And it

signals an early warning against adopting a polarized and over-simplified moral stance against (or for) anything as general as an *undefined*
individualism. It is a point made even more explicit by Charles
Taylor's equally magisterial contributions.[3] As noted in the Introduction, the rhetoric of a reactive age often obscures these vital moral
ambiguities (a charge which can be levelled against both that kind of
political correctness which abhors all aspects of the Enlightenment
legacy of individualism, and those populist attitudes which respond
enthusiastically to the individualistic lure of greater personal autonomy
in every area of life).

So the importance of the attempt to disentangle the various meanings of individualism in theory and practice is clear. The same will
apply to notions of individuality, selfhood and personhood – a cluster
of terms which also require analysis. For it will become clear that
current instability about the individual can only ultimately be understood in a wider context: that is, by considering the interrelation of
broad social trends (such as individualism) and the standing of specific intellectual traditions about particular issues (such as the ontology
of personhood). This point is conveyed especially well by the Chinese
writer Carver T. Yu in his critique of western dualism and individualism. He vividly describes both our existential and social existential
malaise, chiefly through the prism of contemporary western literature:
it is a situation in which 'we find individuals journeying into their
own selves only to find their selves scattered and dissolved'.[4] But
then he goes on to trace its origins ultimately to an ancient Greek
philosophical tradition of ontology.[5] Again, this is an analysis to which
we shall return. For now it simply serves to highlight the range of interrelated issues and terms which require some sort of understanding, or
at least some working definitions for the purposes of discussion.

Hence the first part of this book. It begins with a brief historical
note on the origins of the term 'individualism', then attempts some
sort of conceptual analysis both of this, and of these other related
issues of personhood.

Historical notes

Steven Lukes reminds us that the actual term 'individualism' only
became widely used in the nineteenth century.[6] And it swiftly assumed
a variety of meanings. At the end of the previous century conservative
reaction against the French Revolution was already focusing on the
appeal to the rights of individuals which had fuelled the social

upheaval, and abhorring it: 'individuals pass like shadows; but the
commonwealth is fixed and stable' (Burke).[7] So it is not surprising that
the word emerged, especially in France, with a pejorative connotation.
It implied social disintegration, anarchy and egoism.

On the other hand its characteristic early use elsewhere, particularly
in Germany, was much more positive. It had to do with ideas of originality, artistic inspiration, self-realization. In America it was associated
with equal rights for individuals and *laissez-faire* systems of government which allowed individuals their liberty. In England the term was
used less, and more ambivalently, oscillating between the positive and
negative connotations of Continental thought.[8]

But although widespread use of the word is only recent, the cluster
of ideas it represents can be traced back to almost any number of
sources. The general intellectual ferment of the Enlightenment period
was clearly a key crucible in their development, but it is also possible
to chart a map of their occurrence at many earlier stages.

Robert Hamilton, for example, points to a kind of 'classical' individualism in the fragmentation of Juvenal's Rome; in the self-examination and self-assertion of Cicero's treatises; and in the shift in
story-telling from the public recitation of national epics to private
reading of prose fiction with Homeric emphasis on individual characters. He also draws our attention to the concentration on self-
expression and self-knowledge in the literature of the Latin Middle
Ages. He credits Boethius in particular with 'bringing twelfth century
thinkers into contact with the classical approaches to self-examination'.
Then there is also Dante's towering achievement in the presentation
of individual characters.[9] To be sure, there is a danger of reading back
into this kind of literature a notion of individual identity which only
emerged in fully-fledged form in subsequent centuries. Not least,
many medieval and earlier presentations of character may have been
coloured much more by literary conventions about 'type' than by
modern psychological notions of individuality. There have indeed
been significant changes of perception. Nonetheless, there is no reason
to deny the possibility of some seeds of continuity and connection
between such ideas, whatever their changing nuances of meaning.

Other commentators have traced a similar variety of pathways.
Steven Lukes refers back to Epicureanism,[10] as well as early Christ-
ianity,[11] before moving to the more familiar ground of the Renaissance
and Reformation (especially Calvinism), the rise of capitalism,[12] the
Enlightenment in general, the Industrial Revolution and the rise of
Romanticism.[13] Rather more surprisingly, John Milbank is prepared to

attribute responsibility to Aristotle for some kinds of individualism, and then defends Augustine from other kinds. Here he shares some of Hamilton's assessment of the incipient individualism of the Roman Commonwealth, interpreting Augustine as a significant critic of its tendencies to encourage the pursuit of individual honour and glory.[14] Yet of course Augustine himself is also frequently credited with bequeathing some notions, such as 'radical reflexivity' (the journey inwards to self-knowledge), which can be considered to be of the very essence of modern individualism.[15]

This begins to illustrate my earlier comments about the way alleged sources interrelate and overlap in a complex way. It would be a vast project to sift through them all adequately to strain out the various meanings of individualism, and I do not intend to make any detailed investigation into origins. My procedure will be much more limited. I shall simply sketch out some of the most apposite features of the intellectual and social climate which immediately preceded the emergence of the *term* 'individualism', and which have helped set the scene for its modern form. This will refer us more to the period of the Enlightenment than to any other. Then, as indicated, I will move to a more conceptual analysis of the term – but one which is (I hope) still sensitive to historical considerations. As a procedure this partly follows Steven Lukes' example, though with some differences of emphasis and selection.

Two significant strands of Enlightenment thought:

The attempted justification of morality

It is widely acknowledged that the late seventeenth and eighteenth centuries included a preoccupation with the possibility of establishing an independent rational justification of morality (though this general notion of an Enlightenment 'project' is not without its critics).[16] It was perceived as an urgent necessity in an age where, for the first time, 'moral' meaning was being systematically distinguished from the legal and religious structures of social organization.

In European culture a broad coalition of Aristotelian and Christian ideas had hitherto commanded a wide consensus. Morality had been rooted firmly in a notion of essential human nature, which had a self-evident *telos* (or 'ends') to be fulfilled (Aristotelianism), and in the will of God which was revealed in Scripture as well as nature (Catholic Christianity). But this apparently impregnable basis then came under

withering and sustained attack from a series of sources, often con-
flicting with each other but cumulatively devastating. Broadly speaking
they were both scientific and philosophical. The power both of empirical investigation and unfettered reason combined to undermine the
notion of an essential, identifiable, human nature with certain self-
evident ends to be fulfilled. It also had the effect of relegating the
concept of God, at best, to the unknowable and transcendent source
of all, rather than the immanent one revealed in all. And it all caused
considerable disquiet. After all, if the philosophical and religious basis
for morality is shaken, whence and whither morality itself? (an anxiety
which persisted during the later advances of science in the nineteenth
century as well). Hence that fearful perception, which Pope tersely
proclaimed: 'religion, blushing, veils her sacred fires / while, unawares,
morality expires'.

Thus battle was joined to find some other, more secure, home for
morality. The best known line of philosophical dialogue is probably
that which can be traced through Hume, Kant and Kierkegaard as each
scrutinizes the role of reason, coming to different conclusions, but all
revealing a common goal of justifying morality. Hume found no *reason*
for doing what was right, and so took morality to be rooted instead in
human passions and desires. Kant, by contrast, could find no basis for
morality in our desires, so turned back to the universal character of
reason and proposed that alone as a basis for moral meaning (right
action is that which we consistently will that *everyone* should *always*
do). Utilitarianism, in turn, is an attempt to work out a universal practical system of ethics precisely on the secular foundation of a rational
ordering of desires to a common good. Kierkegaard saw compelling
difficulties in both passion and reason, and became sceptical of any criterion for morality apart from the act of choice itself (a precursor of
modern existentialism and relativism).

Haunting this whole debate was the ancient spectre of Plato's
Euthyphro dilemma, developed in various ways by Hume and others.
What is right cannot be simply defined by the will of God, unless
God's will is already judged moral by some prior conception of what
is right; or unless 'right' simply means 'what God wills', in which case
'value' is an arbitrary function of the 'fact' of the divine will and
appears to lose all distinctive meaning. And where fact and value are
therefore kept distinct (as in the maxim that 'no "ought" can be
derived from an "is" . . .') this served all the more to highlight the
essential homelessness of moral discourse.

Behind these basic positions lie vast acreages of philosophical debate which cannot be entered into here. But even in outline they serve well to illustrate the consistent and urgent quest to find some new basis for morality. What MacIntyre also stresses is how radically new this task was in the Enlightenment period. To understand and justify the category of the moral (abstracted from general perceptions of human nature or the will of God) was, so to speak, an invention of the period. Indeed there is no word for 'moral' in Latin and Ancient Greek (the languages of Enlightenment educated discourse) in the sense it was coming to be used in this emerging debate.[17]

Charles Taylor offers an important qualification in the telling of this story. It would be misleading to speak simply of morality being conceived in a new way, or a quest for 'new' moral sources, as if the Enlightenment generated their availability *ex nihilo*. And perhaps nobody is quite saying that. But Taylor is surely right to remind us of the point already implicit in the brief historical survey already offered: namely, there is a range of views from paganism and ancient philosophy which was always available throughout the period as alternative sources for morality (however hard it is to assess precisely what is meant by 'available').[18]

Nonetheless, granted this qualification, Taylor would still endorse the key presupposition of the story. That is, the most significant (and de-stabilizing) impetus behind the quest for new moral foundations is the bare possibility of a *plurality* of sources from which to 'choose' – rather than the monolithic and unified horizon of religious–metaphysical–moral meaning which had largely obtained before.[19]

It is precisely this possibility of choice which I wish to highlight. It is a key element of the intellectual ferment of the time, and another essential ingredient in MacIntyre's thesis. For it is the climate of choice which formed extremely fertile ground for individualism (of various kinds) to take root. As traditional contexts of belief and behaviour broke down, this made 'space' for the individuals to make their own decisions and develop their own autonomy. Traditional Christian theism and teleological conceptions of a common human nature, which had previously generated apparently binding and unquestionable external systems of divine law and hierarchical authority, could now be queried by the individual. Because their edifice had crumbled, the basis for any moral judgement was now a matter of debate not dogma, and the individual could legitimately take part as an autonomous agent rather than merely as a representative of an externally imposed system.

Moreover, precisely because this great Enlightenment project of

justifying morality consistently *failed*, and each successive attempt
gave way to another, the space for individual autonomy was correspondingly expanded. For MacIntyre the significance of this era in this
respect can hardly be overstated. He is uncompromising: it was the
matrix in which 'the modern individual was invented'.[20]

One other point should also be noted here. It arises more tangentially out of this story and its full significance will only emerge later,
but it needs to be registered now. It is important to note that there
is no evidence here of an *easy*, inexorable shift from a sense of common, objective moral and spiritual truths to a private and subjective
conception. On the contrary, the story was of constant struggle to
reformulate a common basis to connect ourselves with each other (that
is, if reason and religion are inadequate – *what else can be found?*). In
other words, we have arrived uneasily and ambivalently in our state of
privatized and pluralist morality. And the fact that we are still dissat-
isfied, without any new common basis, perpetuates the point: we have
inherited an enduring, deep-seated *quest* for common ground, whether
or not it is possible to achieve. The question of its origin must wait: for
now it is enough to note the force of it.

Social contract

The other feature of this period which deserves particular attention is
a reminder that there was a strong social and political impetus to
Enlightenment thought, as well as a more strictly philosophical one.
This is the theory of social contract – where the interdependence of
the political and philosophical is most striking. It is also particularly
pertinent for understanding modern concepts of individualism, and
'liberalism'. (Liberalism is sometimes used interchangeably with individualism. It is best defined as the specifically political dimension of
individualism: in particular, it denotes the politics of human rights,
and the corresponding limitation on political interference in the lives
of individuals.)

The impetus for social contract lay, again, in this quest to free
human thought and behaviour from externally imposed legal and
religious systems. The rationalism of the era sought to root it instead
in a 'natural' law, universally accessible to human reason. This in turn
assumes a picture of society as a collection of independent and rational citizens, *each one* 'naturally' capable of expressing preferences and
judging for himself or herself. Any organization of society is therefore
built up from a natural state which pre-dates it, and the institution of

government derives any legitimacy and authority it has only from the individually granted consent of its citizens. This implies a doctrine of equality, of universal human rights and liberties, and the representation of individual interests (rather than class interests) in the system of government. As already noted, it also implies a minimal view of the purpose of government. Its legitimate function is confined to creating the conditions in which individuals' interests can be pursued and individual rights protected. It has no right to intervene beyond that.

Again, it should not be implied that such ideas originated in the Enlightenment period. Some form of consent and contract can be traced from Plato and Aristotle, through Roman Law, Stoic thought, biblical ideas of covenant, to Aquinas.[21] But the explosive release of rational enquiry combined with the social, political and economic fluidity of the time to ensure that they took shape in the Enlightenment period as in no other. The 'great age' of the social contract is marked (in Europe) by such seminal publications as Hobbes's *Leviathan* (1651), Locke's *Two Treatises of Government* (1690) and Rousseau's *Du Contrat Social* (1762).[22]

Of these Locke offers perhaps the most sophisticated and defensible account, and one which aptly demonstrates the integral relationship between moral and political philosophy. The immediate political context of the *Treatises* is clear. Locke was setting out to justify the legitimacy of the Whig rebellion of 1688 which had put William of Orange on the throne, and it drove him back to consider the questions posed previously by Hobbes in more general form: whence does any legitimate authority derive? When, if ever, is rebellion justified?

Their analysis of first principles is itself a curiously related nexus of moral and social assumptions. Hobbes had posited an original state of nature in which individuals claimed a natural right to do whatever they liked irrespective of others: an anarchic kind of pre-moral and pre-social state. His 'contract' was thus generated out of self-interested individuals seeking some escape from complete disorder and insecurity. Locke likewise began from a conception of an original state in which individuals are equal, distinct and endowed with natural rights. But he also assumes that each individual already recognized some restraint on his own will. The Lockean 'natural' man recognizes the general right of property, and the right of others to punish transgression, both of which constrain any tendency towards anarchy. His original state is therefore already an embryonic social and moral system, though he would still insist that this is part of the endowment of all simply in virtue of their humanity and not because of any externally imposed system of law or social organization: '. . . truth and keeping of faith belong to men as men, and not as members of society'.[23]

But it is still not ideal. Although all are aware of the natural moral law, they may not give it due attention and will almost certainly misapply it in their own interests. Disputes will inevitably arise, and where there is no impartial arbiter they will escalate to war between the parties. Hence the 'consent' to hand over authority to a civil power which will safeguard the natural rights of property and arbitrate in disputes (property, incidentally, owned by virtue of the labour which has created it).[24] Thus 'I easily grant that civil government is the proper remedy for the inconveniences of the state of nature which must certainly be great where men may be judges in their own case'.[25] So, as already indicated, he is able to justify civil authority, *but only that authority which derives from consent and guarantees individual liberties.*

This does not mean it was always conceived as a freestanding rational system, looking to usurp all religious foundations and motivation. Charles Taylor points out, for example, that rational consent was often wedded to personal commitment of a religious kind (especially important in Calvinist and Puritan societies). This had a theological basis in the idea of covenant: '. . . the importance that Puritans gave to the idea of covenant, the agreement between God and his people, begins to develop into an understanding of society as based on a covenant between its members. In a godly community founded on personal commitment, the two could be seen as facets of one and the same covenant.'[26]

However, the fundamental structure of the theory was rational rather than religious in form, and it is correspondingly open to rational criticism – which can be severe. After all, the notion that authority is justified only by consent of individuals for the purpose of individual liberty is an unwieldy criterion to use in practice, and flawed in its assumptions. Where and when is the original state supposed to have existed? How can every individual ever be supposed realistically to have consented to such a contract with authority? And what specific criteria will be used to judge how well the civil authority is guaranteeing individual liberty and rights? As I have already hinted, Locke is more subtle than some in defence of his own position. He cites Hooker to justify belief in the original state.[27] And he develops a doctrine of 'tacit' consent to make the notion credible, according to which individuals may be said to have consented to a previously established contract with government simply by owning property, or by 'travelling on the highway', or just by residing within the government's territory. Nonetheless, it is clear that contemporary and modern critics have little difficulty in exposing its weaknesses. The question of consent in particular appears to be a fiction (and its direct descendant in the democratic ideal of continuing consent through elections is perhaps not much less of a fiction!).

But although the doctrine of social contract has its obvious flaws as a political theory, it remains a pivotal point in the origin and subsequent development of modern individualism. Consent remains important, albeit in transposed form: we tend to find it both significant and necessary to think of our political society as created by the *will* of individuals, in some sense. And our culture has certainly inherited much of the underlying atomism of the contract theory. It is built out of a concept of humankind as essentially a collection of individuals, each with a distinct source of judgement and with equal access to a universal moral law through his reason. This has entailed, historically if not logically, the concomitant notions of individual rights to liberty, property and fundamental human equality. Following Hooker again, Locke is supremely assured of all this, and of its beneficial effects:

> This equality of men by nature . . . evident in itself, and beyond all question . . . The state of nature has a law of nature to govern it, which obliges every one, and reason, which is that law, teaches all mankind, who will but consult it, that being all equal and independent, no one ought to harm another in his life, health, liberty, or possessions . . . and being furnished with like faculties, sharing all in one community of nature, there cannot be supposed any such subordination among us, that may authorize us to destroy one another, as if we were made for one another's uses, as the inferior ranks of creatures are for ours.[28]

As already noted, the self-evident nature of this equality was not so securely based in universal reason as Locke would have hoped. But the statement remains seminal in tracing key lineaments in the overall phenomenon of individualism.

2

Analysing Individualism (2):
Conceptual Analysis

Some of the most significant strands of modern individualism have clearly emerged already from this brief historical prologue. The next task is to disentangle them, and to offer a more extended analysis of each.

Once more, the limitations of the task must be acknowledged. It is largely an attempt at conceptual clarification of the various ingredients, and how they relate to each other; it deals with powerful and pervasive ideas chiefly as modernity has now received and assimilated them from the past. But as such it does *not* offer a full picture of their historical development in the past, so it will not necessarily do full justice to the nuances of shifting meaning within each stage of their development.

As indicated, this is bound to be an abstract exercise, to some extent. However, I hope there is sufficient contextual awareness to avoid the most arid kind of abstraction. And at least if offers a way of getting some purchase on the texture of the present, without any pretensions to have offered all the intricacies which belong to a full history of ideas.

I should also stress that it is a largely phenomenological survey at this stage in the discussion. That is, I shall not yet offer much explicit evaluation of these key ideas as such (though some, of course, is bound to be implicit). This too is simply procedural: it helps get at least one dimension of the map more clearly on the table, before others are coloured in to give more depth, but also more complexity.

Freedom and autonomy

An obvious and seminal starting point is the idea of autonomy.

22

Broadly speaking this has come to mean that 'an individual's thought and action is his own, and not determined by agencies or causes outside his control'. This entails a capacity consciously to evaluate social pressure and convention, and 'form intentions and reach practical decisions as the result of independent and rational reflection'.[1] It does not, of course, imply the absence of all external constraints and limits to our possibilities of action. Indeed, there is an important sense in which freedom requires limiting factors in order to give structure and meaning to choice. But it does mean that the agent has a capacity for choice: so while it does not entail limitless possibilities in the circumstances surrounding the agent, it does imply some 'potency' within the (individual) agent.[2]

This is clearly incompatible with most strong forms of determinism. It presupposes at least some sense in which the individual can contribute to, and initiate, thought and action (even if the individual is *also* transmitting antecedent causes beyond his or her control). Therefore it entails individual moral responsibility: if we are in some sense and to some degree originators of our actions and thoughts then we are morally responsible for them. However, it does not *necessarily* imply moral constructivism (although it is compatible, as we shall see). That is, our freedom to choose whether or not to act morally does not necessarily mean that we are free to construct fundamental moral values themselves, which may remain 'given' in some way.

Kant has been crucial in the general formulation of this sense of individual autonomy, which has largely survived in spite of greater awareness of the various kinds of constraints which limit it. In knowledge and cognitive skills, as well as in action, individuals are understood to possess at least some capacity in themselves, as well as in relation to others. That element of dependence on others certainly has to be acknowledged as a limiting factor (just as any givenness of ultimate moral values would constitute another kind of constraint). Knowledge clearly is gained from relationship with others and cumulative community experience. But some sense of individual contribution nonetheless remains as one ingredient within that corporate learning process.

There have been various distinct outworkings of this principle of autonomy, in the religious, ethical and political spheres. In religion it is associated with the individual believer's claim to be able to discern the will of God and relate to God without intermediaries. Such a believer need not depend on an external system of belief because his or her own conscience may be a legitimate locus of belief and action. This is most obviously expressed in the Reformation reaction, especially of Calvinism, against the prevailing forms of Catholic hegemony (even though, paradoxically, much Calvinism was also highly deterministic). As perceived by sociologists, '. . . the Calvinist's intercourse with his God was carried on in deep isolation';[3] 'Catholicism thinks in terms of organic unity; it is collectivistic. Calvinism for its part thinks in terms of contractualism; it is individualistic'.[4] (More measured accounts, especially in recent theology, also point quite properly to more subtle points of connection between Catholic and Protestant approaches. But they do not dissent from the broad distinction.)[5]

In general moral philosophy the umbrella appeal to autonomy has generated various trends depending on what precise meanings of the term were sheltering under it. In so far as it was taken to imply that the *object* of moral values was the individual self, then it resulted in a straightforward justification and programme of egoism (especially in the seventeenth and eighteenth centuries, with the shadow of Nietzsche brooding not far behind). But in so far as it meant that the individual was the *source* of moral judgement, which more truly reflects the sense of autonomy we are operating with here, then it may still produce socially co-operative systems of behaviour. However, this latter position also divides, as already indicated, between those who see the individual as final 'creator' and arbiter of moral meaning (moral constructivism), and those who merely see the individual as free to choose or reject, to perceive or misperceive, those moral principles which already have meaning objectively (moral realism).

Kierkegaard stands as a key figure in the development of those who have trodden the former path, although he himself stopped well short of its final destination.[6] Its far point certainly was reached, however, in Sartre's ethical existentialism, at least that of his earlier period. The characters of his novels create meaning by their own actions rather than acting according to some external basis of value: 'Mathieu aspires after a pure freedom in which he acts for no reason, no desire'.[7] Some post-modern forms of deconstruction take this far point further still. The meaning of self is at one and the same time established and annihilated by its power to create a unique but entirely isolating universe of 'meaning' which thereby destroys all other meaning: 'what comes to be celebrated is the deconstructing power itself, the prodigious power of subjectivity to undo all the potential allegiances which might bind it; pure untrammelled freedom' (Taylor, commenting on Jacques Derrida).[8]

By contrast there is the alternative path taken by Kant (followed to some extent by R. M. Hare, and John Rawls).[9] Here the individual's chosen act is only deemed moral in so far as it is an act he or she can rationally will all other people to have performed in the same way in the same circumstances. It is a basis for moral meaning which arises from rational and therefore universalizable constraints, even though the will to conform to it arises from the individual.

What is common to many of these positions, however, is that philosophical assumption alluded to earlier, at least in its most general form: namely, that no empirical or self-evident fact, whether of human nature, or tradition, legal or religious, could itself provide a sufficient and *compelling* reason for moral choice. Fact and value are separated. So it is left to the freedom of the individual to determine that choice, in these various ways.

In political theory autonomy has given rise to those theories of social contract, minimalist government and *laissez-faire* economics whose origin in the Enlightenment period has already been noted. Precisely because the individual's own capacity to choose is so highly prized some doctrine of consent and contract with authority, rather than blind submission to it, is its essential consequence. Modern liberal democracy is its descendant in the political sphere, and the free market doctrine in the economic sphere. These are directly related to a social vision in which people are conceived 'as individual centres of consciousness, as by nature rational and free, as the sole generators of their own wants and preferences'.[10]

John Rawls has been highly influential in this area: he has tried to show how neo-Kantian notions of individual power to shape and pursue our own purposes can be accommodated within a political system which prizes such power and does not override it (for example, for the sake of some overall social utility). Autonomy is therefore specifically connected to most conceptions of human rights. Taylor is explicit about this:

> To talk of universal, natural, or human rights is to connect respect for human life and integrity with the notion of autonomy. It is to conceive people as active co-operators in establishing and ensuring the respect which is due them. And this expresses a central feature of the modern Western moral outlook . . . with the conception of what it is to respect someone. Autonomy is now central to this.[11]

Privacy and inwardness

To place high value on individual autonomy is likely to entail a corresponding value for personal privacy. There must be some area or 'space' in which individuals are free to exercise their autonomy without interference from others in general, or from the law in particular. J. S. Mill's *On Liberty* gives classic expression to this sense of individualism. He argues for liberty of conscience, thought, feeling, in areas of science, morals and theology, freedom to express and publish opinions in these areas, liberty of tastes and pursuits, and liberty to associate with other individuals at will. This region of liberty is '. . . a sphere . . . in which society, as distinguished from the individual, has, if any, only an indirect interest', and individuals may enjoy it at will '. . . without impediment from our fellow creatures, so long as what we do does not harm them, even though they should think our conduct foolish, perverse, or wrong'.[12]

A crucial feature of personal privacy in this sense is that it is positively prized as an aspect of freedom, rather than conceded as an aspect of mere necessity and survival (as one might consider the privacy of the family as a necessity for some things, but an impoverished existence compared to full social and public life).[13] This in turn may be associated with a certain concept of freedom itself, namely that it consists in an absence of restraint, which Isaiah Berlin has characterized as the 'negative' concept of liberty (in his influential essay 'Two Concepts of Liberty').[14] For Mill himself there is no doubt that he sees this negative concept of liberty as a positive value. It underwrites an area of existence in which individuals will have the space to be creative, original and realize their full capacities. Without that privacy they will be constrained and coerced by collective conventions and laws to such an extent that they will sink to the 'mediocrity of the masses'.

We should also note here one particular aspect of this capacity to rise above 'the mediocrity of the masses' which was only systematically articulated much later than Mill. This has to do with the potential for moral idealism. That is, there are possibilities for the individual *qua* individual to dream dreams of altruism and moral heroism – even to live them – which are denied to groups. For there are constraints within the dynamics of social groups which make certain kinds of moral compromise inevitable, even appropriate. By contrast the individual's 'privacy' can set us free from such constraints in our moral aspirations. One has only to think, for example, how individuals might be able *privately* to accept suffering creatively rather than resist it with force ('to turn the other cheek'); whereas within the public domain of social groups such passivity is more likely to constitute a destructive failure to maintain justice. (The general point was made in Reinhold Niebuhr's influential *Moral Man and Immoral Society*.[15])

Clearly this distinction between public and private areas of concern remains important, not least in framing law about matters of personal morality. It lay, for example, at the heart of the Hart / Devlin debate in the 1960s about reforming the law on homosexuality in the UK.[16] In general terms H. L. A. Hart endorsed Mill's position that the 'only purpose for which power can be rightfully exercised over any member of a civilized community, against his will, is to prevent harm to others'. In fact he did add a paternalist clause to allow the law to protect an individual from harm against himself or herself. He also conceded that the organic nature of society makes it very difficult to distinguish entirely private actions which have no harmful effect on society. Yet he was still sufficiently persuaded by the value of private liberty to make the attempt. Thus his concept of harm is correspondingly limited, in order to guarantee the maximum amount of space possible before the law has to intervene. In essence it is only physical harm which must be prevented; he was much more wary about invoking the law against the harm of 'giving offence' or 'moral degradation'. (Lord Devlin, by contrast, considered certain actions which were not directly physically harmful to others might nonetheless weaken the social cement of shared community values; therefore society had the right to protect itself and outlaw [for example] homosexual practices.)

Another way of analysing the concept of privacy would be to relate it to the 'two-tier' doctrines of liberal humanism. In Basil Mitchell's portrait of contemporary culture he describes a characteristically Anglo-Saxon compromise which has emerged between the rationalist endeavour to find universal norms of behaviour by which to order society, and the romantic or existentialist ideal of individual self-expression.[17] This liberal humanist compromise allows for agreement on some minimal social concern with individual behaviour, in so far as it can be rooted in those anthropological 'facts' about human nature and society which are required for survival. But this only provides a basic, minimal code of behaviour. The rest of morality is chosen from ideals which individuals are free to create for themselves. Thus (for example) we might distinguish within the ethics of a prostitute between that element which may be rooted in economic necessity, and that element (if any) which was a freely chosen ideal. The former would be open to rational enquiry and debate, as part of that basic framework of necessity. The latter would be a matter on which we might disagree, but could not be subject to any interference for it belongs to the area of freely chosen ideals (if it does not harm other people's interests, against their will).

Another context in which privacy may be construed and analysed is the religious. Much here may be attributed to Augustine's neo-platonic/Christian synthesis in which the human is united to the divine within oneself through contemplation. It is found variously in other patristic pursuits of the vision of God, the desert fathers, Medieval monasticism, and mysticism generally, where the individual is given 'secret' knowledge and experience of God in his or her own inner sphere. It is also integral to those aspects of the Reformation (Puritanism in particular) stressing self-scrutiny and the internalization of the conscience, which is another form of asserting the positive importance of private space. Contemporary charismatic experience is textured in a similar way. For although it includes some strong corporate elements it depends equally on an intensely private dimension: the word of prophecy may need to be tested in principle, but in practice its origin and authority is often jealously guarded within an area of private certainty.

Taylor devotes a good deal of attention to this turn 'inwards', analysing it in terms both of self-exploration and self-control, both of which are 'important facets of the nascent modern individualism'.[18] He also sets it within the wider context in which it gathered more general philosophical momentum, as well as religious. He perceives it to be inextricably linked with what he calls the disengagement of the self and the disenchantment of the world. That is to say, the locus of thought and value came to be conceived in the mind over against the world. Subject and object are separated, and the object considered in its own right. In short, 'inwardness' may be linked both with Cartesian dualism, 'subjectivism' and the possibilities of scientific method.

Taylor also traces the well-trodden paths between inwardness and social contract theories which have already been mentioned, particularly when that inwardness is allied to a strong sense of personal commitment. Social contract, after all, derives precisely from a sense of validity in the individual's own inner purposes, rather than from some larger order in which the individual is subsumed.

With Augustine cited so strongly there are clearly precedents for some sense of inwardness long before the Reformation and Enlightenment. And there are other pointers to the value of privacy, however embryonic, in Epicureanism, and Roman civilization, as well as early Judaeo-Christian tradition.[19] But there is little doubt that the Enlightenment period constituted a unique *celebration* of these ideas, and therefore bequeathed them to us with renewed vigour and clarity. In any case, whatever their precise origin, and however nuanced, there is this clear common strand: ideas of privacy and inwardness presuppose and confer a value *within* the individual. As such they are therefore essential ingredients in the definition of modern individualism.

Self-realization

Mill's concern, noted above, that a measure of privacy is necessary for creativity, originality and self-development, signals another key feature of individualism: the notion of self-realization. Apart from Mill its importance had been previously grasped by Rousseau, and then systematically developed in the Romantic movement, particularly in Germany.

In fact the notion of self-realization has an ambivalent relationship with privacy (and freedom). Isaiah Berlin, for instance, suggests that some of the most restrictive and disciplined social contexts often breed the greatest creative endeavour. Somewhat like a pressure-cooker, the force of social constraints on the individual may concentrate his or her creative mind, imagination and moral aspirations, more effectively.[20]

However, the idea of self-realization is more firmly wedded to two other notions. And these help explicate it further. First, it assumes a sense of the individual self as a dynamic potential. There are ideals to be realized for individual selves, and we are under some sort of imperative to realize them. Second, these ideals may vary according to the infinitely variable texture of each self. In other words it assumes some sense of uniqueness within each individual.

One of the most influential paradigms for the notion of self-realization, therefore, has been the artist. In Taylor's words,

> Expressive individuation [has become] one of the cornerstones of modern culture . . . In our civilization, moulded by expressivist conceptions, it [art] has come to take a central place in our spiritual life, in some respects replacing religion. The awe we feel before artistic originality and creativity places art on the border of the numinous . . . [21]

When related to theories of social organization the goal of self-realization may also be developed in very different ways. Early Romanticism tended to set individuals apart from society, even against society, precisely to give them the freedom and 'space' to develop. But later German Romanticism transferred the notion from the person to something supra-personal, like a people, nation or state, and saw the self-realization of individuals inextricably bound up in the realization of that larger, organic unit.[22] This is clearly a radically different concept both of self-realization and individualism.

That line of Romantic development also provoked Karl Marx to pick up the notion, and to produce his own particular resolution of individual and corporate concerns. Like others, Marx was profoundly influenced by the artistic ideal. Individuals have an inner necessity to express themselves creatively, and it is precisely the unjust socio-economic structures which have suppressed that self-expression in the masses and concentrated it instead in a few privileged individuals. A proper form of association and community must therefore be developed in which individuals can flourish. Thus, for Marx, communal life is essential for self-realization. This may well be familiar. But it is perhaps less often appreciated that it is precisely *individual* self-realization which therefore counted as one of the chief goals of his social theory.[23]

In modern society a notion of self-development has been influential in various areas. The pseudo-religious role of art has already been noted. It has also had its effect in the shaping of recent educational theory and practice. Christian life has likewise been affected, though more ambivalently. Protestantism especially has embraced the general concern for releasing an individual's full potential in such slogans as 'every member ministry' – although it is more uneasy about accompanying notions of self-assertiveness and self-love.[24]

However, neither the educational nor religious spheres provide the most potent modern symbol of the phenomenon, which is undoubtedly the psychotherapist. When Freud opened up the floodgates of psychoanalysis he was claiming a scientific basis for precisely this dynamic theory of the individual self: namely, the doctrine that the self has potential to be unlocked from within itself, to help realize itself. And although an enormous diversity of theory has since developed, the fundamental quest to explore the inner landscape of the self, with a view to realizing its full potential, is common to all psychotherapy. It has now gained widespread social acceptance, along a broad spectrum from basic counselling to in-depth analysis. As such it represents a particularly powerful expression of this ingredient of modern individualism. Recent preoccupation with diet, aerobics, jogging, beauty treatments, and so on, can be seen as an extension of the same

principle: it is the physical counterpart of the psychological quest. Both
are directed towards the goal of individual self-realization.

Uniqueness and irreplaceability

As already noted, another key notion which links organically with
notions of self-realization is the claim to uniqueness. Thus: '. . . I am
made unlike anyone I have met; I will even venture to say that I
am like no-one in the whole world. I may be no better, but at least
I am different'. So begins Rousseau's *Confessions*[25] – in which this
sense of the self's uniqueness becomes the basis for valuing its creativity and development.

What is meant by uniqueness may vary. It can be conceived in
genetic terms as an irreducible 'given' feature of human personhood.
Or it may be conceived as an aspect of personhood and personality
which is acquired by its interaction with other persons, society and the
natural world (a necessarily unique set of intersections because of an
individual's unrepeatable particularity: the flux of time and change
ensures that no one has *exactly* the same environment as anyone else).
Or, more likely, it is held to arise out of a combination of genetic, environmental and relational factors. There may also be some appeal to a
mysterious aspect of personal identity, 'soul' or 'subjectivity', which is
defined in an *a priori* way as unique by definition (claimed on the basis
of unverifiable introspection, or because of religious assumptions
about God-given uniqueness). This tends to conceive the uniqueness
of individuals in a metaphysical and Cartesian way, rather than by
appeal to empirical or quasi-empirical factors. (All these options will be
considered later in more detail.[26])

In more general terms, uniqueness is conceived (and prized) as an
aspect of what has been referred to above as 'inwardness': that is, the
capacity of an individual to find moral and spiritual truth within him
or herself, independently of the surrounding community and 'web of
interlocution'. And if this community is still deemed necessary for
the *origin* of individuality, then the individual still has the capacity to
transcend it later, out of his or her 'own' inner resources.

This is not new to modernity. Socrates is praised for his ability to
rise above Athenian opinion, and Old Testament prophets for their
stance (with the help of God) over against their own communities. But
it is celebrated more widely in contemporary society. And while the
basic idea of individual differences is hardly new, modernity has
given immense impetus to the notion that these differences should

be a positive determinate in the value of *all* individuals. That is, their primary significance is to help establish the value of every individual, as opposed to justifying a hierarchy of value in which some individuals are diminished.

This last point is crucial. For whatever basis and conception of individual uniqueness is adopted, its significance for the value of individuals is enormous. A unique centre of consciousness and subjectivity generates a sense of value in various ways. In particular, it will be caught up in a nexus of unique relationships. And whether or not these are all healthy, they will nonetheless be *irreplaceable*.[27] For we take it as a fundamental datum of human experience that no one can replace another, and that arises precisely from the unique relationships which we have formed with other (unique) persons. Moreover, although this general perception exerts no strict logical force in bridging the gap between fact and value, it is intuitively powerful in so doing. For there is a compelling connection between the perception of uniqueness, irreplaceability and *mattering* – which moves us irresistibly across that gap.[28] Such notions (taken together) help convey the very meaning of human existence. Thus Karl Popper:

> . . . the unique individual and his unique actions and experiences and relations to other individuals can never be fully rationalized. And it appears to be just this irrational realm of unique individuality which makes human relations important. Most people would feel, for example, that what makes their lives worth living would largely be destroyed if they themselves, and their lives, were in no sense unique but in all and every respect typical of a class of people, so that they repeated exactly all the actions and experiences of all other men who belong to this class. It is the uniqueness of our experiences which, in this sense, makes our lives worth living, the unique experience of a landscape, of a sunset, of the expressions of a human face.[29]

More obliquely, the notion of uniqueness could also be construed through the means–end relationship. This is less specifically tied to the notion of uniqueness and individuality, but it does establish a similar point about the value of the (unique) individual. It was given its most thorough treatment by Kant in his *Moral Law*: 'man exists as an end in himself, not merely as a means for arbitrary use by this or that will . . .' In other words, intrinsic to the very definition of personhood is the nature is individuals as 'objective' ends in themselves, which is in turn a presupposition of value: '. . . persons, therefore, are not merely subjective ends whose existence as an effect of our actions has a value *for us*: they are *objective ends* . . . for unless this is so, nothing at all of *absolute* value would be found anywhere'.[30]

Such is the variety of conceptions by which individual uniqueness is perceived, established and valued. And once again, when efforts are made to trace the history of such notions, it is not surprising to find the story fails to fall in a straight line. It may certainly be seen to have some ancestry in early Christianity. The doctrine that we are created in the image of God has undoubtedly entailed the valuing of individuals; likewise the unconditional nature of divine love embodied in Christ (*agape*), which is biblically focused on all kinds of individuals (not just groups).[31] It may also be true that this kind of emphasis was temporarily eclipsed by organic and collectivist notions of the Christian Middle Ages – when the prevailing doctrines were more likely to conceive individuals existing for the sake of society, right order and the Church, rather than for their own sake.[32] But then it is equally clear that emphasis on uniqueness and individual value revived strongly in the Reformation, Renaissance and Enlightenment periods.

As for its most obvious social implications, the notion has evidently been influential, but again there is no clear, single, line of development in social or ethical theory, even in comparatively recent history. For instance, utilitarian theory began by drawing on the idea to support its doctrines about maximizing pleasure and liberty for the greatest number of individuals possible. It limited state interference precisely on the basis that the state exists to serve individuals, rather than vice versa. But subsequent development of the theory has found itself caught in a paradox. In order to maximize individual happiness in general, particular individuals may have to be sacrificed (the most obvious example is the punishment of an innocent person as a necessary deterrent for the benefit of others).[33] Thus utilitarianism easily slides from valuing individuals in themselves, to valuing only a quantitative notion of individual happiness. This illustrates both how significant and how slippery a notion uniqueness is when incorporated into any systematic ethical or social theory. In so far as all are unique, then we should organize society for the benefit of the greatest number; in so far as each is, precisely, *unique*, no single individual should be sacrificed for that greatest number.

A similar point can be made of the means–end relationship. In principle it provides useful conceptual clarification of the notion of human uniqueness and human value. But in practice it does not guarantee that any single coherent ethical or social programme will or will not emerge. This can be illustrated very simply with reference back to MacIntyre's comments about our own contemporary culture:[34] though fundamentally individualistic (in his analysis), that very same individualism is necessarily manipulative of others. In others words, in order to value ourselves as ends we find ourselves treating others as means.

In terms of Christian religion, a sense of individual uniqueness has likewise given rise to paradox. On the one hand it is held to be the mainspring of a profound spirituality. The Creator's unique relationship with individuals invests them, by grace, with a sense of worth and purpose, and empowers them to offer worthy praise in response. On the other hand it can easily slide into a theological system of extreme egotism. A. N. Wilson's rhetoric is bitter but pertinent:

> Religious egotism is the most potent form of egotism that exists. It can swell and grow and take over the earth. It begins with the simple egotism of believing that the Creator of Earth and Sky is perpetually engrossed in your personal moods, prayers, sins and virtues . . . Anyone who is capable of believing these things has placed themselves, and their relationship with the Almighty, at the very centre of the universe.[35]

Yet however blunt or paradoxical an instrument in the construction of social policy or religious attitudes, the fact remains that uniqueness functions powerfully as an ingredient of individualism. As a necessary, if not sufficient, condition of objective value, and by entailing the doctrine of individuals as ends-in-themselves, it may be counted as one of the most important single features to help define the term.

Human rights and equality

The paradox of investing value in uniqueness is highlighted further by one other key feature of the Enlightenment legacy. This too bears heavily on the status of individuals. It is the imperative to value individuals according to their *common* qualities, rather than their differences.

This centres chiefly around the notion of human rights. It is a notion which came to pre-eminence in its classic formulation in the American Declaration of Independence, and has been enshrined subsequently in the Universal Declaration of Human Rights adopted by the General Assembly of the United Nations in 1948. In broad terms it supposes that there are certain rights which belong to human individuals as such, simply in virtue of being human, irrespective of race, creed, intelligence, or social status. They normally have to do with rights of life, liberty, rights to property, education, health care, rights before the law, and so on.

Some of its origins in social contract theory have already been noted: Locke in particular has a strong concept of what he calls 'natural' rights, not least to property.[36] More recent elaborations have further stressed the role of rights in protecting individuals from subordination to general goals of social programmes: they are 'trumps over some background justification for political decisions that states a goal for the community as a whole'.[37]

It is a notion which has been subjected to vigorous critical onslaught by analytical philosophers. If they are 'basic' human rights this implies they must be absolute, not deriving from some further more fundamental right or value (like the good of a community). But in practice there are always situations in which allegedly basic human rights have to be violated for some greater good, therefore they cannot be conceived as absolute at all. Also, the fact / value distinction is once more wheeled out to do battle. In so far as rights are supposed to derive from the nature of humanity *per se* then they have supposed we can derive 'value' from a very unstable and fluid 'fact'.[38] And they are epistemologically unsafe if they presuppose some (unprovable) normative assumption about intrinsic human worth.[39] More simply, they may be seen merely as redundant intermediaries which obscure the immediacy of the moral judgement at stake: that is, what makes a cruel or negligent act towards an individual wrong is not the violation of some 'right' of his or hers, but simply the suffering he or she undergoes.[40]

But perhaps because the violation of so-called basic human rights has been so gross in recent history (in Stalinism, Nazism, apartheid, to take but a few examples), there have been equally vigorous attempts to rehabilitate and redefine the concept. Richard Wasserstrom offers the following analysis of basic human rights: (1) they are possessed by all human beings; (2) they are possessed *equally* by all human beings; (3) they are possessed *absolutely* in the sense that they are not possessed in virtue of any social status or relationship; and in the sense that no one can claim exemption in virtue of any social status or relationship from the claim of other people's rights.[41] As such they are not being claimed as absolute in the sense that nothing could override them, but only in the sense that they belong to all people over against all people regardless of status. Thus if provision for health care or education, even life and liberty, has to be suspended or reduced in circumstances of war or economic hardship, the decision about who should suffer the deprivation must never be made on the basis of race, creed, social status or intelligence. And when circumstances permit, full provision is necessarily restored to all. The other conceptual objections to the notion of rights have also received detailed response, in a continuing debate which demonstrates the residual strength of the notion.[42]

In post-war Britain the notion has frequently been invoked to back claims from the workforce for increased wages, improved work conditions and job security, chiefly through Trades Union representation. However, as such it has functioned in a more collective sense and, crucially, fails to meet the definition offered above: that is, they are rights which arise out of a particular social role and status (people as workers) rather than common humanity. More apposite in principle (though probably less significant in practice) is the recent invocation of a 'Citizens Charter'. This appears to be part of a sustained effort to grant individuals rights to certain standards of service from public bodies simply in virtue of being citizens. And in so far as some form of citizenship may be seen as an essential concomitant of human life *per se*, then we are closer here to a modern outworking of a doctrine of 'basic' human rights.

In strictly religious terms the notion is invoked more rarely. In general this is because of the moral ambivalence of a notion which can so easily slide into (or arise from) individual egoism. After all, *prima facie* a right appears to involve a prior claim for one's own interests over against community interests – even if it is subsequently qualified. And historically there has indeed been a clear association of rights and individual egoism (given systematic expression, for example, in Hobbes' notion of a 'Right of Nature'). The egoism arises when rights are defined without any sense of correlative duty.

There are also other more specifically Christian grounds for unease. Stanley Hauerwas, for example, sees (and deplores) an integral connection between the notion of rights and mutual estrangement between people. That is, the invocation of rights presupposes that people are 'strangers' and adversaries to one another rather than neighbours; it isolates individuals and groups from each other and skews their relations.[43] There is also theological sensitivity about the doctrine of grace, which will dispose Christians to accept (if not to claim) what may be due to them more on the basis of their status as children of God, rather than because of any socially agreed status or intrinsic worth. Furthermore, under the imperative of *agape* they should in any case be more concerned to meet the claim their neighbour makes on them rather than assert their own (again, on the basis of the neighbour's status as a creature of God, as distinct from his or her humanity *per se*).

Yet even specifically theological discourse can and does employ the language of rights *when suitably defined* (for example, as a protection for the vulnerable – or the right to exercise a conscience, the 'right to be morally good', as Cronin suggests).[44] This simply highlights a problem familiar from other areas of discourse: on the whole, in spite of the efforts of the analytical philosophers, the language of human rights is still used variously and imprecisely. Thus it is employed to justify social and political programmes along a very broad spectrum. It is also used as a catchword to test the moral standing of regimes at the extreme ends of the spectrum (it was a litmus test to judge the collectivism of the Stalinist era and its aftermath, and is still used in the same way against oppressive dictatorships). Equally, it may be used in criminal law, in civil disputes and even in defining domestic relationships. And all these contexts nuance the meaning of the term in different ways.

But in so far as we can generalize, this much may still be said. It certainly functions as that aspect of individualism which vests the worth of individuals in their common humanity rather than their differences. And as such it operates as a regulatory, negative doctrine to establish protection against all forms of discrimination which arise from those 'inessential' differences of race, gender, intelligence, social background and so on.

Such, then, are some of the core ideas which provide much of the momentum and meaning of individualism. It is not an exhaustive list, nor the only way of ordering ideas which clearly overlap and interrelate. But it does at least provide a starting point in any attempt at understanding – and evaluating – such a multi-faceted phenomenon.

3

Beginning the Evaluation

Any attempt to evaluate these notions first begs the question of moral epistemology and criteria. How do we know what is right for individuals and society, and by what yardstick do we measure it? It is a fair question, of course, and any answer will inevitably beg other questions. But I shall simply offer this.

To begin with I shall be operating with very generally conceived criteria of 'natural morality', as filtered through a western post-Enlightenment conscience. In practice this means a tacit appeal to a combination of the self-authenticating and the pragmatic: that is, what intuitively commends itself, and what has 'worked' in history and experience. So I am certainly not claiming any vantage point beyond the complex historical, rational and intuitive process which has formed my (western) intuitions. There is no view from nowhere, and we have to begin somewhere.

This starting point means that I am not yet appealing *specifically* to the Christian theological tradition in the process of evaluation. Of course, the general western tradition and Christianity are so formed out of each other that there is bound to be more than a trace of the latter making its presence felt, even at this stage of the discussion. But this is simply to be acknowledged as one ingredient (however important) in a more general evaluative approach.

The purpose of beginning like this will be clearer as the book later moves on to its explicitly theological analysis. Essentially the point is first to map out the moral issues on a terrain which is at least recognizable to the widest spread of contemporary opinion. This may help show how far consensus might (or might not) be achieved, without specific allegiance to any particular moral or religious tradition (something which will matter in any pluralist situation). By the same token it will also lay bare some of the vulnerable areas in all such attempts at general moral consensus.

Prima facie moral force in core ideas of individualism

The preceding analysis of core ideas did not set out to be explicitly evaluative. Nonetheless some of it was inescapably value-laden, and this needs to be acknowledged straightaway. After all, just as headline titles, it is hard to deny the *prima facie* moral attractiveness of such notions as autonomy, privacy, self-realization, uniqueness, human rights and equality. And the further analysis offered under each heading suggested at least some respects in which they could sustain that moral scrutiny. Here is a brief recapitulation of their most evident moral strengths, so far conveyed.

Some basic sense of *autonomy* is the precondition of any moral responsibility; it is also a key presupposition in all social and political doctrines which respect and require the individual's consent, rather than subordinating him or her too swiftly to a 'greater good'. Autonomy presupposes an area of *privacy* or inner freedom in which to operate, and in which (arguably) creativeness, originality and moral vitality flourish. Moreover, when the subject has the 'space' to distinguish itself from object, there are new possibilities (as well as pitfalls) for technology and science.

The notion of *self-realization* is also an essential condition for human creativity, dynamism and moral vitality. As both a possibility and an imperative it releases and drives individuals to new levels of personal aspiration and achievement. Its organic connection with a sense of an individual's *uniqueness* and irreplaceability is also morally significant. To believe that each individual self is variously textured and dynamically structured provides a crucial objective basis for valuing each individual.

Finally, the notions of *human rights* and *equality* provide essential protection against exploitation and discrimination. They trump the totalitarian tendency to assimilate and subordinate the concrete individual to an abstract whole.

Small wonder such basic ideas came to command wide consensus. Lukes, in his largely conceptual survey, has few doubts about their positive status. He sees an essential and organic link between respect for individual dignity and the notion of equality; between autonomy, privacy, self-development and the notion of liberty:[1] and within this nexus of interrelated ideas he takes it as self-evident that we are operating with some basic moral axioms. Thus he claims of individual dignity (closely related to uniqueness): 'This idea . . . has the logical status of a moral (or religious) axiom which is basic, ultimate and overriding, offering a general justifying principle in moral argument'.[2] Of autonomy he claims: 'It has ... been widely held as a moral value ... central to the morality of modern Western civilization'.[3] As regards self-development: 'In general it has the status of an ultimate value, an end-in-itself'.[4]

Furthermore, these core values have commended themselves by their relation to, and incorporation in, a wide variety of social programmes. They have demonstrated themselves to be capable of embodiment in actual social practice, and to effect real change. And in some cases, historical verdicts of this change have been massively positive. On balance, the explosion of these ideas, particularly through the ferment of the Enlightenment, unleashed a vital moral reformation and reorientation in a period which urgently required it. Hence Sir Ernest Barker's uncompromising conclusion about social contract theory as the effective embodiment of some of these ideas. It was (he claims) an historic factor in the cause of freedom and civil liberty:

> If it were judged by its fruits, on a pragmatic test of truth, it could bring to the bar of judgement a record of rich achievement ... It was . . . a way of expressing two fundamental ideas of values to which the human mind will always cling – the value of Liberty, or the idea that will, not force, is the basis of government, and the value of Justice, or the idea that right, not might, is the basis of all political society.[5]

Granted, subsequent assessment of any particular set of historical circumstances may be more circumspect. Even so, there undoubtedly remain some social achievements of modernity to which few would wish to deny moral status, and which bear obvious marks of the pressure of these ideas. They hardly need elaborating: religious freedom, the abolition of the slave trade, universal suffrage, the rise of feminism, democracy itself, post-Second World War impetus to provide equal opportunities for health care and education, United Nations efforts to transcend nationalism, the end of race segregation in the US, the race discrimination act in the UK, the end of apartheid in South Africa, the collapse of repressive Soviet-style communism.

The possibility that some of these achievements are now, paradoxically, under threat from social philosophies which have claimed the individualist mantle must also be addressed. That is all part of the conceptual and moral incoherence of our current situation, and so part of the agenda of this book. But for now it should not obscure the fact that many of these moral advances were motivated by these core 'individualist' ideas (always remembering that such ideas have a compound origin and meaning in antique, Christian, as well as Enlightenment thought).

Less obvious, but equally pertinent, is the relation of some of these ideas to a more general social attitude which I also want to suggest as a moral achievement. This is the modern affirmation of 'ordinary life' as a locus of true value, a context in which we are encouraged to find personal fulfilment in the broadest terms, including our moral and spiritual good. 'Ordinary life' here means economic life, work, friendship, family life, marriage, child-bearing. Generally, it is the labour and form of life which has to do with personal necessities and survival, but it might also include play and sport (and it involves the whole person including the body). It is therefore distinct from the Aristotelian ideal of the good life as an 'élitist' activity of contemplation, deliberation about moral excellence and the (political) ordering of laws. For Aristotelian ethics ordinary life was only a kind of substructure to sustain these higher activities. But western culture has come to value ordinary life in itself.

The impetus for this valuation derives in part from a Platonic, then Augustinian, vision of the goodness of all things. There is a synthesis here between some Greek thought and longstanding Judaeo-Christian spirituality which affirms the goodness of creation, and God's love for all of it. But it received renewed momentum particularly in the Reformation era when *all* people were credited with the capacity to relate to God, and the mediation of the few was rejected.[6] Neither special people (priests) nor times, acts, places (mass, the Church itself) were considered strictly necessary for access to God.

Charles Taylor devotes considerable attention to this feature of modernity, and links it (interestingly) with a corresponding revulsion for suffering.[7] A concern for ordinary life is bound up with ordinary human welfare. That is evidenced, he claims, by the fact that we are much more inclined to avoid and prevent suffering than previous civilizations. He traces this in part to the decline in belief systems which depend on cosmic order and balance. That is, we no longer see the *point* in inflicting suffering simply as a 'balancing' punishment for crime.[8] By the same token, the individual is not to be callously or senselessly sacrificed as a pawn to any such spurious higher order of things. This is why we find *some* forms of utilitarianism inveighing powerfully against needless suffering inflicted in the name of such systems.[9] As indicated, there is a general debt here specifically to Christian belief and spirituality, with its traditions of concern for human welfare arising out of its theology of creation and redemption.

The connection of these important social attitudes with the core ideas of individualism therefore becomes apparent. Historically they clearly form a close nexus, not least by virtue of their common bond with Judaeo-Christian belief, and with some forms of utilitarianism. Conceptually, too, there is a clear relationship. An affirmation of ordinary life, and a concern for ordinary welfare, presupposes ideas of universality, equality, and the common capacities, rights and dignities of *all* individuals – not just of a spiritual, intellectual or political élite.

Taylor himself does not spell out all these relationships in detail. But he is no less confident about the significance of these social attitudes themselves. The affirmation of ordinary life has become 'one of the most powerful ideas in modern civilization': it underlies bourgeois concern for 'welfare'; it powered Marxism, with its preoccupation on man the *producer*; and when taken together with the corresponding sensitivity to suffering, 'it colours our whole understanding of what it is truly to respect human life and integrity. Along with the central place given to autonomy it . . . is peculiar to our civilization, the modern West'.[10]

This kind of accolade, and Taylor's juxtaposition of this idea with autonomy, may suggest that 'valuing ordinary life' should itself count as another core idea of individualism. In fact this might not be strictly appropriate – it is probably best conceived in a secondary relationship to those other core ideas. But it can certainly be claimed as an immensely valuable consequence of them in actual social attitude and practice.

Of course, there is always the possibility of moral ambiguity in the way even this notion is developed. Taylor's reference to Marxism raises one such issue. Even the general notion of human welfare itself can be criticized, if it is taken to imply the avoidance of suffering *at all costs*.[11] Nonetheless, *prima facie* an affirmation of ordinary life must surely count as a positive fruit of individualistic ideas, and its concomitant revolt against suffering even more so.

Another significant indicator of the moral power of these ideas is found in the way they function as benchmarks to test and criticize overall social doctrines and programmes. This is a point already made in respect of human rights. But it also applies more generally to the core ideas of individualism as a whole. This is obviously true in relation to collectivist and / or totalitarian societies. In Dostoevsky's Russia, for example, Ivan Karamazov's celebrated protest against the oppression of the Church is based on core ideas of individualism. This is all the more notable since he is also operating within a strong sense of 'sobornost' (a sense of mutual solidarity, communion and responsibility amongst people). What it reveals is that the corporateness of true sobornost nonetheless depends on individual consent – which is what the Church has crushed for the sake of overall harmony and stability. Hence Ivan's protest. And while this is not primarily expressed in abstract ideas, but in narrative, it clearly embodies them. This is most vivid, and the protest most profound, when at one point he rejects not only the institutional form of the Church but God himself, *in the name of the value of a single, individual, suffering child.*[12]

A similar appeal is made, with equal dramatic force, by Arthur Koestler in relation to Marxist forms of society.[13] In the narrative of his book an individual finds he can no longer consent to the dialectical laws imposed by the state in the name of historical necessity. He resists and is imprisoned. For there is no trace of Kantian ethics in the state system which might give him any status as 'end' in himself, in order to save him. He is only an expendable means to a greater whole, and has been taught to consider himself as such ('I'-ness is a 'grammatical fiction', referring to no substantial reality). Yet it is precisely that obstinate fact of his self-consciousness, the worth and reality of his unique individuality, which haunts him in his cell and vindicates his stance to the reader. Core ideas of individualism, made concrete in narrative form, are clearly the basis of the protest.

Less marked, but equally significant, is the way ideas of individualism also function as a criterion of criticism in relation to forms of society which are themselves self-consciously individualistic. MacIntyre's observations quoted in the introduction provide a telling, if unconscious, example. One of his most damning criticisms of contemporary 'bureaucratic' individualism, as we have seen, is that it is manipulative: that is, it inclines us to use other people as means, not ends. But this, of course, is precisely an appeal to a fundamental *idea* of individualism in order to check a particular development of individualistic culture. This also clearly operates in Charles Taylor's more balanced and eirenic assessment of our present situation, especially in his *Ethics of Authenticity.*[14]

Another example is implicit in the paradox of utilitarianism, already noted. As we have seen, utilitarian theory in origin was an expression of individualism, seeking to maximize the liberty and happiness of individuals. But by producing social programmes of rational calculation about quantifying pleasure and pain it can lead to gross violation of individual rights, riding roughshod over concepts of particularity and uniqueness. Not only the punishment of the innocent, but also infanticide and compulsory euthanasia, may in principle be justified by utilitarianism, and have been[15] – *unless it is rescued and regulated by precisely those core ideas of individualism from which it developed.*[16]

Similarly, more recent social visions which are partly constructed out of a radical *critique* of contemporary individualistic culture are notable for their selective appeal to those very ideas of individualism as *positive* ingredients in their own enterprise. Feminism is a case in point. Thus Susan Parsons, reviewing feminist ethics: 'Many feminists are still persuaded that decisions regarding justice for women are best formulated in relation to the principle of treating persons as ends in themselves and never as means to an end, and have affirmed the notion of personal autonomy upon which that principle relies.'[17]

The *prima facie* case for these fundamental notions is therefore powerful. They are proven positive ingredients in moral and social advance, and vital regulators against oppressive or lop-sided social programmes. If we abandon them in wholesale fashion, it appears we would do so at great peril.

The corruption of individualistic ideas

But then it is also possible to generate a very different picture. The shadow side of these ideas is never far away. At best they can be morally ambivalent, and at worst corrupting and socially pernicious. It was noted at the outset that the developed phenomenon of individualism in its great variety of social, cultural and religious aspects is often referred to pejoratively and critically. Some of the reasons have already emerged in our initial analysis of the constituent ideas. Here again is a brief recapitulation and development of what has already been mentioned or implied, this time about the negative consequences of individualistic ideas.

It was made clear, for instance, that emphasis on *autonomy* may lead to the creation of egotistical values rather than a measure of freedom to accept or reject given values; to extreme *laissez-faire* government (with all the casualties that implies) rather than a guided market economy. Paradoxically, it can also lead to the deconstruction of the self, in so far as the purely autonomous self becomes so isolated that it destroys all relations on which it depends for its own meaning.

An area of *privacy* may precipitate a disintegration of the social cement and widespread corruption rather than simply allowing for freedom of taste and self-expression. The drive to inwardness can divide subject from object, creating not constructive possibilities for science and technology but artificial and potentially alienating dualisms.

Self-realization can transfer its ideals to the state in a totalitarian way, suppressing rather than stimulating the development of the individual; or it may imprison individuals in isolated introspection rather than liberating them in creative endeavour. It may encourage self-assertion at the expense of others, rather than for the sake of others or proper self-confidence.

Stressing the *uniqueness* and value of individuals can generate the cruel paradoxes of utilitarianism already noted, whereby concrete individuals are sacrificed for the sake of an abstract, quantitative notion of individual worth. Treating the individual as end rather than means likewise gets distorted. For when the dictum becomes self-referential (or just selective) then it is all too likely to justify manipulating some as means in order to serve others as ends. It can certainly lead to extreme forms of religious egotism.

Even the notion of equal *human rights* may be wielded unrealistically to feed greedy self-interest at times when restraint and responsibility is required, rather than securing protection for those exploited and discriminated against. Instead of establishing justice, it may have an alienating and adversarial effect on human relations.

Notions of individual *equality* can also give cause for complaint when they ride on the back of a genuinely 'universalist' but correspondingly abstract ethical viewpoint. For this can compromise the concrete particularity of individual persons, and devalue their differences. This echoes the utilitarian paradox: it begins by asserting the value of all individuals, but ends by restricting their actual individuality by an abstract framework of impartiality. It is an ethical vision which presupposes individuals to be simply separated selves in competition, needing to be held in check. Feminists in particular have criticized this as the expression of a largely male conception of human personhood.[18]

More generally, as we observe how these ideas may be taken up into social programmes, we need to remind ourselves of the origin of the term 'individualism', especially in the ferment of the French Revolution and Counter Revolution, where its ideas appeared to be embodied in chaos and anarchy as much as liberation and creativity. Lamennais was as uncompromising about that time as Barker was later when he wrote of the social contract – but with an entirely contrary evaluation. Of individual autonomy and reason, he wrote '. . . the same doctrine which produces anarchy in men's minds further produces an irremediable political anarchy, and overturns the very bases of human society . . . Individualism destroys the very idea of obedience and of duty . . . and what then remains but a terrifying confusion of interests, passions and diverse opinions?'[19]

Marxism, too, is a wayward child of some individualistic ideas. Marx's own concern for the artistic ideal of self-expression has been noted, along with the affirmation of ordinary productive life which became a central pivot of Marxist social theory and practice – and these may well count positively. But of course the complete story of Marxism is a much more ambivalent one, in which individualistic and collectivist ideas have jostled symbiotically, uneasily and sometimes destructively. In so far as Marxism as a whole can be accorded a moral verdict it is hardly likely to be uniformly positive. It spawned too many cruelties and entailed too much oppression.

The Nazi experiment, more obliquely, was another aberration of core ideas of individualism (though likewise parasitic on collectivist dreams as well). In this case it was the idea of autonomy which assumed a pivotal and particularly pernicious position. Partly through its Nietzscherian basis the philosophy of Nazism followed a romantic ideal of autonomy to its terrifying extreme, free to create its own criteria of 'value' out of power and racial supremacy.

More recently, if we consider contemporary post-communist and post-fascist social programmes, the balance of ideas and the manner of their embodiment has changed radically, and assessment is by no means straightforward. In so far as the countries of the former Soviet Union struggle to implement political programmes of democracy and economic programmes of free enterprise they seem to be employing at least some core ideas of individualism. Yet it is a change which has unleashed grave social instability, inequality, exclusive nationalism and burgeoning criminal chaos. So while the jury has not yet returned its verdict, it is unlikely to be wholly favourable. The same is broadly true of the post-colonial processes in Africa, in which core ideas of individualism are being grafted unhappily into different cultures. Again, the causal relationship of this process with the devastating turmoil apparent in some contemporary situations is complex and arguable. Likewise, any assessment of its overall necessity, value or disvalue, must always be provisional and tentative at this stage. The stories are open-ended, in full-flow as this book is written. But in both cases there are at least sufficient traces of Lamennais' nineteenth-century diagnosis of the French experience to cause moral alarm. These ideas are explosive. They appear to have potential for great harm, as well as great good.

Finally, there is our own contemporary western/northern society in which we have been shaped by these ideas even more directly. Here too the effects are adverse, with MacIntyre's comments quoted at the outset suggesting that we shall not have to look far for a serious critique of how they have functioned for us. And it is this which now deserves much closer analysis.

Before that analysis, however, just one point about methodology which begs further mention here. For what has now become clearer are both the limitations and possibilities of this process of *abstracting* moral ideas for evaluation.

On the one hand it is easy to see how we have already slidden inexorably from core moral concepts to their embodiment both in ethical theory and fully-blown social programmes. This is both inevitable and right. It exposes how difficult, if not disingenuous, it is to evaluate basic moral ideas in abstraction from the way they function in actual social order.

Yet on the other hand there is a sense in which the discussion has justified a procedure of conceptual clarification which *requires* some measure of abstraction. This is because we have had to note both the inspirational and regulatory power of ideas *qua* ideas. This is the power of ideas to bridge – and criticize – different cultures. So to talk only of morality in actual social embodiment risks diluting that inspirational element which properly belongs to ideas. In other words, what a consideration of concrete social programmes may gain in moral realism, it loses in moral motivation and transcendence: it is an inevitable result of their nature as complex, organic, entities. Their constituent moral ideas, by contrast, travel light and travel further; they have a vital role to play especially in the process of initiating change. So the attempt to abstract them, to some extent, remains crucial.

All this surely justifies a decision to maintain some sort of dialectic and distinction between ideas and their social embodiment.[20] The point remains that we are bound to assess these ideas as they are received, embodied and re-expressed in any particular culture and social order. Yet they must also be allowed to function as potential tools of 'transcendence'. Both sides of this point need to be kept in mind as we turn to portraits of our own culture in more detail.

Individualism, expertise and fragmentation: more detailed portraits of a current culture

So now to the substance of MacIntyre's analysis – as a useful point of entry to our own situation (although writing at the beginning of the 1980s in the USA much of his analysis remains apposite for the UK in the late 1990s, as we shall see).

MacIntyre suggests we have reached our situation of bureaucratic individualism not least because of the process outlined above, in our historical account of the attempted justification of morality. That is, because our moral values and meaning have cut loose from either a revealed will of God or a teleological view of human nature (fact and value divorced) we have been set loose to find our own moral way without any objective authority. The only rational justification, there-fore, for preferring one action over against another will be its *effective-ness* in achieving any end which is chosen (the end itself is a-moral, and cannot be a matter of rational discussion, in the sense that there is no agreed objective framework to root it in). This preference for effectiveness or expertise provides the specifically bureaucratic element in our culture (here following Max Weber). It produces the paradoxi-cal situation already noted, that although we are all supposedly set free in ourselves as individual moral agents we are constrained in social practice by the managerial system of bureaucratic experts.[21]

Thus as 'free' moral agents we are isolated and fragmented from each other. We can create our own ideals, but have no common 'fac-tual' story to relate it to, either in our past or in our contemporary culture. Because all our moral choices are expressions of attitude, pref-erence or choice (rather than rooted in a common sense of human nature, history, religion) then we are selves '. . . with no given conti-nuities'.[22] On the other hand, as agents in the social world, we have to relate co-operatively in *some* way – and the only mode of social practice we are given is precisely this bureaucratic system governed by the criterion of effectiveness.

We have already noted that this social practice is necessarily manip-ulative. What must be added now is that it also separates the moral self from his or her social role. For when social practice is governed by efficiency and expertise, without discussion of overall ends, there is an inevitable dichotomy between the private life and social context of the moral agent. A person may be highly successful in terms of social expertise (as a schoolteacher, soldier, civil servant or farmer), but this concept of 'success' will bear no necessary relation to his or her private ideals or lack of them.

MacIntyre goes on to contrast this with the ancient Aristotelian concept of the virtuous man in which it was impossible to separate the notion of being a good schoolteacher and a good person. Because the common sense of ends, purposes and ideals was so strong, because social roles were so integrally related to that common story, and because personal identity was so rooted in that common story rather than fragmented in a private self, there could be no such division. Thus:

> In much of the ancient and medieval worlds . . . the individual is identified and constituted in and through certain of his or her roles, those roles which bind the individual to the communities in and through which alone specifically human goods are attained. I confront the world as a member of this family, that household, this clan, this tribe, this city, this nation, this kingdom. There is no 'I' apart from these.[23]

He finds something of this sense in the world of Jane Austen too, but crucially absent in our contemporary culture. And as it is frequently the absence of something which helps define the complexities of a cultural ethos, his positive characterization of the ancient, medieval and Christian social worlds are as much part of his analysis of our modern post-Christian world as the critique itself.

This still short-changes the scope and full force of MacIntyre's analysis. But it summarizes at least some of his most telling charges. It indicates in more detail how he sees the prevailingly negative effect flowing from the particular form of individualism which has become incarnated in our society. And it deserves the seriousness with which it has been received.

To be sure, it has received sustained criticism as well. This has mostly related to his historical and philosophical methodology; the manner in which he has established his history of ideas; or to his particular account of the Aristotelian virtues; and to his grim proposal for the future, with which I shall also take issue at a later stage.[24] However, his actual diagnosis of our current situation, to the extent it can survive or stand apart from methodological criticism, remains acute. The point I wish to emphasize now is how far it is *recognizable*, if somewhat impressionistic, as a portrait of our contemporary culture.

It is recognizable in the attitudes of some of the young males who roam our streets violently (or who ransacked the money markets so ruthlessly in the 1980s, purely for personal gain). Immediate causes (for the former) may include the forces of global economics which seem to have forced a permanent wedge of unemployment into many of our housing estates and inner cities. But the attitudes of both groups may also be products precisely of a culture where they feel no common truths compelling enough to bind them to the rest of society. They belong to no wider community of values but are isolated in themselves, or in small packs.

It is more generally recognizable in the way we have been inclined to handle (and define) matters of personal morality. In such issues as marriage and divorce, drug-taking, abortion, or homosexual practice, our inclination is to assert a right to private judgement according to individually chosen ideals and values. There is little sense that judgement about such issues is to be made out of some community of values rooted in an agreed view of human nature or religious system. This may well be beginning to change. That is part of the reactive situation to which I alluded at the outset. But the pendulum (or spiral) has far to travel, for the instinct to private judgement is deeply rooted. There is certainly little evidence of any new common ground on which it may lay down and rest, in spite of the best efforts of communitarianism.

It is also recognizable in the fragmentation and isolation of individuals, evidenced in the significant increase in stress, mental illness, and the growth of the therapy and counselling industry. This arises precisely from the strain of having to carve out our own individual sense of meaning and values without the resources of a wider, communal 'story' or religious community. It also arises from that separation of our private selves and our social and work roles which MacIntyre highlights. When we operate with different criteria in our place of work we set up an internal sense of alienation from ourselves, and mental strain is the price that is paid. So MacIntyre is surely right to pinpoint the therapist as another of his paradigmatic characters of our culture (along with the manager, and aesthete). And I suggest this is not only because our society requires the therapist to pick up the pieces of the fragmented and homeless selves it has created. It is also because the therapist's characteristic mode of operating actually reinforces the underlying causes of the initial breakdown: that is, the therapist fights shy of presenting any common and external values as part of the healing process, but has concentrated instead on integrating the client *within himself or herself* (an aspect of 'non-directional' coun-selling).

In public affairs our society is also recognizably MacIntyre's when we preoccupy ourselves primarily with means and efficiency, rather than engaging in discussion about common ideals and ultimate ends. It is instructive, for example, to analyse political debate about educa-tion and health care. The debate in the 1980s and early 1990s in the UK *may* have assumed certain common ends, but has been very wary about articulating them and relating them to any wider community of values. Instead, it has been much more confident in discussing cost-efficiency as the chief guiding criterion for policy.

Another test of this tendency might be to mark the changes in the meaning of 'professionalism'. It is being represented as a social virtue, and being extended into nearly all areas of social practice (including church life).[25] But as this happens its characteristic use now has less and less to do with the ultimate ends and values of the enterprise, and much more to do with the effectiveness with which the enterprise is carried out. In other words, its meaning has become elided with man-agement expertise.

Granted, a point could also be made about counter-reaction, in relation to all these issues. Under the acute and often bitter gaze of the novelist (for example) the therapist is now sometimes being dethroned.[26] And, arguably, recent work practices have now begun to stress the relationship of an enterprise with a wider community of values (such as environmentalism). The debate about health care has also taken a step back from the *language* of cost-efficiency. Indeed, much of the language of bureaucratic individualism in general is being moderated. As indicated, the language of communitarianism is bid-ding to supplant it.

However, it is hard to assess the status of this reaction. A new language can (cynically) still be driven by and mask other meanings. And it must be said that the social attitudes against which any reaction struggles are still deeply ingrained.

Moreover, in other areas the evidence is still increasing in support of MacIntyre's analysis. Perhaps most significant, I suggest, is the oblique but telling evidence of increasing civil litigation, particularly in matters of compensation and damages. Just because expertise and efficiency is prized and open to rational debate then the public also expects redress for any proven negligence and inefficiency. The relent-less quest for truth after public disasters such as Zeebrugge, Pipa Alpha, Clapham (in the UK) and the 'friendly fire' incidents of the

Gulf conflict, may be represented to us simply as the emotional needs of distraught relatives of the victims. But in fact the intensity of it is also being fuelled by these powerful social expectations for efficiency. These arise precisely when a culture has become 'bureaucratically individualist': that is, a culture where the only area of public accountability left for individuals to pursue has to do with managerial expertise, rather than those ultimate ideals and ends which now belong only to the preference of individuals themselves. In other words, the emotional intensity of the quest for legal redress has become morally charged: we are to 'blame' for any negligence in the same way (almost) that the hooligan is to be blamed for his deliberate violence. It is as though the moral energy of individuals is so frustrated by the confines of the private self that it is being diverted into the public arena according to one of the few common criteria still allowed: efficiency.

This is a specific instance of the more general disposition of blame, accusation and conflict in our common discourse, which is hardly abating. Attitudes of young males in housing estates and increased litigation are therefore equally symptoms of this much more broadly-based phenomenon. The point is essentially the same for both, and still arises plausibly out of MacIntyre's analysis. That is, where there is no common rationality or morality, competing groups develop internal criteria of discourse to serve their own interests. This leads inevitably to the rhetoric of mutual suspicion, accusation and hostility between groups (and especially against authority, if power or privilege is under threat).[27]

Clearly, if this is anything like a fair portrait of our culture it is a cause for grave concern. Its assessment is overwhelmingly negative. MacIntyre himself does not hide his despondency, nor withhold his judgement. But – *is* it a fair and balanced picture?

Charles Taylor provides a useful complement to the analysis. To a large extent he endorses the view that we are caught in a modern malaise of individualism. We are no longer 'locked into a given place, role and station' which 'gave meaning to the world and to the activities of social life'.[28] These orders and hierarchies are now discredited, and although we may have gained a sense of individual freedom we have concomitantly lost meaning, purpose and the 'heroic' ideal of living (and dying) for something greater than ourselves: the world has suffered 'disenchantment'.[29] Taylor also characterizes the prevailing preoccupation with efficiency and cost-benefit analysis of actions as another, closely related, malaise. He calls this the primacy of 'instrumental reason', and acknowledges its moral ambivalence; when wedded to technological and bureaucratic power it becomes threatening, not liberating:

> There is . . . widespread unease that instrumental reason not only has enlarged its scope but also threatens to take over our lives. The fear is that things that ought to be determined by other criteria will be decided in terms of efficiency or 'cost-benefit' analysis, that the independent ends that ought to be guiding our lives will be eclipsed by the demands to maximize output.[30]

Returning to some of the basic ingredients of individualism he specifically warns against excessive concern with self-realization. Centering on the self 'shuts out' the self from greater issues and 'flattens' or 'narrows' the quality of human existence. Likewise, certain kinds of individualism lead inexorably to extreme forms of relativism, which again cut us off from each other and reality beyond us. All this echoes much of MacIntyre.

Yet he also softens the analysis and evaluation in some respects, and balances it by other concerns. He is more willing than MacIntyre to point up the moral gains made by some aspects of individualism. The notion of self-fulfilment, for example, has moral force behind it which distinguishes it sharply from mere egoism. When people feel 'called' or obliged to fulfil themselves they are using the language of a truly moral discourse. This arises from the uniqueness of individual personal identity which we have already identified in the conceptual analysis of core ideas: that is, the differences between individuals have a moral significance, and it is a moral ideal to be (uniquely) me, and to be 'true to my own originality'.[31] And there are other examples which Taylor uses to give due weight to the positive contribution individualistic notions have made, not just historically but also in some of the prevailing tendencies of contemporary society.

Furthermore, although Taylor clearly remains concerned to check the excesses of individualism, it is interesting to note how this is often done precisely by appeal to the moral force behind its own core notions. That is, he shows how extreme forms of individualism are self-contradictory in terms of their own (moral) goals. Thus he grants that self-realization and originality *are* goods to pursue. But because self-fulfilment is also defined (in part) by relations with other people and their originality, it cannot be pursued or construed in isolation. Egoism cannot therefore *sensibly* follow from a *proper* understanding of individualistic ideals. He offers a similar analysis of the self-defeating nature of extreme relativism. For the possibility of *significant* personal choice, required by the ideal of autonomy, actually depends on acknowledging a common horizon of *shared* significance.[32] This constant appeal to the moral force of core notions of individualism therefore provides a useful rider to the overall thrust of MacIntyre's polemic, and echoes much of the initial analysis of individualism which was positive.

Nonetheless, in the final analysis Taylor is still employing these positive ingredients of individualism as part of a critique of a society in which they have become corrupted into something distinctly threatening. So while he may be adopting a mediating position it is still a position which signals a serious criticism of our society.

Moreover, there are also similar critiques being offered from experience of other cultures. There is acute observation of our western malaise, for instance, from Carver Yu who writes out of Chinese origins. His theological critique of western dualism and individualism may be somewhat neglected, but it focuses well some telling points of connection with MacIntyre and Taylor.[33]

Foremost for Yu is the way in which western culture has become an extreme expression of materialism and objectification. This too implies false isolation of individuals – who are separated from their external environment, each other and their own selves. They are technologically able to dominate and control these 'externals', but precisely by treating them as external. We are therefore alienated from any unifying context of meaning (unlike Indian culture which largely rejects the external altogether, and Chinese culture which takes its place as the mean between these two extremes).

Yu finds the symptoms of this predicament most evident in the pessimism of modern literature. From Eliot's *Wasteland* to Auden's *The Age of Anxiety* he sifts out symbols of the self's fragmentation and isolation. More specifically, through Kafka, Camus, Joyce, and back to Eliot's *Prufrock*, he identifies the familiar themes of dislocation and loss: fractured meaning, personal identity and personal relations.

These are hardly new insights, and some of his analysis is portrayed with perilously broad strokes of the brush. But it reinforces much of the previous picture. And what is perhaps more notable is the attention he draws to particular philosophical developments in his critique of individualistic ideas. For he insistently earmarks that particular Greek tradition of thought which conceives of the 'really real' as being '*in itself*', an individual thing apart from its relations with other things.[34] According to Yu it is this, ultimately, which issues in the human being's isolated search inwards in his or her own individual self for all truth, value and capacities for understanding.

By referring to this seminal Greek tradition of ontology, Yu therefore vindicates further our previous caution about oversimplifying historical origins. Notions of the autonomy of individual reason, and inwardness, are key actors in a long drama. They have taken the stage of our history in their modern guise quite recently, but were always incipient in the previous acts. And it is this drama as a whole which has issued inexorably in our modern malaise. Even more important, this reference to ontology also raises the specific question of alternatives. That is, is there any *other* ontological basis of personhood – one which can sustain the moral power of core ideas of individualism, but without encouraging their development in disastrous social consequences? This clearly needs more attention.

So there is more to come. But at least this much can be said now, as preliminary evaluation. The core ideas of individualism are profoundly ambivalent. They have the capacity to be powerful ingredients in a positive moral and social vision, to regulate pernicious social tendencies. At the same time they have been embodied in destructive and self-defeating practices. They can be handmaids to injustice and catalysts to fragmentation. Our current situation of instability and reaction reflects their ambivalence acutely. It drives us, therefore, to examine further the basis both of social unease and the nature and ontology of individuality itself.

4

Individualism and Definitions of Personhood:
Extending the Analysis

Widespread and profound dissatisfaction with contemporary culture is hardly unique to our own. It is endemic to the processes of civilization. And it provokes the obvious question of whether our particular state of unease (about individualism) merits radical reaction, or whether it deserves a more measured appraisal. The question is sharpened by the very ambivalence of our moral framework which has been highlighted. How are babies and bathwater to be safely separated out in any process of change?

Addressing this question leads inexorably into further analysis of the situation itself. For a start, the question might seem to imply that change can be consciously intended, or resisted, and that either could in some way be politically *managed*. But does our current situation allow this?

To some extent it does. I have already indicated that there is a growing consensus of anti-individualistic rhetoric from media, political, social and theological commentators. There is much talk now of being in community, belonging and individual responsibilities to the community, as distinct from rights over against it. In the political arena this can cross traditional party boundaries and battlelines. It is by no means all rhetoric, but includes serious attempts at recasting political philosophy.[1] All this can inform and change policy. There is therefore an important sense in which reaction *is* calculated, calculable and conscious.

But there is also a sense in which it may be precipitated and driven by uncontrolled and unconscious dynamics of our situation. After all, if the preceding portraits of our culture are anywhere near accurate, then they carry within them the seeds of *inevitable* change. If indeed our individualism has driven us into fragmentation and isolation; if we are therefore suffering metaphysical unease about our very identity; if we have been forced to become fractured people flailing around desperately for new horizons of meaning and relation; then these profound conceptual and ontological confusions will also have made us psychologically and socially unstable. So the reaction may not be just contained and rational; it may not be just a matter of measured disapproval of some unfortunate by-products of excessive individualism; it may not just involve some managerial fine-tuning to curb the manipulative or depersonalizing effects of the efficiency drive: it might be convulsive and extreme. It might well rule out any managed or rational re-ordering of our common life. It might mean that all constructive proposals to re-awaken *any* tradition of common life might be impossible (a criticism often levelled at MacIntyre's positive proposals about the revival of some sort of Aristotelian–Thomist world-view).[2]

In fact a more sanguine appraisal of our current situation is possible, as I have already noted (and I shall return to this). Nonetheless, I have no doubt that there is evidence of at least some sense of convulsion, which certainly operates at the level of *ideas*, as well as at other levels. Some of the more extreme deconstruction of post-modernist ideas is already evidence that we are being driven by just such subterranean reaction. Stephen Clark has commented astutely that we have not yet recognized the extent of the self's instability at the intellectual level of interdisciplinary discourse: 'political philosophers have not quite caught up with the radical dismemberment of personal unity that is occurring nowadays amongst psychologists and philosophers of mind or action'.[3] My point now is that this multi-levelled evidence of instability about the self may be reinforcing a kind of cumulative reaction, as each level of experience and discourse feeds off the other.

One theoretical outcome of a such deep-rooted reaction is all too obvious. In any situation of extreme instability it is palpably easy to lurch from individualism into collectivism. There is, after all, a notorious historical and conceptual link between the two. We have already noted the way in which core ideas of individualism have been grafted, paradoxically, into Marxism; and how Nazism elevated autonomy into a kind of collective egotism for the master race.[4] Conceptually it is easy to see why such apparent anomalies occur. Both Yu[5] and Gunton[6] have made the point forcefully that an atomistic conception of fragmented, unrelated, particulars actually means they *lose* their differentiating value: they have become the same, precisely because they are all 'unrelated particulars'. As such they are therefore much more susceptible to fusion: that is, to the collectivist programme of uniformity and the morally disastrous goal of subsuming the part in the whole. It has long been recognized that the extremes of individualism and collectivism are not far from each other.

But before even beginning to suggest alternatives to that far point of reaction, Clark's point needs picking up. What has happened to our fundamental ideas and beliefs about the self and personal identity? What theories of individual personhood have undergirded the kind of culture we now inhabit – and what beliefs about the self are emerging from it? Is total deconstruction inevitable, or is there some possibility of constructive consensus, at least at this level of discourse? This is an aspect of individualism which our discussion has not yet addressed directly. Yet it is clearly integral both to the phenomenon as a whole, and to our reaction to it. In other words, extending the conceptual analysis of individualism at this deeper level may help both its evaluation and the wider task of identifying a way forward.

To begin with this task will be fairly straightforward. The basic understanding of individuality which has burgeoned in an individualistic culture is easily characterized, and just as easily criticized. It embodies a widely acknowledged flaw, which it will be simple to identify. A viable alternative which commands some sort of consensus may be much harder to secure. But at least the map can be laid out. For if any kind of stability can be found here, in our fundamental definitions of individuality and personhood, then we would have vital terrain on which to stand ground and stake out the outlines of a positive social vision. In so far as we are looking not just for a clear-minded critique of where we are and how we travelled here, but a positive vision to work towards, then this is at least worth the attempt. Reactions, after all, are much better controlled by what they are *for*, than what they are against!

Defining the individual

Critique of the abstract individual

The flaw in much recent portrayal of individuality is a familiar one, and has emerged implicitly throughout much of the preceding analysis. The modern sense of self has been consistently characterized as isolated and fragmented, divided within, and cut off from any wider community of values (apart from the bureaucratic). *And this arises inexorably from a particular and entirely inadequate assumption about how the individual is formed: namely, as self-originating, in all his or her most significant characteristics.*

This has been evident throughout the discussion. A tendency of much social contract theory and subsequent utilitarian theory makes precisely this assumption. As we saw, it is based on a view of the individual as a self-sufficient independent centre of consciousness, the *sole* generator of his or her own desires, preferences and choices (social organization is therefore an external contrivance constructed by individuals to serve their needs and wants). It is an a-historical and a-social definition of individuality, sometimes dubbed as the 'abstract' individual (or the liberal self).[7] It allows little or no sense that the individual may be formed by, and a bearer of, historical and social forces, in addition to his or her own self-generated thoughts and actions.

Such an understanding of individuality has been nothing if not pervasive and influential. And it simply will not do. There are no such things as individuals conceived apart from their historical and social setting. We are formed as individual persons, at least in part, by our conscious and unconscious relationship with the past and with other persons and social realities in the present. This is a massive consensus verdict of both sociological and psychological anthropology (and certainly not one from which most Christian theology would dissent, as we shall see). Concrete processes of recent history also contribute, however paradoxically, to this consensus. As Marx was already observing in his own penetrating critique of eighteenth-century tendencies:

> . . . the period in which this view of the isolated individual becomes prevalent, is the very one in which the interrelations of society . . . have reached the highest state of development. Man is in the most literal sense of the word a *zoon politikon*, not only a social animal, but an animal which can develop into an individual only in society.[8]

Nor is such consensus easily disturbed by the anxiety that only some kind of abstract individualism can safeguard the basic ideas of individualism against collectivism or tyranny. On this point Stephen Clark remains unimpressed, and implacable in his critique:

> I remain baffled that anyone should suppose that the only way of avoiding Marxism (or in times past the Bourbons) is to believe in the existence of abstract individuals. The institutions of a free society, which I wholeheartedly support, are best served by acknowledging what we really are: nodes on a web, elements of a wider whole, creatures utterly dependent for their lives and minds and

welfare on the communities of which knowingly or unknowingly
they are a part. 'The patriot', so Berkeley said, '. . . considers
himself as part of a whole, the knave considers himself as the
whole'.[9]

Exactly so. And Clark presses home his attack on the abstract individual equally in response to more recent liberal theories of justice and
utilitarian calculations of happiness:

> We live and act and have our beings in established crafts and
> communities. There is nothing humanly recognizable that human
> individuals *would* be like if they had not grown up in a community,
> and we cannot sensibly ask ourselves what wholly deracinated, soli-
> tary, uninformed 'intelligences' would agree on if they had to . . .[10]

The onslaught on deficient definitions of individuality has also
received momentum from recent reflection on specific political programmes. John Gray chastizes the 'New Right' for failing at just this
point: that is, for swallowing uncritically the assumptions of social
contract theory and neglecting the 'historical basis of political allegiance in a shared history and a common culture . . .'. This arose
'because they had imbibed from liberal individualism the denatured
fiction of the person, the Kantian subject that lacks any particular
identity and has a history only by accident'.[11] He insists that in fact we
are *not* 'Mill's sovereign selves, parading our individuality before an
indifferent world . . . that human individuality is not a natural fact
but a cultural achievement . . . The matrix of human individuality is
a cultural environment in which people are *formed* [emphasis mine] as
choosers with responsibility for their actions';[12] 'human individuals
are not natural data . . . but artefacts of social life, cultural and historical achievements . . . exfoliations of the common life. Without
common forms of life, there are no individuals.'[13]

Historical, political and conceptual critiques of the abstract individual may also be married to anthropological observation. Language
and custom reveal that our sense of self is radically different depending on how we are placed within a cultural framework by others. It is
in acquiring language and other social practices that we thereby gain a
sense of self (argues Harré, for instance), and the evidence for this lies
precisely in cross-cultural variations in self-awareness. Thus Eskimos
have a weaker sense of self than western individuals, and their language is correspondingly deficient in proper personal pronouns (their
sense of *individual* responsibility, as distinct from corporate, moral

responsibility, is consequently weak). The Japanese tend to 'compart-
mentalize' their sense of self (and therefore their moral responsibility
or obligation) according to particular social situations, and their
language reveals a correspondingly high degree of complexity in self-
referential expressions.[14]

These are just a few examples of dissatisfaction with any abstract
'universalized' notion of the individual. Others could easily be added,
especially from sources in psychology. Together they give a fair indication of how it appears to fail the test of empirical evidence, common
sense and conceptual analysis. And taken in conjunction with the
preceding discussion about our current situation, it is clear that recent
history has indeed discredited it. As we have seen, its chief characteristic of isolating the individual from his or her social history, in order
to preserve private ideals in a distinct world, describes just the symptoms of our own malaise. It is one of the most significant factors lying
behind MacIntyre's summary claim, that 'twentieth century social life
turns out in key part to be the concrete and dramatic re-enactment of
eighteenth century philosophy'.[15]

Its flaws are also apparent in some extreme developments of utilitarian theory. I have already noted that the logic of utilitarianism can
be developed over against the welfare of actual individuals, and this is
due in large measure to the *abstraction* of individuals.

The most dangerous developments of utilitarianism occur like this.
In so far as the criterion of right action is conceived primarily as the
maximizing of pleasure and minimizing of suffering, and if this is calculated on a purely quantitative basis, it can give rise to grotesque
proposals for dealing with large-scale situations. For instance, it has
been suggested that whole populations should be written off without
aid, to wither under the ravages of famine and disease as the only
effective form of population control in certain developing countries.
The utilitarian justification for this is to weigh the suffering it would
permit against the much greater suffering which would ensue for
greater numbers of people if yet more generations were kept alive by aid
merely to live and die in similar poverty.

With origins in Thomas Malthus, this kind of proposal has been
espoused more recently by Garrett Hardin and others.[16] As an ethical
theory it expresses a tough-minded, if terrifying, commitment to help
only where there is likely to be long-term benefit. It is a policy which
received considerable impetus from principles adopted in battlefield
situations: in order to use limited medical facilities most effectively
casualties were divided into those who would not survive even with

aid, those who would recover without it, and those who would only recover with it: only the last of the three categories was treated (the so-called 'ethics of triage').

But however relentless the surface logic, the flaws in the underlying theory are apparent:

(1) It assumes suffering (or pleasure) are quantifiable concepts, transferrable as a 'fixed-price' commodity between individuals. This in turn treats individuals precisely as abstract units, capable of experiencing the same kind of pleasure or pain in the same way, such that it can be added up and compared quantitatively. But in fact individuals are formed out of a complex historical and social web of relations to such an extent that we cannot *simply* compare one individual's suffering with another's: the same outward circumstances will be textured in a different way precisely because individuals' subjectivity is differently formed by our varying communal context. Thus the mathematical calculation of this kind of utilitarian theory is a rational abstraction from actual experience, and cannot work reliably.

(2) It also assumes future possible people are equivalent in value to actual people (and therefore that the greater numbers foreseen in the future must take precedence). This is another form of abstraction. After all, the future does not yet exist so it is intrinsically unpredictable, and unknowable (at least to us). So although we must make provision for the future we cannot possibly relate to it *in the same way* as we relate to people in the present.

(3) Such a policy is also likely to be subject to infinite regress. To put it at its simplest: once we arrive in the 'future', what guarantee is there that we shall not feel bound to apply the same criterion of action to *that* generation? In other words, we might always refer our moral responsibility forwards, and never fulfil it in relation to actual people. Again, this betrays a process of abstraction (and it is hard not to suspect a deliberately hidden agenda lying behind apparently good intentions).

Some of the most basic ideas of individualism (and even of some forms of utilitarianism itself) would certainly check the development of this sort of doctrine.[17] That is why I have spoken of the paradoxes of utilitarianism. The specific point highlighted here, however, is to note the way in which the notion of an abstract individual acts so perniciously in that development. A mature notion of the *actual* social and historical individual is always going to be necessary to act as a salutary check to the construction of such extreme rational theories about abstract individuals. (The crucial question of whether core ideas of individualism can be easily detached from the abstract individual and wedded to more concrete notions of individuality will be dealt with later.)

Post-abstract alternatives

But what of an alternative notion of individuality and personhood? In one general sense this critique of the abstract individual has already generated its own alternative. The individual must be conceived as a 'concrete' or 'corporate' reality formed and sustained out of the social interaction of many causes. Any adequate understanding of individuality must acknowledge this, and the construction of social order must presuppose it. And I suppose that when it is cast in such general terms it would not be hard to claim a large degree of consensus for this sort of portrait of personhood.

But of course this by no means completes the second part of our task. On its own it is too bland. It will require far more rigorous scrutiny if it is going to be of any use. Is it going to be sustainable, particularly in the light of recent analytic work on personal identity? Will not this too deconstruct into disunity and fragmentation? Is it still compatible with the positive moral force of core ideas of uniqueness, autonomy, originality and so on? These general queries in turn generate more specific questions. If our individuality is formed out of a shared genetic and social inheritance, in what sense (if any) is anything uniquely or originally 'me'? Could what is socially formed as 'me' *develop* some capacities for creativity or *gain* some unique value, even though its origin is collective? Would such an 'I' really endure as a unitary subject of experience, or am 'I' just a succession of experiences forged out of the relations which continually make and re-make 'me'? Even though I normally have a *sense* of self as a being with a unique, enduring, personal identity, is this sense itself illusory (or at least unverifiable); is it simply an arbitrary function of our particular social structure and language, with no more claim to truth than that of any other culture which produces radically different senses of self? Would a dualist doctrine of inner soul or substance (highly contentious) be necessary to sustain my sense of an enduring personal identity?

Such questions have to be addressed not merely to secure the theoretical underpinning of any definition of individuality: they also bear directly on the credibility of the moral ideas we have been dealing with (and so, indirectly, on any positive social vision which may emerge). For example, if the genetic and social formation of the concrete individual is construed in wholesale, radical terms, then we may have reconstructed him or her *simply* and *solely* as a complex transmitter of preceding causes. This would amount to a strong form of determinism, incompatible with any significant sense of autonomy. A core moral idea of individualism would be discredited *in itself* (and could not even be used in a inspirational or regulatory way). So the possibility of canvassing some less radical sense of determinism would become essential. Likewise, if an individual's uniqueness is still to count as a core value, it would need to be demonstrated that what arises out of a complex of other causes is no less irreplaceable than that which is purely or mostly self-generated. If not, what theoretical basis is left to secure the individual against dangerous devaluation? In other words, as Clark's swift move (above) to defend a free, non-collectivist society implies, there is at least a *prima facie* risk the corporate coup against the abstract individual will replace one tyranny with another. Only further definition will determine whether that is necessarily the case (Clark clearly thinks not). And only additional analysis will show whether the variety of possible answers to these questions entirely confounds the prospect of consensus.

In offering some further comments in this area I should immediately make a couple of disclaimers. I am making no pretence at original insight. Nor can I refer here to the whole field of enquiry – which is vast and complex. My aim is far more limited: only to stipulate some definitions to determine whether there is any possibility of stability or consensus; also, to clarify the logical relations of such definitions with some of the moral ideas and values we have been discussing. In short, it is simply an introduction to the range of possible positions and prospects.

Broadly speaking the debate at the analytical level divides in these ways. There are those who maintain that personal identity (which distinguishes one individual from another) consists in a simple unanalysable 'centre', unique to each individual person: a 'substance' (or soul) of a different order or category to anything else. As such it is distinct from body, brain, or even psychological continuities and connections (such as memory). On this view these latter categories certainly relate to personal identity, and may in some measure count as evidence for it, but do not constitute it. This notion therefore establishes a basis for enduring personal identity regardless of physical or psychological changes in a person, however radical. It can allow for the fact that our *sense* of selfhood may indeed be fluid and fluctuating across cultures (or, in some cultures, even within the life span of a single individual), and that this is a consequence of social interactions with others, transmitted in various ways. Nonetheless, there is an enduring, unitary ground to this socially formed self which transcends the flux and secures the self in its fundamental uniqueness, originality and ultimate identity. The view has its ancestry in Cartesian dualism, but has been refined considerably to meet sustained anti-dualist arguments over many years. It remains as a minority report, but vigorously maintained.[18]

The challenge to it is issued at various levels. Most radically, there is straightforward materialism. This denies that mind in general, and consciousness of selfhood in particular, is anything other than a function of neurophysiological events in the brain. Nor is there anything else to personal identity. So individual personal identity is defined only though a physiologically constituted channel which has itself been determined by preceding natural causes. This might be unique, but only in the trivial sense that any particular configuration of atoms (like a tree or stone) is unique. It certainly has no capacities for autonomy or self-origination. In these terms the only sense in which personal identity would have continuity would have to depend on the contingency of physiological resemblances recurring through time.

This sort of outright reductionism should also be filed as a minority view. But there are various mediating positions. John Searle is a case in point, offering a non-dualist, non-materialist 'naturalism'.[19] This is best described as a coalescing of concepts, whereby the phenomenon of consciousness compels us to re-categorize the mental and physical as real concepts which define each other, rather than defining distinct 'substances' or the one reducing to the other without remainder. For our purposes the key notion this permits is that consciousness (and therefore a potential sense of selfhood) emerges out of the brain, but *then also has causal properties itself.* Although Searle himself is wary of pressing this too far, it at least lays the conceptual groundwork for a notion of personal identity in which a particular causal account of its origin does not necessarily preclude its capacity for originality and autonomy.

Then there are other major contributions about the nature of personal identity which are grounded neither in ultimate dualism nor materialism. Most of these have some ancestry in Locke's seminal views about the significance of memory in which the key criterion of personal identity is the capacity to recall experiences and actions of the past *as one's own*: that is, to report them in first-person memory claims.

Some obvious flaws in this (not least amnesia!) have required the criterion to be revised significantly: that is, it is some form of psychological continuity which constitutes personal identity, rather than simply the specific phenomenon of conscious recollections. This is summarized by Noonan like this:

> Besides direct memories, there are several other kinds of direct psychological connection. One such connection is that which holds between an intention and later act in which this intention is carried out. Other such direct psychological connections are those which hold when a belief or desire or another psychological feature, persists. These direct psychological connections are accessible to consciousness, but others need not be. Thus we can count as direct psychological connections the links between childhood experiences and adult character traits, fears and prejudices . . . [20]

And even this needs further elaboration if the position is to out-flank the logical problems posed by the hypothetical possibility of reduplication (that is, the same psychological continuities apparently existing in more than one 'person', for example after brain bisection and transplantation into another body).

But, granted such refinement, the basic position is quite widely held to be sustainable. As such it would allow some principle of continuity in personal identity persisting in the interplay between its self-creation and its constitution by social relations.

On the other hand, there are other notions of personal identity, appealing to different senses of psychological connectedness, which offer a far less secure account of the continuity of the individual person. The most influential of these recently has been championed by Derek Parfit.[21] What matters, for Parfit, is not that 'I' exist throughout time (or beyond) with enduring personal identity: rather, it matters only that persons should exist in the future who have the same psychological characteristics (thoughts, concerns, desires, intentions and so on) as I currently experience. So if, hypothetically, these could be transferred into some other future person (as a kind of replica), then this matters more than 'my' survival.

There seem to me various ways of reading this sort of proposal, but with a common outcome. One is to take it as a definition of personal identity which (notionally) separates it off from that bundle of psychological characteristics which is transferrable, and in so doing trivializes its significance. It really doesn't matter if 'I' survive at all (in that sense).

The other is to assume that the Parfitean project is not primarily concerned with defining what personal identity consists in, only with its significance. In effect it is asking existential rather than onto-logical–metaphysical questions: not so much what I am but rather 'what is it about myself that matters to me now?' And the answer is not some intuited notion of an enduring irreducible personal identity, but simply that 'mind-set' which constitutes my current experience. Provided some person is connected to *that* then I am content that should exist, whether or not it falls under the usual definitions of what constitutes 'me'. Of course, this too diminishes the significance of personal identity. In so far as such mind-sets might change radically through time, then on this view there would be successive (different) personal identities. But there would be no enduring 'I' to own them.

If widely accepted this would certainly dissolve any notion of secure, enduring personal identity, at least in theoretical terms. But there are powerful objections to it, morally, intuitively and conceptually.

After all, if 'I' do not exist (or do not care whether I exist) in the future with the same fundamental personal identity as I now own, then to what extent need I acknowledge responsibility for my actions with long-term consequences? Moreover, so far as our attitudes to others are concerned, this is a notion which might allow value to other persons in the present, but fails to provide a secure basis for respect-ing that particular individual in relation to his or her past or future. So it has a strangely flattening effect in human relations (and a potentially chilling one of we reduced the very young or elderly to their purely present personhood – unrelated to the wider narrative of their lives). If that criticism fails to carry weight, then there is always robust common sense – which reminds us amongst other things that we subscribe to pension schemes (presumably on the basis that we think we *shall* be the same person in the future!). Common sense also reminds us that we simply *cannot* sensibly think ourselves out of being some sort of enduring, unitary subject of experience. After all, our very capacity for conceptual thought presupposes an ability to correlate and compare particulars (to gain a 'universal' or generic sense), *over a period of time*. It is not so easy to see how this could occur merely on the basis of successive replications of bundles of experiences.

By contrast, and more promisingly, MacIntyre bases his definition of individuality and the unity of personal identity precisely on that wider narrative through time. This is conceived both in terms of the

past and future of the person concerned and, crucially, how that
person is formed and shaped within the wider narrative of the community to which he or she belongs. This gives a certain continuity of
meaning to the identity of individuals, while allowing that they are
also subject to change both in their own inner consciousness and their
'outer' circumstances. It is when the individuals are isolated from that
wider narrative of the community that they lose a sense of their
personal identity (though without necessarily losing all actual continuity of selfhood) – the very nub of MacIntyre's analysis of what is
occurring in our contemporary culture, as we have noted.

Paul Ricoeur provides a similar though not identical view, again
through an analysis of narrative (which for Ricoeur includes fictional
narrative, much more than for MacIntyre).[22] He offers a penetrating
critique of Parfit's position based chiefly on a distinction between
personal identity as *sameness*, and as *selfhood*. The former can certainly
dissolve, provoking Parfit's question: that is, 'Does my personal identity *matter*, when it is so subject to change and decay?' But this in
turn invites the further question, 'To whom does it not matter?' This
question implies that there is still a self to whom that question can
be addressed. In other words, there is a still some unitary sense of
personal identity (selfhood) which persists through the narrative of a
changing life. This remains the case even when both the narrative and
the sense of identity (as sameness) break down completely together:

> Even in the most extreme cases of the loss of sameness-identity of
> the hero, we do not escape the problematic of selfhood. A non-
> subject is not nothing, with respect to the category of the subject.
> Indeed, we would not be interested in the drama of dissolution and
> would not be thrown into perplexity by it, if the non-subject were
> not still a figure of the subject . . . [23]

In short, an analysis of narrative leads Ricoeur to posit some sort of
unity of selfhood, whatever fragmentation occurs in some aspects of
our identity. It is also through narrative that he unfolds the particular
nature of this self as that which is constituted by otherness. This is
elaborated in three ways, as the otherness of one's own body, of other
persons and of the self to its self ('conscience'). Such dialectic between
selfhood and otherness is fundamental to selfhood (even more fundamental than the contrast between sameness and selfhood). It signals
a relational and dynamic ontology of personhood but, as we have suggested, without denying the possibility of a persisting unitary self as
well.[24]

To be sure, the appeal to narrative as a basis for understanding personhood does not of itself presuppose or predetermine any particular kind of narrative. The question of which particular narrative tradition we can or should belong to is not settled by this analysis alone (and MacIntyre has been hard-pressed to justify the apparent arbitrariness of how that 'choice' is determined).[25] So this means that the task of charting the logical relations of a narrative concept of personal identity with moral ideas and social order can only be done in a contextualized way. It will require scrutiny of a particular narrative tradition considered in its own terms (the task of the second half of this essay). But given this contextualization, a narrative understanding of self certainly takes its place as another possible approach to personal identity.

All this therefore maps out something of the diversity in the post-abstract world of personal identity. What it also reveals is at least one underlying reason for such variety: a disagreement about ontology.

Thus the substance dualist who defines personal identity according to Cartesian antecedents (however revised) is likely to be operating within a tacit ontological framework in which the 'real' is that which exists 'in and for itself'. As we have seen, this can be traced back to a certain kind of Greek ontology, reflecting a basic view of reality in which introverted or self-contained subjectivity necessarily becomes the locus for all truth, value and reality.[26] Given such an ontological framework individuals find their identity easily and essentially to be a solid, stable reality. Fluidity, or any claim that identity is constituted or diminished by relations with other realities, is possible to sustain, but harder to accommodate. I have indicated that such relational notions *can* ride on the back of this sort of ontology. But they tend to relate to the main definition of personal identity more as epicycles than essence.

By contrast, much of post-modernity has become deeply suspicious of ontology in general, and especially any ontological basis to individual personhood and subjectivity. As we have noted, much recent analysis of subjectivity and selfhood demonstrates that it does not exist in and for itself but is essentially constituted by otherness and relation. And as such this may both presuppose and confirm a dissolution of *all* ontological frameworks. It characteristically cuts the ground from under the feet of substantial definitions of personal identity. At its most radical it offers little or no possibility for understanding the individual as an end in himself or herself or an enduring self on the basis of some fundamental view of what is 'really real'. The self is only 'really' individualized at all in response to other realities, none of which have any substantial identity themselves. This naturally issues in understandings of personal identity which begin at the opposite end: the given is flux, transcience and shifting relations; any stability or continuity has to be found. (Levinas is particularly instructive in this respect.[27])

This means the ontological question is often simply sidestepped. Commitment to ontology is declined, even where it is not explicitly disavowed. It is enough, for some, to construct an understanding of personal identity out of an amalgam of phenomenological methodology and moral intuition, without explicit ontological commitment. This itself allows for considerable diversity: without the constraint of any particular ontological framework, conceptual pluralism abounds.

So does this leave any basis at all for some stability or common ground, at least at this level of conceptual analysis? Complete consensus clearly is out of the question. But are there at least some points of connection to get hold of? Tentatively I suggest there are, and that the following *has* emerged:

(1) All positions outlined above acknowledge some social constitution of our *sense* of selfhood (while disputing whether that sense is an essential and sufficient definition of individual personal identity, or merely partial).

(2) At the same time most positions, though not all, attempt to offer some basis for a measure of continuity and stability in their definitions of personal identity. For even if they feel they have sloughed off the shackles of outmoded substance ontology, there is still some constraint from the 'primitive' first-person experience of subjectivity and narrative notions of selfhood which requires *some* sort of principle of unity. (And where even this much seems unwanted, by Parfit for example, then there are powerful criticisms of the kind I have outlined.)

(3) Apart from extreme materialism, many positions are still defined to some extent by the possibility of an individual's originality, uniqueness, autonomy, self-realization. This was evident, for example, in John Searle's notion of emergence: that which is created out of a complex of various other causes may still have unique causal capacity of its own; it may therefore be conceived as original or irreplaceable, no less than the purely self-generating causality of the abstract individual. (This parallels a point made in our original analysis of autonomy – which can bear a sense implying a measure of freedom to accept or reject

certain values, even though it does not require or claim sole control in the *creation* of all values.)

(4) Finally, although disagreement about ontology is fundamental, the vacuum it leaves need not be the last word. For previous points at least raise the question of canvassing an alternative kind of ontology rather than abandoning it altogether. Their suggestiveness here lies in the evident need to wed a relational definition of individuality with equally profound instincts for principles of continuity and ultimacy. That calls for an ontology in which relation itself participates as an ontological category – which might provide just that basis for stability which is required. So what is 'really real' (for want of a better term) is 'being-in-relation', rather than being in and for itself. This might lead us to rehabilitate some of the conceptual world of the Greek Fathers of the early Christian Church. It picks up Yu's point, and was signalled by Ricoeur's willingness to use some sort of ontological language, albeit in a different way.

This is an issue to which I will be referring more extensively in the next part of the book.[28] For now it is sufficient just to acknowledge its potential significance as a rallying point. We are not necessarily impaled on what would be for many the horns of an impossible choice – between traditional substance ontology and total ontological scepticism.

Reaction and a positive social vision

So what now of the nature of our reaction to the discredited individualism of modernity? I suggest that this brief foray into underlying theories of personal identity helps unravel the reactive web at a number of key points.

In the first instance, just at the intellectual level, wholesale deconstruction of the self and individuality is neither necessary nor dominant. So far as conceptual possibilities are concerned, the resources outlined above are available and potentially constructive. They may well be able to offer some sort of alternative which is at least credible, if not compelling, in the current ferment of modernity and post-modernity. Such an alternative will begin with full acknowledgement that individuals can and must be conceived as social realities: they are only properly and fully formed and sustained by a network of relationships and interactions; persons are only fully found within community (and if it helps to talk more of 'persons' than individuals to reinforce the point, then so be it). But, equally and crucially, it will also sustain some sense of continuity and stability in this notion of personhood, in which each individual endures uniquely and irreplaceably within the flux of changing relationships.

This is the simple but nonetheless sustainable response to the paradox of our current situation in which an abstract understanding of the individual – which originated in the attempt to value individuals – has actually resulted in the reverse: that is, the isolation, fragmentation and 'flattening' of individuals who are reduced to interchangeable units in a rational or bureaucratic system.

As such, this highlights the moral and practical urgency, as well as the conceptual possibilities, of re-conceiving persons in this kind of way. For it is the flawed, abstract understanding of the individual which has been specifically exposed by this analysis as the real poison in the culture of individualism. It is this which has been the chief catalyst in the corruption of core moral ideas into cultures of fragmentation and egotism, or the rationalistic horrors of extreme utilitarian theory. So its concrete alternative must surely help draw the poison.

By the same token, however, this analysis also helps to absolve the core moral ideas of individualism (*qua ideas*) from complete complicity in the flaw of the abstract individual. In fact it further endorses them. For although the nature of the abstract individual associates easily with some core ideas, nothing in this analysis has demonstrated an essential link with them. On the contrary, those core ideas have again been seen to provide a profound moral *critique* of social orders and attitudes which the abstract individual spawns (particularly in relation to some extremes of utilitarianism).

Indeed, far from linking core ideas with the abstract individual, the analysis suggests instead how they are integral to most relational notions of the individual. They actually require such a notion. After all, respect for the unique individual in his or her *concrete* reality depends on full acknowledgement of the unique nexus of relations in which individuals are constituted. And something similar is true for the relationship between the value of self-realization and a social nature of the individual: each entails the other (Taylor's point, noted before).[29]

Moreover, it is clearly these same core moral ideas which would continue to *safeguard* relational ideas of personhood. They do so by preventing them from collapse into mere flux and meaningless deconstruction. This is because a strong sense of autonomy, uniqueness, creativity and so on, requires a measure of stability and continuity in personal identity. A 'person' who is constantly slipping away into another, or subsumed within a whole, has little opportunity to exercize self-realization or original causality in any significant sense. Nor will such a person necessarily command any significant commitment of love and loyalty from others which would help give them a sense of meaning and identity. Core ideas of individualism stand as a bulwark against such reductionism. This emerged particularly in criticism of the Parfitean persons.[30]

So in these ways the moral value and potential 'transcendence' of core ideas of individualism is highlighted again. And because this may be controversial, I must labour the point. They need only be considered controversial if they are deemed to be *irredeemably* infected by their corruption in individualistic culture and their association with notions of the individual as being-in-itself. But the point of this analysis is to show that this is not the case. It only carries weight as a psychological, rather than logical, association of ideas. The fact remains that they may be conceptually divorced from the abstract individual, and are demonstrably eligible for marriage with the social individual instead. It also bears repeating that these core ideas are the very notions which offer the most powerful moral *critique* of abstract individuality and the corruptions of an individualistic society, and so offer a creative impulse for change.

In particular, we should also note how peculiarly apt they may be in precisely this reactive and unstable situation in which we find ourselves. For if indeed there are complex, powerful forces of fragmentation operating in our current malaise then, as already indicated, we shall need more than a renewed vision of the nature of personhood at the intellectual level – important as that is. We shall also require something very much like these ideas to drive such a vision. They are compelling, simple, graspable. They resonate with the deep instincts and influential traditions of the past (both religious and secular), but also demonstrate a capacity to transcend any one particular culture or tradition. They can function as vital moral regulators against extreme reaction; but they are also positive catalysts for change. As such they can help carry a strained, pluralist, society forward in its moral and social vision without requiring the sort of radical severance with the past that merely turns strain into chaos.

To put it more starkly: any reaction which wholly deconstructed them, dismissing them as pernicious abstractions, or as irredeemably contaminated by their context, must find something of equal power and persuasiveness to replace them. It would also be turning its back completely on the narrative and intellectual traditions which have helped generate them. And we have to remember that it is such traditions which help provide the sense of belonging, shared meaning and identity that individuals desperately need for their own fulfilment as relational beings.

So the case for reinforcing and redeeming, rather than rejecting, these core ideas of individualism, when properly wedded to a relational understanding of personhood, remains powerful. Of course both the ideas themselves and any particular view of personhood must also be embodied in a wider tradition, if they are to be truly effective (and we have already acknowledged the difficulty of that). Nonetheless, a start has been made. These core ideas of individualism together with a relational definition of personhood present themselves as clear priorities.

A general conclusion to this analysis and evaluation of individualism therefore looks something like this. A society based chiefly on the isolated individual, which is ultimately locked into its own fragmentation and (paradoxically) destroys the individual too, must and will pass into a new form of social order. This is irresistible. But the process of change and the shape of the new order need not be left unmanaged and uncontrolled by the past. A future order must be based on a more cohesive community of values and relationships, which is the only effective crucible for individuals to be formed, flourish and belong (so narrative traditions and subcultures will have a critical part to play); and this cannot come about without a more corporate and relational notion of individual personhood. But it may also depend on renewed confidence in the core ideas of individualism, for all the reasons given before. *It is therefore the wedding of such core ideas to a relational understanding of individuality which forms the vital pivot on which both stability and change can operate successfully.*[31]

5

A Step towards Practice

What has been offered so far remains at the level of general comments, expressed mostly as abstract possibilities, based on the history and relationship of ideas. And this essay is not presuming to offer much more than this. But if we were to fly a kite in the direction of more practical implications, where might it go? That is, can we say anything more about the general *shape* of social practice, attitude and political structure which might emerge from and sustain these ideas?

To attempt this, even in a rudimentary way, would begin to test the validity of these ideas against a number of present realities. In particular, it would compel us to face the issue of pluralism in more practical terms – as the likely constraining context of any future social vision. That is, we may have to accept that we shall continue to experience an overall social framework within which a variety of subcultures will persist and flourish. And if so, this certainly will affect the shape of the social vision we might wish to construct.

The persistence of pluralism is itself a large assumption. But it follows realistically from the situation we now inhabit. This includes at least one (paradoxical) element of relative stability, which arises out of the following combination of factors. On the one hand we are in some degree pluralist and fragmented, at various levels, as we have seen. We also inhabit a situation of liberal democracy (the relation is complex, and not a necessary one, but it is a concrete historical fact). However, a liberal democracy has at least one resemblance to a lobster pot. While it might just sustain a strongly inherited cultural homogeneity (but only just), it is highly unlikely to create and mould any such homogeneity *once pluralism has entered in*. In other words, what democracy lets in does not get out so easily. Hence the likely persistence of pluralism. (Naturally, some extraordinary socio-political convulsion or religious revival is possible, and the events of the last decades of this century have punctured all certainty and complacency:

75

I have already expressed unease about the peculiar power of unconscious forces of reaction in a situation of fragmentation. So neither
liberal democracy itself nor its pluralism is set in tablets of stone.
Nonetheless, they must remain firmly in view. They are certainly part
of a foreseeable balance of probabilities.)

So much for the assumption. It is significant in so far as it raises
this question. Does the inevitability of *cultural* pluralism of itself necessarily entail the *individual* isolation and fragmentation, which is so
characteristic of our culture? To put it another way: will the theoretical
possibilities of advancing relational definitions of individuality *which
require stable communities of belonging* founder on the practical realities
of pluralism?

I do not think so. For overall homogeneity in every respect is not
necessary. On the contrary, the first step would be to positively affirm
*sub*cultures, *local* communities and *particular* traditions as the legitimate locus of belonging. This is now becoming a familiar plea, but
none the worse for that. Individuals should indeed be encouraged to
be more firmly rooted within such subcultures, to seek their social
identity and reintegrate their social role and private selves within
them. A pluralist situation may well mean that they are less able to do
so in relation to any *overall* social 'stories' or values which purport to
be common to society as a whole. But failure to achieve this latter form
of integration will be less devastating to the extent that the subcultures
are properly valued.

MacIntyre himself seems to be offering something like this proposal at the end of his book. In a celebrated, controversial, and somewhat visionary passage he appears to abandon all hope in the short
term of our society rediscovering a positive moral and cultural cohesion as a whole (he compares the rootlessness and disintegration of our
society with the decline of the Roman Empire). So he looks instead to
small subcultures to keep alive our hope of personal integration: 'what
matters at this stage is the construction of local forms of community
within which civility and the intellectual and moral life can be sustained through the new dark ages which are already upon us'.[1]

In fact this step alone is hardly sufficient – and along with others
I part company with MacIntyre at this point. Put in this way his is
too chilling a counsel of despair, carrying its own dangers of justifying 'ghetto' sect-like communities which cease to relate in any positive
way to the overall political structure of a society – or to other communities within that structure (some churches are only too ready to
withdraw in such a way). It appears to abandon all hope of such a

wider network of shared meaning at a higher level. In effect it replaces an individualism of persons with an individualism of traditions or sub-communities; it risks the creation of new conflicts between traditions, nationalisms and religions.

But if another step is taken such a far point of pluralism need never be reached. This further step must relate to the more difficult task of establishing an overall social framework, rather than a subculture. But I do not see this as impossible, even in a pluralist situation, *precisely when the persistence and potential 'transcendence' of core moral ideas can be so fruitful*. For, as we have seen, when they are divorced from their flawed history (and especially from abstract notions of individuality) they can operate as a cohesive rallying point, commanding widespread allegiance. They provide an overall moral framework which resonates with particular narrative traditions and stories, but they are not themselves an exclusive or divisive 'story'. Moreover, we have also seen that they actually *entail* a general affirmation of the social needs of individuals. In that sense the rationale and value system of that overall framework can and should still include an explicit commitment to enhance, not undermine, the cohesion and effectiveness of sub-communities. This reverses the common perception that cohesive and distinct sub-communities (and traditions) are a *threat* to the wider community of meaning. Instead they are constitutive of it. The state must come to see the flourishing of subcultures as essential to its own rationale.

In this way the overall shape of the social and political vision emerges. For a start, it will require redefining and reining in the parameters of what the state can realistically claim, require, or expect to offer its citizens. It is now primarily related to them as a secondary, supporting framework, operating through the sub-communities which it supports. As John Gray expresses it, it is 'a strong commitment to the intermediary institutions in which individuals are formed and in which for the most part their lives find meaning'.[2] This therefore provides a ready criterion to test the legitimacy and value of any policy or programme operated by the state on behalf of the wider community: namely, does it permit and contribute to the flourishing of local, sub-community life, or does it restrict and constrain it? In effect it is an appeal to *social* consents, rather than individual consent, as a basis for legitimacy.

At the same time it is a form of government which gains authority from a clearly defined and widely accepted set of moral and social values and priorities (and in that sense it is sharply distinguished from economic dogmas of extreme *laissez-faire* policy, and from extreme forms of social pluralism). These priorities, to recapitulate, are to sustain a lively sense of local community and traditions in which individuals can find integration, value and identity; but at the same time to unite the sub-communities in a shared structure of responsibility and citizenship, centred around common core moral ideas – precisely in order to realize this (common) end of personal integration. Thus there remains this crucial structure of moral commitment at the overall level which is also ordered precisely towards the local. The balance is therefore maintained coherently, with local and national concerns reinforcing rather than competing with each other.

To elaborate further: the level at which the most significant social practice will occur, the locus where values and traditions must be cherished and where individuals will best *belong*, will be in a network of local relationships. However commonplace these may be, they actually have immense importance (as the commonplace often does). This is expressed uncompromisingly by Stephen Clark:

> I am indeed suggesting that the 'pre-political' life of human society, the network of families, baby-sitting circles, residents' associations, parents' associations, children's gangs, church guilds, business and informal friendships, colleges and choirs and grocers' shops and pubs, is the most important part of human society. It is this network of 'voluntary associations' and their corresponding obligations – obligations which are not simply what any individual chooses that they should be – which continue to provide us all with a sense of who and what we are.[3]

Such local networks do not fulfil this potential simply through their structural form, as should by now be clear. They are informed, implicitly or explicitly, by particular traditions of belief, usually narrative, religious or 'mythological'. But the essential point remains: this is where personal identity is most obviously and securely celebrated; so there is a clear imperative to endorse actively and celebrate this kind of social interaction at the local level (something, incidentally, which the Church *has* characteristically been involved with). *However*, because all this is pre-eminently the imperative of the state itself as well, it cannot be taken as the description of a self-contained ghetto subculture. Rather, it describes a network of local communities which interpenetrate with others and depend to a considerable extent on an overall structure of social order to sustain (and defend) them.

Such are the general contours of a social vision which might sensibly emerge from the preceding analysis and evaluation. It will be in just this sort of terrain that the best seeds of our inheritance of individualism will flower, and the worst will be held in check. It will provide a context in which the identity and value of individuals can be nurtured and nourished. Local communities of tradition and narrative can and do give that sense of an enduring and irreplaceable self which our deepest intuitions about the nature of personal identity require. Yet they do so precisely through a strong relational view of the individual person which cannot collapse into the black hole of abstract individualism. At the same time, because they are also integrated within the overall purpose of the wider social order, through its core moral ideas, then these local traditions will not in their turn be sucked into sectarianism – another kind of abstraction.

And how does all this translate, if at all, into current terminology? I suppose some of it could be construed as a form of communitarianism. Its acknowledgement of the significance of small communities and their critical role in the formation of persons is certainly characteristic of the movement. On the other hand, its insistence that no local community should exist solely within its own framework of values and tradition sits awkwardly with the more radical relativism of at least some forms of communitarianism. Also, there are clear strands of liberalism in the limits it implies on the role of central government ('liberalism', as already noted, is normally associated with the specifically political dimensions of individualism). And in its general concern to redeem, rather than revoke, core ideas of individualism, it straddles both liberalism and communitarianism. In short, it is not an easy translation.

But I suspect this simply demonstrates the notorious difficulty in defining all such broad movements as communitarianism and liberalism (and individualism itself), rather than betraying any particular incoherence in the discussion itself. Such movements, after all, tend to delineate a coalition of ideas and practices, not all of which are self-evidently mutually exclusive, particularly when their actual policies are compared.[4] So while labelling a vision is always tempting, especially in the cause of communicating it better, perhaps it is a temptation best resisted. This discussion, as with many others, must take its chances: it must stand or fall without making any claims for itself about its precise position within the normal terminology of social and political philosophy.

Limits and requirements

One haunting question remains, however – one which has become even more pressing in the light of this brief foray into social order and practice. Can we even begin to think of working for this sort of shape to society in practice, when the preceding analysis suggested such powerful pressures pulling in the opposite direction? Is the merely theoretical possibility of reinstating core moral ideas and establishing agreed definitions of personhood really sufficient to cohere society at the overall level? And is there sufficient credibility in any particular narrative traditions to provide even 'local' cohesion?

The counter-pressures which force these questions have to do with the wider diagnosis of our modern situation, stressed time and again by MacIntyre, Taylor, Yu, amongst others. For the whole point of what they have been saying is to highlight the extreme difficulty in maintaining precisely those effective networks of community and common values on which persons depend.

This was variously expressed. For MacIntyre the perception that we need to sustain a common narrative tradition of values, *but cannot*, lies at the heart of his diagnosis of the current (western) human condition. For all the reasons enumerated before, including fundamental metaphysical uncertainties, the common tradition has disintegrated and we are cast adrift. There is no truly common tradition, but many traditions *which are themselves largely insecure and isolated*. In other words it is not only the individual self that is fragmented, but the credibility and sustainability of traditions: the very medicine which could heal us is itself seeping out from broken bottles. That, perhaps, is why he advocates the withdrawal of a tradition into relative isolation. It may only survive by paying attention to itself and licking its own wounds.[5]

Taylor is more sanguine, as we have seen. He fully acknowledges what he calls our fractured horizons of meaning, in which common (largely theistic) sources of meaning and moral discourse have splintered, but also wishes to demonstrate that some common 'inescapable' frameworks of meaning can be retrieved. Yet the essential point remains: this is a task to be achieved, not an easy inheritance to be simply received.

Another way of sharpening this practical question is to consider the sheer extent of the personal sense of alienation which has resulted. The splintering of metaphysical certainties into a plurality of transient and 'shallow' traditions has, according to some commentators, led to quite *radical* personal fragmentation. Here it is Yu who offers the most useful summary statement to remind us:

> The three recurrent themes, which we find to be pervasive in modern literature in the West, point to Western man's experience of his ontological uprootedness, to the fragmentation of his personal identity and to the failure of human relation. The three are closely interrelated because they all refer to the condition of the human person. To have a distinct personal identity, one has to maintain a distinct and unified structure of meaning, for one exists in and through one's intellectual and emotional commitment to that structure of meaning. When the structure of meaning is fragmented, one's personal identity becomes ambiguous. At the same time, personal identity and human relations are dialectically connected. One's authentic existence is actualized and manifested in and through one's relation with others, and one's personal identity emerges also in the context of human relations. Thus the failure of meaningful relations is symptomatic of the problem of personal identity . . .[6]

This presses home the difficulty of the task from the other end. Not only are received traditions of meaning and value so fragile – so are we. And that affects our capacity to reintegrate. In other words, have we travelled too far within ourselves from the experience of belonging to *any* shared tradition? Both the traditions of shared meaning and social relations, and our own sense of self, are too insecure – and they are so interrelated that they reinforce that instability within each other. In such a situation is not the proposal, such as it is, simply inadequate? This question returns us to my earlier comments about the extent of our instability and state of reaction, and to the unease expressed about MacIntyre's positive project: is *anything* possible in such a situation?

Such a question is not intended to be rhetorical. I do not believe it begs an unequivocal answer one way or the other. Nor should it paralyse us. For in the first instance it may lead us again to some of the moral continuities and possibilities for consensus we have been searching for – and finding. In other words, the diagnosis of radical fragmentation and instability may simply be overstated. Taylor might be a better guide than MacIntyre. And this could be reinforced by recalling the sheer weight of moral energy within the human condition which appears to operate 'centripetally' rather than chaotically: that is, those fundamental moral intuitions which press for *some* form of public, shared, expression, rather than remaining private and individual. I referred to this briefly in relation to the displaced moral energy which is poured into litigation.[7] It was also the point raised earlier in relation to the Enlightenment project of justifying morality: that is, the quest for common ground, even when it fails, is deep-rooted, restless, persistent. (And there is some important theological ground for this too, which will emerge in the next section.)

In the second instance, even if the question begs a bleaker kind of answer giving much greater weight to the forces of fragmentation, this still does not lead inexorably to retreat. It could lead us instead to examine more carefully the most vulnerable aspects of continuity, consensus and cohesion – simply to see how they can be strengthened. And it is this line of enquiry which again takes us into the second part of the book. For it is precisely, and perhaps only, when a particular tradition such as Christianity is considered in some detail that these weak links *can* be addressed effectively.

In this context there is the specific question of ontological scepticism and metaphysical uncertainty to be considered. Although I have tried to suggest provisional rallying points for consensus in definitions of personal identity, and in some core moral ideas of individualism, the question remains: how can they survive, motivate and provide stability without a more secure ontological foundation? To the extent that they have emerged from a variety of sources, but now function largely as free-floating ideas, they may seem dangerously one-dimensional. So here, certainly, we must look to Christian theology, which has such a profound ontology to offer.

We are also bound to consider Christian belief as a response to the more general problem about the credibility of *any* particular tradition. Traditions of common belief and practice are vital for subcultures and persons to flourish, but they are fragile. So Christian faith cries out for consideration specifically in these terms: that is, we need to know whether it can still lay claim to be a *credible* and communicable tradition of belief at every level: metaphysical, moral, social and existential. In particular, does it generate and sustain the sort of moral and social vision of personhood which can connect with what has been proposed so far? Or does it set a different sort of agenda altogether which can only be sustained in isolation from the other discourses of this discussion?

If it does prove to have a radically different agenda then a centre will have failed to hold, things may fall even further apart, as Yeats famously foretold, and the Church may have to live out its own vision separately after all – an offshore island in a MacIntyrean world-view. But if the Christian agenda *is* recognizably related, then the Church will want to lend its resources in promoting the overall vision. And in that sense it will function not just as a subculture but as a vital ingredient in the wider framework of our social order.

The only way to answer these questions is to step inside the tradition as fully and fairly as we can. And so we shift from a general survey of an individualistic culture to a much more specific consideration of Christian belief as it bears on these same issues.

PART TWO

6

Individualism and Christian Belief:
Introduction

The first part of the book has engaged in an enterprise in which many would profess to be involved. Politicians, social commentators, artists and writers, as well as philosophers and theologians, are all contributing evaluations of our current culture on the basis of historical sense, pragmatism and the general moral intuitions of a western conscience. But the question now is more specific. How does explicit Christian belief address us?

In one sense a groundwork has already emerged, at least in embryo. As already indicated, a general analysis of western culture is bound to include highly significant strands of explicit Christian belief. The specific matter of individualism has proved to be no exception. It has already become apparent that Christian beliefs have, as a matter of fact, contributed to some of the core ideas of individualism, historically and conceptually.

A summary of these links that have emerged already would include the following points. The notion of autonomy of the individual before God was noted as a strong strand in the Reformation reaction against religious and state heteronomy. The sanctity of an individual's privacy and the importance of introspection and inwardness received similar impetus from Augustinian and Puritan traditions of Christianity. The originality and uniqueness of each individual is a presupposition of Christian belief in our createdness, and of prophetic ministry. Our capacity to exercise free consent is promoted in the biblical notion of covenant (and made much of by both Aquinas and the Puritans). The high value given to *all* individuals, including 'ordinary' people engaged in their common tasks, derives in some measure from the Judaeo-Christian belief in the goodness of all creation (elaborated by Augustine). It was then given new momentum in the Reformation when all individuals were credited with the capacity to relate to God without special mediation by a privileged few. The notion of *agape*, expressing an unconditional dimension of love for any individual, was also noted: it too has made a distinctive theological contribution to our moral discourse.

But all such contributions and connections need more than this sort of summary statement to establish whether they make the Christian tradition still credible or constructive in our current situation. And this sets the agenda for what follows in this part of the book. It needs to be demonstrated whether, and how, these theological ideas function within a coherent tradition of wider beliefs which can still command respect, motivate allegiance and engage positively with our present state.

In the first instance this means setting out more clearly the general possibilities of theological language and belief engaging with the wider world at all. The point was raised briefly in the Introduction. These possibilities depend on certain theological and philosophical assumptions – which must now be properly acknowledged.

The assumptions begin from the internal logic of basic Christian claims about the universality both of creation and the apparatus of redemption. In the doctrine of creation itself, in the *logos spermatikos*,[1] in the 'law written on the hearts of the Gentiles', in Paul's speech at the Areopagus,[2] in the reversal of Babel at Pentecost, we have examples of conceptual, symbolic and historical definitions of at least some kind of *universal* basis of divine action and communication. In some way or another God ordains a relationship with all, and amongst all, his creatures. That is an essential part of Christian self-understanding.

This implies that we are operating with an ultimate realism in our theological ontology and, likewise, a corresponding realism about the notion that there is a common good for humankind. For by insisting that we are all made in the image of the same God and set within the same created order, we assume that there is some sort of objective order of things with which we should accord. In other words, there *is* some sort of natural ethic. It is not simply a matter of what we choose or construct, individually or collectively, but of what we encounter in a common reality which transcends us and relates to us all. This remains the case even granted a significant element of change in that transcendent reality (whether this is change within creation or within God himself). For however relativized and particularized the application of God's will (and our perception of it) in the twists and turns of changing circumstance, it remains the will of the one God relating to us all with consistency. This is the unyielding Christian bedrock for belief that connections are ultimately there to be established. Here are crucial grounds for believing that our restless quest for a common life (noted previously)[3] has an inner resilience born of a *divine* origin and goal, not just of the necessities of survival and co-operation.

To be sure, our grasp of this order is disordered and distorted through finitude, fallenness and fallibility. It is also relativized, partial and particularized through all our historical and cultural contingencies. The very disconnectedness and fragmentation we have analysed in our current culture is ample testimony to this. So our realism must always be critical, not naive, and the possibilities of realizing our ultimate connectedness always limited.

This too is reflected in the internal logic of the Judaeo-Christian tradition. That is why it has strained out this tension in a variety of distinct but overlapping categories of paradox. This is expressed in the paradox of Israel's election and its mission to the nations; also in the New Testament tensions of a Church set squarely within, but not of, this world. It is expressed further in the relationship of the two Cities (Augustine), the two Kingdoms (Luther) and the relationship between natural and revealed law. It surfaces similarly in the relationship between 'Christ and Culture' (Niebuhr), and more generally in the vexed but creative relationship between gospel concerns and secular systems of thought (medieval Aristotelianism in Thomism, modern Marxism in Liberation theology, and so on). These all bear witness, in one way or another, to the *limits* of our connectedness.

So much for the broad assumptions. What follows from them is therefore double-sided. In the first instance they offer a mandate at least for *attempting* Christian communication (and action) in relation to a wider world of discourse. For they mean that when we explore the inner landscape of the Christian tradition we are not travelling in a wholly different country from the rest of God's creation. It therefore becomes a matter of moral and theological responsibility not to act as if we are. Habermas is surely right in this: anyone whose tradition excludes them totally from such a basis of communication clothes himself, and imposes on others, a dangerous kind of silence and an isolation of the very kind we are trying to overcome.[4] In such isolation nothing can be contributed: the world could not be served by the faith (only ignored or despised). And in gospel terms, we are not given this option: we are to be salt or light, not simply a community which speaks only to itself. In doctrinal terms the nature of this ontology, rooted in the personal God of all, revealed in Christ, has the same effect: it drives us to make this attempt to speak and act beyond our selves. For as he acted in Christ to realize our common connectedness so must we, so far as we can within our constraints. That is why we cannot acquiesce in our fragmentation, even though we may properly rejoice in our differences. That is why the Dominical commands cannot be re-written even in the most dislocated circumstances: we are always to 'go into all the world and make disciples': to work for his will 'on earth as it is in heaven'; to be sent into the world as the Father sent him.

But then there is this reverse side to the assumptions as well. They also forbid us to be naive or over-sanguine about our likely degree of success in the enterprise. The constraints of change, finitude and fallenness remain, in both the Church and the world. At any one stage in history there is no guarantee that we shall be particularly effective in realizing our fundamental connectedness. In terms of the questions posed at the end of the last chapter, that is why we cannot presuppose that Christian perceptions of individuality and social order will fit snugly into more general perceptions at this particular time. When the tradition is scrutinized it will not *necessarily* commend itself as credible or compelling: the agendas *may* differ significantly. What the logic of ontology (in creation and redemption) leads us to expect and work for, the logic of epistemology (in our finitude and fallenness) can still undermine at any one point in time.

To some extent this might seem to define the task more as 'witness' than apologetics. That is, it includes an exploration of the internal landscape of Christian faith and theology in order to commend it and make what connections we can, but without supposing this will constitute a decisive argument to transcend relativism. This is the force of Hauerwas's position:

> the task of the Christian is not to defeat relativism by argument but to witness to a God who requires confrontation . . . The command to witness is not based on an assumption that we are in possession of a universal truth which others must implicitly possess . . . If such a truth existed we would not be called upon to be witnesses but philosophers.[5]

Furthermore, just because we have to concede these limits to communication, it might seem that we are always more likely to be persuading ourselves in this sort of discussion, rather than persuading others who stand outside the tradition altogether. As such, this self-persuasion may still function indirectly as a form of witness, for by reintegrating ourselves more deeply within our own tradition we may well reinvigorate Christian confidence in commending it more widely.

But it still cannot be a decisive demonstration of the precedence of Christian truth claims.

Yet our first assumption about the logic of creation must also be allowed its full weight. If we are also committed to underlying possibilities of communication, even at the 'philosophers' (*sic*) level, then we should not concede too much to Hauerwas. His complete dismissal of universal truth is too summary. So in that sense this task of demonstrating whether and how Christian belief can provide a coherent and credible perspective on individualism *does* retain an element of apologetics.

In any case, granted any possibility of either witness or apologetics, the moral and theological imperative remains in force: if we can, we are bound to seek connections and contribute to the wider world. Indeed, we are bound to *evangelize*. For in a world of lost and fragmented people any tradition which can offer a substantive narrative of meaning, motivation, belonging, which can engage credibly with our current situation and deepest moral intuitions, *any such a tradition should seek allegiance.*

In these ways the task must therefore be deemed both possible (in some degree) and necessary. But how is it to be undertaken?

Here we shall need to refer again to the terms set by the first part of the book. There, for a start, it became apparent that an effective tradition of belief will need to include a credible *ontological* basis, particularly in relation to the nature of personhood. This is a crucial area of vulnerability in current instabilities, and clearly needs addressing.

What was also required is some demonstration specifically of *moral* credibility in any tradition. A tradition must be able to contribute to a sound social vision. In particular, it will need to demonstrate whether it exemplifies core moral ideas of individualism, and how they are nuanced. Above all it will be important to show whether this is a tradition which can not only generate and sustain core moral ideas, but can also 'control' them; that is, to prevent them from developing perniciously, as they clearly have tended to do on the wider stage of history. This too was a clear requirement of the preceding analysis.

There were also more general pressures voiced in the Introduction. That is, the tradition must also demonstrate that its intellectual and moral vision is charged with *existential* power. It must engage the whole person. It must have to do with human motivation, imagination and passion, as well as human reason. For we are clearly not going to be bound to traditions or communities by intellectual bread alone, but by the *mysterium tremendum et fascinans* of what satisfies our souls.

So this is the task which has been set, with just these final disclaimers and further points of clarification to register. First, it should
again be clear that this is an attempt to assess the moral credibility of
the tradition of Christian *belief*, as distinct from its history of *institutional practice*. There is another story to be told about the latter. This
is a sad story which often mimics the more general history of ideas
traced in the first part of the book: that is, a story of the corruption
of moral ideas when incorporated in actual social programmes. It
includes Christian complicity in moral outrages from the Crusades to
Auschwitz. And it is vital that this story should be told. Nonetheless,
it is not the task of this essay to do so – though it is just because of
this potential corruption of moral ideas, in religion as elsewhere, that
the capacity for 'control' and self-regulation within the Christian tradition will be emphasized so much in what follows.

It should also be noted that this is not part of a comparative exercise with other religious traditions. So it is not an attempt to commend
Christian moral belief *over against* other religions or cultural traditions,
nor in explicit dialogue with them. That would require a knowledge of
other religions – and space – which I do not have.[6]

As for methodology, it should emerge clearly enough as the discussion proceeds. In the first instance, so far as ontology is concerned, the
issues will be dealt with in direct response to the concerns raised in
the first part of the book. So this is an attempt to correlate the
Christian response to the 'secular' question, in a specific way (following Tillich, therefore). Such an approach lends itself readily here: it
seems to do no violence either to the form of the question, or the
manner in which Christian resources must be appropriated for the
'answer'. But thereafter I shall attempt to let the Christian tradition
of belief determine the agenda more in its own terms. So rather than
seeking Christian perspectives specifically on the particular categories
of the core moral ideas of individualism (autonomy, privacy, self-
realization, and so on), I shall offer a survey of key biblical and doctrinal themes which bear generally on such issues. Thus (for example)
Christian beliefs about the nature of autonomy or freedom will emerge
tangentially out of such doctrines as 'grace' and 'love', rather than
from a specific attempt to extract Christian teaching on the notion of
autonomy *per se*. This will correlate less directly. But it will prevent
imposing categories on the Christian tradition which do not naturally
belong to it in quite the same terms.

It will also be clear that I am not offering this survey of biblical and
doctrinal themes through the lens of one particular philosophical-

theological tradition (such as Thomism, Neo-Orthodoxy or process theology, for example). Part of the credibility of the tradition as a whole depends on its capacity to yield its insights variously throughout its history by straddling a variety of such sub-traditions.[7]

And what if this task succeeds, at least in its own terms? The conclusion would be straightforward. It would commend the Christian faith *at least* as a plausible, persuasive and responsible subculture within our current situation. But it would also go beyond that. For if it is shown to be contributing creatively to precisely those core moral ideas and notions of personhood which will cement an overall social framework, then it ought to be accepted more widely. Even without the presuppositions of its own theological imperatives, it should be sought out to provide a positive role within that wider social order. The tradition will have been shown to have something to say – not just to itself but to others, and it must always strive to do so.

7

Theological Ontology:
Christian Foundations for
Individual Persons

Ontology has to do with ultimate questions about being, what may be said to be 'really real'. What is now called for is a theological account of ontology in general, and the ontology of personal identity in particular. To compress this with any precision into a wider argument is a tall order. Any attempt will be strictly limited in the ground it can cover, and what follows is only a selective sketch of a huge field. But the task clearly cannot be sidestepped.

Without any explicit appeal to theology, as we have seen, the sort of ontological stability which could be construed for individual persons seems strictly limited. There are some definitions of the narrative and social self (as distinct from discredited notions of the abstract self) which could allow for some measure of unity and continuity. But because there is also widespread wariness about specifying ontological foundations to these notions, they are hard to sustain. By contrast a firm, realist, theological foundation secures the identity of persons in the most radical way conceivable. For if *God* is the inescapable ground of all being, and if God-given personhood is the irreducible and unique aspect of each human being, then there is stability indeed. If God wills it, identity can endure through all kinds of flux, and can even be restored after death itself. Such, in brief, is the uncompromising traditional claim of Christian faith.

This needs a good deal more elaboration. What is being maintained is an order of reality in which the being of a transcendent, personal God determines the being of human persons, as a creator determines his creatures. We are brought into being and held in being not just as an accidental collocation of atoms with an evolutionary by-product of consciousness, nor just by our social, cultural and linguistic

conventions and constructions, but also by an ultimate and transcendent personal reality. Taken together with Christological doctrines
of redemption and resurrection, in which God's love underwrites (and
remakes) human personhood into eternity, this therefore begins the
sketch of a systematic ontological framework which secures the continuity and value of human persons (as persons-in-relation, not only to
others, but to God).

As such, it provides an essential basis for those values and meaning
of the human person which common intuition has been willing to
affirm, but fails adequately to justify. Without it, as we have noted, the
self is always likely to be unstable, transient, diminished. Thus Keith
Ward: 'if there is no such God as the foundation and goal of being,
then the soul becomes an inexplicable anomaly in the universe . . . and
once you start to think that, any sense of the unique dignity and worth
of human life is in danger of collapsing'.[1] Likewise Stephen Clark, even
more polemically: 'If God is dead, so also is the Self. Philosophers who
question Descartes' "proofs" of God also deny his proof of that lesser
god, the spiritual substance that endures through change and illusion,
Ego.'[2]

The form of this kind of argument oscillates between the logical
and the psychological. It follows logically that this sort of realist theistic ontology entails security for the individual person, its uniqueness
and value. As such it also has the potential to offer psychological security about the self (and motivation to respect other selves) – at least to
the extent that we are adequately embedded in the Christian tradition
and the plausibility structure it provides.

The point is further strengthened by considering what happens if a
deconstructed or non-realist 'God' is preferred, and located wholly
within the self. *Prima facie* this might seem to provide even sounder
warrant for a strong sense of self, personal autonomy and individual
value. But in fact it simply becomes vulnerable to further deconstruction of the self itself. For with nothing 'beyond' to hold the self in
being it too becomes subject to deconstruction, in spite of being
buttressed by religious language. Hence the critical role of a realist
ontology of God: 'If God is dead . . . so also is the Self'.[3]

Granted, none of this demonstrates any *proof* of this sort of realist
Christian ontology (which remains an assumption). As already indicated, we are not expecting that level of decisive argument in either
witness or apologetics. But it does constitute good reason for considering it to be plausible. Plausibility here derives from the basic
congruence between the self's intuitive quest for stability (which is

widely acknowledged) and general Christian belief in a transcendent and personal creator God (which may be supported on other grounds as well). Such congruence helps render such a belief intuitively persuasive, as well as existentially reassuring. Because it is also helping to provide a more secure basis for the sort of satisfactory social order outlined before, then it can claim to be morally compelling as well. And all this remains significant for broadly-based truth-claims, even though it is certainly no covert recovery of the old proofs for the existence of God.

But that is only the beginning. How far can this still be sustained and elaborated in a post-Aristotelian, post-Newtonian, post-Kantian world? This is a world, after all, in which all definitions of ultimate reality seem subject to revision. Either they seem to require a dynamic and relational interpretation. Or, more radically, they are ruled out of court altogether because of extreme epistemological and metaphysical scepticism: that is, we simply cannot *know* of any ultimate reality beyond that which we construct from within our own resources of language and meaning. Hence the non-realist alternative.

In such a world it is not surprising that Christian theology has responded with its own state of ontological diversity, if not disarray. Thus Milbank outlines a huge spectrum of modern and post-modern theological response to the problem of ontology. This ranges from the modified, critical realism of the sort I have been adopting, which still seeks to defend the objective existence of God; to a kind of parallel universe of religious meaning, where the Christian experience of 'God' and the Greek experience of 'Being' are held to be so incomparable that we cannot sensibly relate the two at all; to that position of wholesale anti-realism, where God refers to nothing transcendent at all, but only to the passing creation of transient human selves.[4]

So far as the extremes of anti-realism (or non-realism) are concerned, I can do little more here than draw attention to the nature of the realist assumptions which I outlined earlier. A truly radical non-realist epistemology would indeed deconstruct all possibilities of maintaining this sort of realist ontology. But then this would also deconstruct all possibilities of theology itself, in the way I have presupposed it. So, in my view, all recent attempts to revise 'theism' to accommodate non-realism only succeed by a gross distortion of God-language, worthy of Wonderland (such attempts do not in fact recast *theism*: they reinterpret religion instead).[5] In short, theological ontology is by definition realist, so that while it can always be challenged by non-realism it can never be absorbed or radically reinterpreted by it without meaning something entirely different.

The only substantial point of debate with this challenge which might naturally emerge here arises when this simple question is pressed: on what grounds could the relative merits of extreme episte-mological scepticism, and the critical realism it seeks to displace, be judged? One obvious answer is their general explanatory power in illuminating the self's intuitive claims to enduring significance, stabil-ity and the possibility of a real communication with other selves. And these are the very grounds on which a realist theism can perform particularly well, as I have already suggested. So in that sense the burden of proof lies squarely with the non-realists.

However, while theism can hardly engage with its own wholesale deconstruction (only confront it with an alternative vision), it is a dif-ferent matter with other more significant aspects of modernity and post-modernity. For the most dominant intellectual trends in our culture have not been those which explicitly deny all possibilities of thinking about ultimate reality; they are those which are driven to strain such concepts through the language of flux, historical change, relationality and relativity. Here, theism can and does engage fully, drawing creatively on its own internal resources as well as others, in a constant dialectic of reinterpretation. Here, it *is* possible to elaborate a theological ontology which incorporates such perspectives without entirely deconstructing itself as theology.

Thus we find classical theism's conception of a timeless, immutable and impassible deity now commonly qualified, or at least 'expanded' – but done so in a constructive way, without abandoning all sense of transcendence or realism. Under pressure both from modernity and post-modernity theism has recovered what are, in fact, traditional biblical insights of a supremely personalist, immanent, active God of 'changing' will, temporality and 'new' incarnational experiences. It is true that the attempt to wed these with classical attributes has not always produced a happy marriage (the dipolar God of process theism is one such instance which I have reviewed in some detail elsewhere).[6] But there are other more promising doctrines of God which provide a better bridge between modernity's concerns and Christianity's own ancient insights. And here we need to return in more detail to the project of joining personalist priorities to the ontology of the Greek Fathers, already noted in Yu's analysis.

Milbank offers the most radical step down this path. He wants to introduce the 'relational, productive, responsive' into our conception of the Godhead. This Godhead retains some neo-platonic or Christian sense of transcendence: that is, it is an *infinite* and *absolute* coincidence of 'goodness, truth, beauty and Being itself', lying beyond our finite and partial approximations.[7] So in that sense he is clearly speaking of God with meaning beyond us, not just constructed by us, and to that extent it implies a kind of realism. However, it is crucial to note that the notion of relationality and movement is not just being projected into this being of God: it *is* God's being. Ultimate Being (God) *is* therefore an infinite relation and movement of creative power and goodness, a 'relation between *act* and *act*'.[8] And that means there is little room for the notions of enduring substance or particularity within God. All is determined by the ontologically prior category of relationality. Accordingly, it means that the being of the created world and its persons is radically determined by the same categories of flux and relationality: 'Just as God . . . is not a "substance", because he is nothing fundamental underlying anything else, so also there are no substances in creation, no underlying matter, and no discrete and inviolable "things" . . . There are no things, no substances, *only shifting relations*' (emphasis mine).[9]

Here Milbank has surely gone a step too far, and unnecessarily so. He describes it as 'an ontological scenario which is not *exactly* Greek',[10] but this is understated. It actually departs a long way from that strand of Greek thought which can sustain a dynamic and relational notion of being but without dissolving so much into 'mere' relationality. And the consequence of Milbank's position, as it relates to our chief concern, is evident. It casts doubt yet again on the possibility of conceiving persons as enduring particulars. They (we) are adrift once more as a shifting and unstable set of relations with little prospect of any significant continuity in our identity.

However, there are other reformulations of Christian ontology which do not take us so far down this path. They share the same concern for a dynamic, relational view of God himself, and human personhood, but they have resisted Milbank's more radical conclusion. The major modern figure lying behind most of these is Karl Barth.

For Barth the concrete revelation of ultimate reality (that is, God) which we see in Christ is clearly a revelation of relatedness. It is a relatedness in which there is both union and differentiation between persons. This relatedness constitutes the transcendent God as God (in his Trinitarian reality). It also (derivatively) constitutes human persons. We become persons by virtue of our relationship with God and with each other. As such neither the persons of the Godhead, nor human persons, can properly be self-sufficient or self-centred. Humanity simply cannot be *homo incurvatus in se*.[11] Thus there is certainly dynamic process and activity at the heart of God's being and ours: being is in becoming.[12] It has been dubbed as eschatological realism, in the sense that our security in ultimate reality depends on a realization of reality which is still in the process of becoming (though also given already in Christ).[13] *Nonetheless*, what is constituted in this way is still particular persons and differentiated being. There is no sense that we (or God) are reduced solely or simply to shifting relations or processes of activity.

The influence of Barth's massive theological enterprise is undeniable. At the same time it does not always relate easily to other positions, not least in this matter of ontology. This is because he charts his own 'grammar' of theology and theological terms, so that the meaning of being, substance, persons, relation (for instance) are determined as much from within his own system of thought as from outside.[14] So in that sense it may be easier to pursue its implications through others who have parallel concerns.

The most fertile development can be traced through Zizioulas,[15] closely followed by Gunton.[16] Their fundamental concern is similar: to provide a conceptual and theological framework in which substantial particularity and relationality are mutually constitutive, rather than mutually exclusive. The 'substantial' being of particular persons here does *not* necessarily mean there is an entirely unchanging, simple, 'substratum' of being underlying particularity. It simply means that particular things and persons have a distinct (and potentially enduring) identity and being, even though this is constituted by relationship with others. In that sense both God (through the persons of the Trinity) and human persons can and do have distinct, concrete, particular identity, which can be held secure within the various relations which help constitute that particularity.[17]

The historical background to this kind of position is best charted by Zizioulas. His argument is that the notion of personhood as the concrete and substantial reality of a free relating individual is, historically, a creative insight of Christian patristic thought. It was forged out of the early Trinitarian debates about the nature of God, which were in turn a direct response to the pressure of the Christ event (and the wider biblical cosmology) as it engaged with contemporary intellectual resources. In short, we owe the very idea of relational but particular personhood to the Christian revelation.

This is explained further by reference to its classical background. Prior to this struggle of the Christian intellect, both Platonism and Aristotelian philosophy had represented individuality as a tendency to non-being. Their conception of true being and ultimate reality was driven by the quest for overall unity, not differentiation and individuation. In so far as a free 'person' exists, it is therefore nothing but a mask, someone playing out a transient role in the theatre of society, but with no substantial, ontological basis. The underlying necessity of things must ultimately dissolve such illusions of freedom and concrete individuality. *But* given the biblical cosmology of a created order in which humankind is freely willed to exist, and interacts freely with personal deity; and given this further insight through Christ that the very nature of God himself is a reality constituted by the free relation of 'persons'; then (and only then) it becomes possible to think of ultimate and enduring reality in terms of the relations between 'real' persons rather than some monist unity of all things.

Zizioulas' historical argument is not unchallenged. But this overall conception of a relational view of reality in which persons are secure in their particularity *and* constituted by their relations, remains convincing. Flux and stability cohere in us because they are held together in God himself who gives us being. A doctrine of Father, Son and Holy Spirit, when conceived as *perichoresis*, is a doctrine in which each eternally interpenetrate, interanimate and constitute each other's being. It is as such that God is God, and it is as such that the nature of our being is determined. We find our being only in our relationships, but therein we really do find our being: 'he who loses his life . . . will find it'.

All this is culled from the debates between early Christian thought and antiquity. But it is nonetheless apposite for our current climate. It offers just that basis for a secure but relational view of personhood which is being sought. In its relational concern it coheres well with insights from social anthropology and psychology about how human persons are constituted and sustained: we are not 'abstract' entities existing in individual isolation, but essentially relational.

Equally, it provides an ontological framework which will sustain narrative notions of personal identity. That is, a notion of individual identity in which the relational self is formed, known, changed, through the narrative of life, yet also retains *particularity* and *continuity*. For in this kind of Christian ontology the stories of our individual and corporate lives derive their shape and meaning as sub-plots within the wider story of the Trinitarian life – revealed pre-eminently through the pivotal Christian story of Christ himself. It is precisely because the Trinity is conceived in the dynamic relations of enduring particulars, which project into history, that such a narrative is possible.

In more general terms it might also cohere with contemporary natural science, in so far as it employs similar ideas of relationality in its attempt to describe the 'ultimate' realities of the physical universe. This is part of what is meant by calling the Trinity a transcendental truth: that is, a mark of all reality. As such it reinforces the general credibility of the ontology being claimed.

At the same time it provides a concept of transcendence which, while undoubtedly realist, cannot be dismissed as the conception of naive realism or anthropomorphism. That is, it is not a picture of God painted simply as the projection of the human individual (or human society) writ large in the sky. On the contrary, it expresses the ultimate in categories which may connect with our human understanding of being and personhood, but which also stretches it. Perfect *perichoresis* lies in some sort of determinate relation to personal experience but also pushes our conceptions beyond anything we have actually experienced. This element of 'strain' in our conception of God is far from being a deterrent to belief. It is a vital ingredient in the credibility of revelation. The Trinitarian God of relatedness is credible just because he is not easily dismissed as a simple projection onto reality, but is a sophistication forced out of a revelation of ultimate reality.

This, incidentally, introduces a further point in relation to theological realism. So often those who complain they cannot believe in a personal God, when pressed, actually mean they can no longer believe in an individual Father-figure in the sky of childhood picture books. But of course they do not have to, for 'He' is not the Christian claim. The Trinity is the claim. In short, when Feuerbach or Cupitt want to deconstruct the Christian idea of God 'out there as an individual person' they are deconstructing an Aunt Sally who was never there.

Ontology and particularity: pressing the implications

If we now turn more specifically to Gunton's development of these issues there is further useful elaboration. Not least, it takes us into more direct dialogue with the sort of position signalled by Milbank, where there is a fundamentally relational view of reality, but one which threatens rather than secures the substantiality and particularity of our personhood.

This merits more detailed discussion. We need to be quite sure we can sustain an ontology which is not only relational but which also buttresses individuality and enduring particularity. It is crucial not least because part of the paradox of our confused culture is that we are as much in danger of losing particularity as we are of failing to grasp our essential relationality. This danger does not just arise through fragmentation but also through the homogenization which (paradoxically) that fragmentation entails. It is a feature of our current situation, already noted, which arises out of extreme individualism. It is precisely when individuals are so spuriously 'exalted' and isolated in themselves that they lose the concrete distinctiveness and differentiation which a social or relational context would help to give them. They therefore become abstract and interchangeable units (that is, 'homogenized') just because of their individual isolation.[18] To put it more simply: I am less likely to value persons who are conceived solely or chiefly as self-created, self-contained, unrelated. These (common) characteristics make them individually unremarkable and nameless. I am much more likely to value a 'Sara', 'Stephen', 'Fatima', whose identity is conceived to be given and differentiated (in part) by a family, culture and particular context of relations.

Trinitarian ontology, as we have seen, *does* secure particularity and differentiation within relational reality (ultimately in God, derivatively in human persons). As such it becomes a bulwark against both fragmentation and homogenization of individuals. In this way, therefore, we have been given good grounds for accepting relationality as a mark of all being, and without losing hold of individuality. It is a proper Christian reaction both against Cartesian notions of unrelated substance, the abstraction of an 'underlying' substance, and post-modernism's fragmented view of unrelated particulars.

Yet this also marks the point where further clarification is needed. Just because the importance of relationality is (rightly) being presented so persuasively, its totalitarian tendency must continually be noted, and resisted. In other words, none of this should be taken to mean that relationality is in itself the prior ontological category. This would mean that substantial particulars might dissolve after all into some kind of unreality. And this is where Gunton explicitly takes issue with Milbank. Although persons are constituted by relations (they are not prior realities who then enter into relations), neither do they dissolve into a 'mere haze of homogeneously insubstantial relationality'.[19] On the contrary, 'the chief affirmation to be made here is that if persons are, like the persons of the Trinity and by virtue of their creation in the image of God, *hypostases*, concrete and particular, then their particularity too is central to their being'.[20] ('*Like* the persons of the

Trinity' is important here, incidentally [emphasis mine]: although human persons derive particularity and relationality from the being of God, the form of relationality between things, people and the persons of the Trinity, compares only analogously, not univocally.[21]) In other words, while we are wholes constituted by (relational) parts, we are more than the sum of our parts. So while relationality is essential it would be more true to say that particular-being-in-relation is ontologically prior, rather than relationality in itself.[22]

By resisting any tendency to substitute the ontological priority of (non-relational) substance with the priority of relationality *per se* we are therefore reducing the risk of this reaction which constantly threatens us: the deconstruction of any enduring sense of the self. The importance of this can hardly be overstated. It is, after all, a reaction in which intellectual positions are all too easily driven by personal convenience. We are highly susceptible to sliding out of any commitment implied by substantial and enduring personal identity (in respect of the elderly, the marginalized, and marriage, to take a few obvious examples). And such evasion is precisely what a *purely* relational understanding of ontology might collude with. For this reduces personal identity to a succession of intersecting 'moments' within a shifting flux of relations, giving rise to a perception of identity only if the relations themselves exhibited common patterns of interaction. It would beg the old questions about stability, continuity and the commonsense experience of persisting identity: what common factor (if anything) holds 'me' *or anyone else* together? If there is no substantial self which is constituted by these relations there would be no satisfactory answer to the question. The moral imperative for loyalty and commitment would be dangerously undermined.

The point is so critical that it needs to be pressed further. It is not sufficient simply to affirm that we have a substantial self and personal identity constituted by relationality, as if it is something that relationality brings about on its own. It requires a constant reminder and further elaboration of the essential interpenetration of relation and substantial being. For if we simply talk of my personal identity as that which is made out of a dynamic flux of relations (as if being and relation were separable) then my identity would still itself be in constant flux. We could then be subject once more to a version of the Parfitean nightmare in which there are many different 'I's throughout 'my' life, all concrete and particular, but still lacking any significant principle of unity and continuity.

Alistair McFadyen addresses this to some extent. He likewise wants to emphasize the social and dialogical formation of persons, without reducing persons merely to relations,[23] and offers the notion of 'sedimentation' to meet the point. The 'I' which responds in the flux of unfolding situations and relationships includes a 'sedimentation' of previous such moments of response which together form a unique and stable cluster within the structure of the developing personal identity;[24] he also appeals to the notion of a 'deep self' as a core 'at some remove from the immediacy of particular relations and their effects'.[25]

These categories certainly offer some point of purchase for a continuing identity though time – once constituted. Yet so far as I can see even these may be insufficient, at least in one respect. They fail to provide any clear notion how to resist what might be termed an infinite regress to abstraction. With what does the process of sedimentation *get going* (so to speak), apart from relations with others whose sedimented selves also beg the same question? Whence the resources (or 'substance'?) with which the deep self organizes and distances itself, apart from that which has been received and formed by relations with others (about whom, again, the same question can be asked)?

These questions are provoked partly because MacFadyen and others *do* sometimes appear to abstract relations from being, by giving them historical precedence. Thus MacFadyen points to the fact that historical and chronological questions are distinct from the ontological, and relations have historical priority over individuals (he says) 'because it is by, in, and through *antecedent* networks of relations that individuals are born and formed' (emphasis mine).[26]

In fact MacFadyen's footnote about this then goes on immediately to redeem the point I am making: 'but that need not imply ontological priority: as bipolarities of a single process ... individual and relation must be considered ontologically coincident'.[27] Exactly so. But I would want the point raised well above the status of footnote. The notion of historical precedence must not be taken to confer on the category of relation some kind of totalitarian hold on ontology. Otherwise the question of infinite regress will continue to press. That is, if relations with other people are the sole constitutive categories of personhood then it is hard to get a grip conceptually on how they can constitute anything other than other relations-in-relation. Or, to put it another way, how would communion-in-communion ever constitute *being*-in-communion?[28]

So to safeguard Gunton's general concerns in this area it must consistently be reaffirmed that being and relation are to be welded firmly together - so that they never fly apart or reduce one to another. The basis for this is precisely where we began: it is the Trinitarian God in whom there is enduring substantiality of particulars within a relational structure of being. He just *is* active being-in-communion, without antecedent. And as the ground of all being he is the incontrovertible bedrock of our own being-in-relation, and the buffer against any kind of infinite regress.

This returns us to the main point of the discussion. A specifically Christian doctrine of God matters inescapably in any quest for a coherent ontological basis for a personal identity which is enduring, substantial and relational. As I have indicated, it is a credible ontology, and one which resonates with a number of current perceptions in other fields of knowledge. The Christian tradition certainly need have no reticence in offering it as a broad conceptual basis for social order.

We should also note again that such ontology does have clear, concrete implications for practical living. It profoundly underwrites obligations of long-term *loyalty* towards other people. Neither the passage of time, the reality of change, nor the ultimate transience of temporal existence is sufficient reason to revoke such loyalty and commitment, once we truly believe that all persons are substantially rooted in God and his eternal being. Our attitudes towards the marginalized and outcast, the care of the very elderly, marriage, employment, should all be significantly affected by this assumption of enduring, substantial, personal identity. (These are issues which will all be raised again later.[29])

Gunton's own proposals for practical implications relate more to the wider form of social and political order. Negatively, he suggests that the absence of a proper Trinitarian ontology permits the kind of unitary view of deity which is 'commonly associated with totalitarian or repressive forms of social order'.[30] This is true when deity is conceived transcendentally, and is even more likely to be true when it has been reconceived immanently as the state.[31] Such conceptions allow no 'space' for free interrelation; any free relation with otherness is perceived as threat. Positively, by contrast, a proper Trinitarian theology and ontology provides a warrant to order society quite differently: that is, as the free relation of individuals who are constituted by their relations. In this scheme of things the otherness of particularity, whether of the transcendent God or fellow creatures, is constitutive of our being and freedom, not subversive of it.[32]

In fact this founders somewhat when we begin to specify actual historical circumstances. A graph tracing relations between monotheistic/

deistic / unitarian societies and repression on the one hand, and poly-theistic / Trinitarian / pluralist societies and tolerance on the other, will not yield the unequivocal evidence that Gunton might wish – and he concedes as much himself.[33] There are obvious reasons for this, to which I shall refer later when the doctrine of the Trinity is considered in its own right. Nonetheless, it remains plausible in principle however skewed in practice and in need of careful qualification.

Finally, we should also note specific implications for some of those core ideas of individualism identified previously. The most obvious has to do with equality. All persons are constituted and held within their relationship with God by their unique particularity, whatever the changing flux of their existence through time. This is an ontological reality which does not admit of degrees or exception. It is therefore a clear basis for all people mattering equally (a point which will be devel-oped later in relation to the doctrine of *imago dei*).[34]

More oblique, but just as important, is the particular nuance this sort of ontology also gives to the notion of rights. For in so far as we are all constituted by such a relationship with God, and by our rela-tionships with others, then there is at least this one primary 'right' that we may claim: access to those relationships. In its most fundamental ontological sense this is, by definition, already given. We would not *be* at all if there were not some sort of relation given. However, the full realization of such life-giving relationships in our experience may not be granted automatically, certainly not in this life. On the contrary, it is often blocked by the contingencies of life, and by its evils. That is the essence of tragedy. It happens equally when a child is deprived of the possibility of faith in God, or the love of its human parent. So the full existential and moral force of the notion emerges here, as we realize ourselves to be under a primary duty to remove that block wherever possible: it is a direct response to this most fundamental human right of *access to relationship*. (This is a socially and theologi-cally orientated concept of rights which escapes the obvious criticisms of the notion, such as Hauerwas' claim that rights make other people into adversaries and strangers.[35] Here it is quite the reverse: it makes other people into friends.)

Interestingly, McFadyen expresses this even more specifically as the right to communication, and develops the notion in concrete terms. It leads him to propose specific social priorities such as equal opportu-nity in educational strategies.[36] This in turn reminds us that such priorities should also, in Christian terms, extend to evangelism (that is, the communication of the gospel, understood specifically as the realization of relationship with God). Naturally, possibilities of effective evangelism will be limited; but we have already noted how a realist theological ontology must still hold us to the *attempt*. For while barriers to communicating the gospel universally clearly exist they are provisional and contingent, whereas the transcendent reality in whom we all subsist is ultimate and universal. Thus we are bound to make this attempt to communicate, knowing that we are not irrevocably fragmented and cut off from our common source. It is a commitment clearly reinforced by what we have now seen in this more detailed account of our ontology. We can and must communicate, as God himself does, for therein lies the very constitution of our personal identity, and our salvation – if not fully in this life, then certainly in eternity.

8

Biblical Belief, Doctrine and the Individual

Such theological ontology commits us unequivocally to valuing persons. If personal being (defined as particular being-in-relationship) is the very ground of all reality (that is, if God is), then we have the strongest possible reason for valuing all personal being. Hume's baleful gaze does still come between fact and value, at least for some. But the moment we dare talk of God's being at all, this supposed category mistake is hardly likely to detain us. God, by definition, is value-laden. And because God's being is both personal and the ground of all being, then all personal being is value-laden. People matter.[1]

Yet although some general sense of personal value is established like this, it says little on its own about the specific nature of that value: that is, how individual value is determined in relation to corporate or social needs, and the extent to which it can and should be expressed through those 'core' ideas of individualism with which we have been dealing. In other words, the relational individual may be presented as secure and substantial in and through the relational being of God – but that is only the beginning of working out a more substantive Christian anthropology and social ethic.

This now requires a much broader theological perspective: an enquiry into a history of Christian stories and ideas from biblical foundations, through doctrinal developments across the whole range of theology. We need to trawl the narratives and beliefs through which this ontology is expressed, if we are to uncover specific implications for issues of individualism. What follows is therefore an attempt to sieve biblical and systematic theology through the specific questions which have emerged: is there any balance of emphasis offered between abstract and relational views of persons, and (more generally) between individual and corporate identity? Is any kind of endorsement – or control – provided for what have come to be called the core ideas of individualism? As I have previously warned, these questions are not always directly answered, because the tradition has not always asked them in quite these terms. But they remain a general reference point.

Broad brush biblical perspectives: responsibility and solidarity

In the first instance we could simply ask whether there is any evident *overall* biblical foundation for any of these issues. In other words, is there any consistent or normative biblical picture of God's dealings with individuals or groups which crystallizes the relationship between the two? One primary focus for dealing with this question is the matter of moral and spiritual responsibility. Notions of responsibility are clearly present and highly significant in the biblical narratives (for example, in the notion of covenant). And they are never entirely eclipsed even in the face of divine sovereignty and some strands of pre-destination. But to what extent does the biblical witness locate this in the individual, considered in isolation, or in the corporate body?

At this point hermeneutical paralysis is almost bound to set in. All questions asked of the Bible on such a huge canvas beg others. Just to pose such questions might seem to imply both a spurious unity about the biblical tradition as a whole, and a spurious capacity to interpret it with any authority when we are bounded by our own limited horizons. In particular, the very form of the questions we put is more than likely to distort the texts' own categories of (for example) the individual person, or the soul. It will be hard to avoid reading into them our modern assumptions about personal identity and ideas associated with modern individualism. Cultural anthropologists have issued their own sharp warning about this, which theologians would do well to heed. So Bruce Malina, writing specifically about some of these issues, suggests this:

> In our culture, we tend to consider a person's psychological make up, his or her personality . . . individuality and uniqueness . . . as perhaps the most important elements in understanding and explaining human behavior . . . Yet if you carefully read the New Testament writings . . . you will find an almost total absence of such information.

Thus he concludes that our understanding of an individual is wholly different to that of the first-century Mediterranean world.[2]

Clearly such warnings should lead us to be wary of naive exegesis.

At the very least I shall therefore try to draw on exegetical debate which incorporates this kind of awareness in its conclusions, both in this section and in the subsequent survey of systematic doctrine. In practice this means that I can only offer generalized answers out of a complex debate.

However, I also believe that Malina's particular warning may be overstated, and his picture of the first-century Mediterranean world is itself over-simplified.[3] Furthermore, to the extent that we are driven to generalize from wide debates, this may not be so bad. For it is precisely within a broad range and diversity of traditions within the Bible, and in all the exegetical debate which is filtered through our different hermeneutical horizons, that theological knowledge is mediated. We can hardly escape some form of broad-brush perspective. And while this reveals a particular methodological presupposition (even a sort of foundationalist one), at least it is one which counters the paralysis and enables us to *get going*. We have to begin somewhere, and it is these sorts of generalized biblical foundations that we choose. They are generalizations which have been made about the specific question of individual and corporate responsibility, as they emerge through the dialectic of exegetical discussion which has surrounded them.

So we begin where we can. For a start that means we must surely acknowledge *some* sense of corporate responsibility in Hebrew anthropology. This has been expounded most forcefully in Wheeler-Robinson's celebrated claim there was a concept of 'corporate personality'.[4] It was expressed in collective cultic remedies for sin, and a shared sense of responsibility in which 'the sins of the fathers would be visited upon the children'. The Yahwist stories of creation and fall, likewise, may be taken as expressions of our corporate nature:

> man's offence . . . is not the act of an individual, but the act of man in community . . . The Yahwist then, by uniting in one the stories of man's creation and man's defection, can present an outline of a philosophy of man . . . summed up in one sentence: no man can be isolated from his fellow. (So says Westermann.)[5]

But if that is a commonly accepted starting point, there is also a widely acknowledged movement away from it. There is a discernible shift, particularly under pressure from the prophetic religion of the Exile, from corporate aspects of responsibility to individual moral and spiritual responsibility. God's justice must be worked out in and for each individual, not relegated to subsequent generations, and there must be correspondence between individual act and consequence: 'the righteousness of the righteous shall be upon himself, and the wicked-ness of the wicked shall be upon himself'.[6] This shift is often taken to be endorsed and deepened in the New Testament preaching of Jesus, in which 'God seeks out each individual lost soul with infinite love . . . and individuals decide the eternal meaning of their lives without regard to their membership in a people'.[7]

However, the instant this generalized view of a biblical pilgrimage from corporate to individual responsibility is stated, this too needs to be qualified. In the first instance, it is by no means clear that there was ever a *comprehensive* concept of corporate personality in the way that Wheeler-Robinson expounded. In its legal aspects at least, and specif-ically in relation to moral responsibility, it has crumbled under J. R. Porter's scrutiny. There always was at least some significant element of individual responsibility.[8] In its more general anthropological and psy-chological aspects (for example, if it is taken as an assertion that the Hebrew mind did not distinguish subject and object or the self from other selves). John Rogerson has also questioned the evidence with similar scepticism. Wheeler-Robinson's notions seem to be derived more from Lévy-Bruhl's (arguable) anthropological theories than from any reliable data about Hebrew life and thought.[9] Moreover, even to the extent that corporate aspects of responsibility were significant (especially in cultic theory and practice), they certainly did not disap-pear entirely under the onslaught of the prophets. So the supposed change of emphasis is softened from both sides of the shift: there was never an exclusively corporate culture in Israel, nor an exclusively individualistic culture, nor any straight line of progression between the two.

Within the New Testament world there is a similar oscillation, with no obvious movement from one clear conceptuality to another. On the one hand the starting point might seem to have shifted to the indi-vidual. Jesus' call was to individual disciples. But this cannot simply be elevated to a new covenant of individual responsibility. It needs to be qualified immediately by the new reality of the corporate body of Christ into which they were called and through which they were being newly formed. Nor were they called entirely out of, or apart from, their original *sitz-im-leben*, as if they could be treated as deraci-nated individuals. After all, the theological depth and variety of Gospels and Epistles is actually (in part) a consequence of the interplay between Jewish and Gentile 'pasts' which persisted and coexisted in the present new reality of the Kingdom. And the Kingdom itself certainly has a corporate dimension, whatever else may be drawn out of it (as we shall see later).

Both the figure of Christ, and the matter of our relationship to him, have also been conceived both corporately and individualistically. One of the more extreme theses of the corporate Christ has been John Robinson's proposal that Paul's faith and apostleship was founded on encounter with the resurrection body of Christ conceived 'not as an individual but as the Christian community'.[10] More generally, exegesis of Paul has tended recently to move away from the individualistic reading of the isolated, introspective soul struggling with his own conscience, to the one who is saved by incorporation into a new community.[11] (Both these issues will be pursued later, in discussion of Christological and soteriological doctrines.) Yet it is also true that the dialectic can always to be reopened from the other direction. As C. F. D. Moule warned over thirty years ago, we must not allow the ideological lens of our reaction against Enlightenment influences to blind us to the forms of individualism which are celebrated in the New Testament (particularly the Fourth Gospel).[12] Thus the oscillation maintains its own momentum.

Even theologies of the Old and New Testaments which attempt some unifying and systematizing perspective reveal the irreducibility of these biblical tensions. Walter Eichrodt, for example, begins at one point from the personalism and individualism of prophetic religion:

> Moreover, this God, who had encountered [the prophets] in their own lives with consuming immediacy . . . they now set over against any form of autocratic national self-will as the sovereign will compelling men to ultimate personal decision . . . The person of Man, as a Thou called by God, acquired a unique value; and this in turn gave the sphere of ultimate personal decision, namely the moral, that quite distinctive majesty from which derive both the dignity and the limitation alike of cultus and of law . . . [13]

But he immediately feels compelled to add 'even so, the solidarity of the nation in responsibility is maintained'.[14]

He then goes on to suggest that this emphasis on individuality actually created possibilities of new forms of interpersonal solidarity and forged new links across old boundaries (an echo here of the capacity for 'transcendence' we noted in some core ideas of individualism). Thus: 'it could dare to bridge the gulf between Jew and Gentile'; and 'the individual called by God's word is shown the way into a new house of Israel'; '. . . out of the profound convictions and decisions of individuals a common pattern of conduct is arrived at . . . leading to the creation of a congregation of God's people . . . Here the confrontation of collectivism and individualism is transcended, and the individual ego discovers an encounter with God which is identical with incorporation into a new relationship to his fellow men'.[15]

It is a conclusion broadly echoed by Paul Hanson's more recent study, *The People Called. The Growth of Community in the Bible*.[16] Individual responsibility, championed by prophetic literature, is certainly cherished and liberating: thus in Ezekiel 'the fatalism of the one resigned to a life of iniquity due to the weight of past [that is, collective] sin, or the smugness of the one who drew comfort from past righteousness, were both nullified by the principle of personal responsibility'.[17] But, equally, this liberation of the individual is not just for his or her own sake but, interdependently, for the health of the community: '. . . the individual finds full personhood not through self-indulgent personalism, but by becoming an unstinting contributor to the vitality of the whole people'.[18] Likewise in wisdom literature: 'although the general gnomic style of the proverbs tends to focus on the qualities of righteousness and compassion in the life of the individual, it is clear both implicitly and explicitly that these qualities are deemed the only reliable basis for a healthy life *in community*'.[19]

Within the New Testament a similar dialectic prevails, even from a theology which begins clearly at one end of it. Thus Whiteley flags up the chief polemic of his *Theology of St Paul* like this: '. . . many of St Paul's fundamental doctrines can be properly understood only if we realize that he took for granted the presuppositions of human solidarity';[20] 'members of the Church are not linked only with Christ individually; we are joined to Christ and we are joined to each other in mutual functional dependence'.[21]

Yet even with such a programme as this he also finds himself bound to resist J. A. T. Robinson's thesis (that is, that Paul's faith and apostleship was founded on the resurrection body of Christ understood only as the Christian community). And while he wants to assert that there is (through Christ) a 'general transcending of the separateness of normal human individuality', he also feels bound to assert there is no 'swallowing up of human personality', especially in eschatological terms.[22]

Hanson is similarly constrained. He finds he cannot settle in any one pole of the dialectic in the New Testament as in the Old. In his summary of his study of both Testaments he acknowledges the important biblical focus on specific individuals, and the value of individual identity. He further stresses that, while this identity is not self-generated but God-given, neither is it obliterated either by God or the covenant community.[23] Yet he also depicts the fundamental dependence of these individuals on God and others:

> It would be inaccurate to characterize the members of a true community of faith as solitary heroes of righteousness in the world. In fact, the faithful in the Bible are not portrayed as invincible individualists, capable of single-handedly vanquishing the foe. Moses, Jeremiah, and Jesus are portrayed as humans with genuine needs for comfort, encouragement, and support.[24]

In short, personal identity remains relational, even when it appears exceptional. But then again, this relationality can provide a basis for equality and personal freedom, in relation to others and in terms of access to God.[25] So the dependence and relationality of these individuals also gives something back to the autonomy of the individual (a reciprocal movement we noted before, specifically in relation to some of the core ideas of individualism). In this way the restlessness of the dialectic continues.

The point in citing these particular snapshots of biblical theology is not necessarily to endorse the balance they have settled on (and certainly not to imply they are exempt from the conditioning of their own *sitz-im-leben*). It is simply to indicate how centrally the issues raised by the previous conceptual analysis feature within the flux of biblical theology, and how resolutely they resist any simple reduction into exclusively individualistic or collectivist tendencies. It demonstrates how biblical exegesis can uncover some basic ideas of individualism (moral responsibility, personal value, personal freedom, and so on) as positive ingredients in religious piety, social liberation and integration, and as safeguards of personal identity. But it shows equally that biblical theologians have been offered no clear mandate in either the development of Israel's faith and social life, nor the new covenant itself, for the kind of individualism characterized by fragmentation and isolation. This much, even if it seems an obvious and minimal point, is perhaps a *terra firma* on which a biblical theology can begin. Thus far it resonates with, and endorses, much that emerged from the more general evaluations of natural moral instinct.

Creation, the image of God and the fall

However, biblical exegesis on specific issues is only the beginning of theology. In its interrelation with culture, and specifically in its contribution to the history of ideas, Christian belief engages even more through its systematic doctrinal developments. Here an obvious anthropological focus for systematic doctrine to begin with is creation. More specifically, there is the doctrine of the *imago dei*. For here we see particularly clearly the reciprocal relationship between the datum of the biblical images and narrative, and the prevailing philosophical and social climate of the exegetes, expositors and makers of doctrine. As the meaning of the doctrine is variously shaped within this relationship it becomes all the more evident how it bears on our particular concerns about the individual.

Westermann is insistent on this. He makes two parallel points, which combine with a single effect. Within doctrinal history the image ('man in the image of God') has been abstracted from the narrative (which is the event of God's creation); then, once abstracted, the image has been taken to refer chiefly to individual persons, statically conceived. The consequence is that attention has been focused far too much on construing some special quality belonging to individuals which mark us out as the image and likeness of God. Hence the quest through doctrinal history to derive the meaning of the image in certain attributes, such as spiritual capacities (Philo), powers of memory, intellect, love (Augustine, and some nineteenth-century Protestantism), religious and moral capacities (Schleiermacher), external appearance (Gunkel) and so on.[26]

Westermann, largely following Barth, prefers instead to interpret its meaning through the narrative. It is the event of creation which vests humanity with a special significance in relation to God. This significance belongs to humanity as such, and not because of certain particular qualities which may or may not be found in the different individuals in different degrees. Creation in the image of God is therefore primarily a general and collective concept applicable only derivatively to individuals. In Barth's (disputed) analysis it is also a relational concept, specifically defined through the reference in Genesis to the relationship of male and female: 'God created man in his own image . . . male and female he created them'.[27]

Of course, these reconceptions themselves beg a few pertinent questions. It is hard to give any definition to the general notion of our 'createdness' without reintroducing certain specific qualities. If we are made to relate to a creator God, then the form of that relation must be further specified if it is not to collapse into a merely trivial doctrine which leaves the *imago dei* applying univocally to stones, cabbages and fruit flies, as well as to the foetus, the comatose, the believer and the unbeliever. Yet if the form of relation *is* then defined it risks the very dangers the reconception sought to avoid: it is likely to become exclusive and divisive. If the form of relation is defined primarily through mental or spiritual capacity it may divide the human individual with him or herself (mind from body); and it may divide the different sorts and conditions of men and women from each other (according to our differing degrees of mental and spiritual potential); it may also divide humankind too radically from our relationship with the rest of the created order (a notable contemporary concern).

In response to these concerns there has been a recent but sustained attempt to offer a more defined theological anthropology, based on the ontology of persons-in-relation. In general terms this is what we have already referred to in the work of Zizioulas and Gunton, amongst others.[28] But they have also developed it specifically in relation to the doctrine of the *imago dei*. At the heart of this is the view that human being (as distinct from any particular qualities belonging to human individuals) is defined and constituted by the relations we have as *whole* persons, minds and bodies, with others and with God. These relations may be characterized like this:

(1) They are inclusive rather than exclusive. That is, they include what we give and receive consciously and unconsciously, in all aspects of our being, from and to the natural order around us, other persons and God.

(2) They are distinctive and asymmetrical, in so far as the relations of human persons have a different quality to those of other creatures. But they are not ultimately divisive, in so far as *all* reality is nonetheless bound up together in a network of mutually constitutive relations (that is, the dust has no mental capacity, *pace* some process philosophy, but has still contributed to human reality: so everything is to be valued in *some* way).

(3) As we have already seen, they may be derived from a Trinitarian doctrine of God in which he is himself conceived perichoretically, that is, as a community of mutually interrelating 'persons'.

(4) For some they are also eschatological: that is, these relations may take shape and develop towards a transforming future. Such a future

may be conceived within history as well as eternity (Moltmann's great concern). But either way the future is essential if we are to make any sense in Christian terms of being conformed *into* the image of God through Christ, as part of a redemptive process (already noted as an aspect of Barth's eschatological realism).

If the question is now pressed about the extent to which this conception of the *imago dei* has remained thoroughly corporate (as Westermann wishes), or whether it has tacitly reverted to something more individualistic under pressure of greater definition, we shall find echoes of much the same oscillation as before. Certainly it is a *relational* concept. Our reality is constituted by our relations with God, others and the natural order. But, equally, the reality which is thus constituted (and maintained) is of a unique individuality which is necessarily particular and 'other'. This follows from the second mark of the *imago dei*, above: that is, the distinctiveness of human persons *qua* persons. For without such particularity and otherness relatedness itself would collapse, the possibilities of personal giving and receiving (and love itself) would cease, and the category of personhood would disintegrate. This is the logic of Gunton's position which has already emerged in the general discussion of ontology, worth quoting now in full:

> Of crucial importance is the matter of the way in which the structure – the taxis – of human community constitutes the particularity, uniqueness and distinctness of persons: their free otherness in relation. To be a person is to be constituted in particularity and freedom – to be given space to be – by others in community. *Otherness* and *relation* continue to be the two central and polar concepts here. Only where both are given due stress is personhood fully enabled. Their co-presence will rule out both the kinds of egalitarianism which is the denial of particularity, and leads to collectivism, and forms of individualism which in effect deny humanity to those unable to stand on their own feet.[29]

I have already indicated broad sympathy with this position, provided the relational particular is adequately safeguarded against a slippery regress.[30] With that proviso, it represents a valuable marker in the debate on theological anthropology to illustrate some of the issues we are pursuing. That is, it indicates a significant and salutary tradition which sharply challenges any concept of an abstract individual. But equally, it maintains the individual in the dignity of his or her unique particularity. As we have seen, it also offers a clear basis for equal value of persons, with no difference of degree. For the fundamental onto-logical fact that each human individual is constituted as a particular human being by relation to God and others is common to all, regard-less of the degree to which this is realized in experience.[31] It also helps define the value of 'inwardness': the image of God may be found with-in the individual, but only if we look at the individual person-in-relation.

Of course, the fact that this ontological truth about the image of God is not fully realized in existential reality is also highly significant. The *imago dei* has been seriously distorted within the struggles of our freedom and our finitude.[32] That is the doctrine of our fallenness, and our sinfulness, integral to our understanding of creation.

So what of this?

Chiefly, the fall speaks of disordered relationships and impover-ished identity, as an inevitable aspect of the human condition from earliest times. (The chaotic nature of Hobbes' 'original state' was just one political–philosophical echo of this fundamental Christian dogma.) For whether we adopt an Augustinian or Irenean account of the origin of evil (that is, whether evil is conceived as a privation of good for which we are corporately culpable, or as a virtually inevitable condition for free persons to grow to maturity), either way evil is being charac-terized in Christian tradition as a deep-rooted sense of disorder and fragmentation in identity and relationships (just those symptoms of malaise highlighted in part one of this essay).

Thus we find in the Genesis myth that a key consequence of fall-enness is, undoubtedly, the disruption of right *relations* – between persons and God, each other, and the environment. There ceases to be a sense of belonging. There also ceases to be a clear sense of iden-tity ('Am I my brother's keeper?'). Indeed, death brings the terrifying prospect of *no* identity. Even within life there is a profound sense of alienation (Adam and Eve are driven from the garden). In another of its stories this is accompanied by wider social fragmentation, symbolized powerfully by the broken language of Babel.[33] Finally, in the pivotal revelation of the nature of evil which we reach in the New Testament story of the crucifixion, all these themes are recapitulated and sharp-ened: a fallen condition means forsakenness.

As with other doctrines, the variety of interpretative development which follows from these narratives is considerable. Evil has been perceived to be embodied in different forms throughout the history of the theological enterprise: within devils, individual persons and social structures. A more specific analysis of how *sin* has been perceived yields a similar history of diversity (and controversy). In part this reflects some of the oscillations already noted in biblical notions of responsibility: conceptions of sin have ranged (for example) from Reformation concerns with individual sinfulness to the corporate and structural accounts of more recent liberation and feminist theologies. Paradoxically, they have also oscillated between Reformation and Protestant emphasis on sin as a *collective* condition, and Catholic emphasis on sins as particular transgressions identifiable as individual actions.[34]

There has also been recent scrutiny of traditional tendencies to characterize sin as pride and the will-to-power. These have been criticized as a distorted male perspective which fails adequately to recognize the corresponding sin of servility and total passivity (a sin because it colludes with the domination of the powerful and proud). The tension here is between sin as self-assertion, and sin as a failure to realize a self at all.[35] (This obviously raises the specific question of how Christian tradition has understood the notion self-realization, one of the important core ideas of individualism – something which will be dealt with later in more detail, in relation to *agape* love.)[36]

To be sure, these debates about the nature of evil and sin do not settle our particular concern about the status of the individual: they imply no clear-cut assumption either of wholesale individualism or collectivism. However, the fact that they remain restless with either extreme is once again significant. It is a direct correlate of what we have seen the positive *imago dei* to entail – a profound concern for individual persons *in their relationships*.

More generally they affirm precisely this fact that evil is manifested most characteristically in broken relationships, lost identity and forsakenness, which is therefore the constant backdrop against which Christian belief struggles to realize the true image of God. So it certainly confirms this agenda for Christian concern, as for all human concern: in one way or another we are looking to reintegrate individuals as secure persons in a wider web of right relations.

The Trinity and the Spirit

But what if we now turn to the doctrine of God, and the Trinity in particular? This has already featured to some extent. It provides general ontological foundation for all talk of individuals-in-relationship.

However, we also noted how it provides only an ambivalent basis for reading off more specific social and anthropological implications. So is there anything more that can be said here?

In fact the causes of this ambivalence prove well worth investigating. It arises first from the fact that the doctrine is itself already an organic development. It is mutually constitutive of other doctrines, which themselves are subject to revision and reconception. It has also adapted to, and been shaped by, its more general cultural, intellectual and social environment, as well as reacting upon it. As such it is no immutable dogma issuing a fixed moral and social agenda, but a slippery notion susceptible to a plethora of interpretations and bound to spawn as many ethical and social implications.

Yet within this wide field of interpretation, there are still some generalizations which can act as signposts. At the very least it is worth recalling how the most celebrated doctrinal debates of the early Christian centuries oscillated between the pressure to conceive plurality (and equality) within the Godhead, and the concern to resist straightforward tritheism. Two features of Augustine's presentation of the Trinity illustrate the problem of being caught between these two imperatives. It is an old and familiar story.

First, in order to safeguard the singularity of God as a source of being, Augustine conceives the Son and Spirit as derivative from the Father; and in order to distinguish the Son from the Spirit he also conceives the Spirit to be in some way derivative from the Son; he further describes the Spirit as the 'bond of love' between Father and Son (just as he is the ground of our union with God). Immediately, however, this appears to subordinate the Son and Spirit to the Father (and the Spirit to both); it also might seem to reduce the Spirit to 'mere' relation; but, equally, the schema also appears to compromise God's divine singularity by elevating 'Son' alongside 'Father' as a double source of being. Greek Trinitarian thinking objected strongly, both to the implied duality of the divine source, and to the tendency to de-personalize the Spirit.

Augustine's thinking has therefore been duly qualified heavily, refined and revised. But it is worth noting that his characterization of the Spirit as the ground and catalyst of relationship has proved to have a particularly durable and adaptable role in theological thinking. Not least, his potentially depersonalized conception of the Spirit has nonetheless drawn attention to the category of relation. For the dynamics of a tradition which would not allow the Spirit to be side-lined has rallied to its defence, so to speak, not so much by denying the Spirit's relational role and character as by elevating the category of relation itself to a new significance.[37] What Augustine has not necessarily intended he has, paradoxically, helped to provoke.

The second pertinent feature of his thought is his appeal to analogies drawn from *within* the individual human person to illuminate the nature of the Trinity. Here it is the mind, knowledge and love, or the memory, understanding and will, of an individual, which provide some sort of picture of the three persons of the single Godhead. Such analogies arise for Augustine, in part, from neo-platonic assumptions about the significance of the human mind as a focus of the creative imprint: it is there that we shall find an image of God and a trace of the Trinity.

However, it is the consequence of looking (only) there which concerns us, more than the epistemological basis. Clearly, the individuality of the one God has overwhelmed the plurality of the three persons; once the chief referent for the analogy is the human individual, rather than human relations, then this outcome is inevitable. *And it is here again we find the dynamics of the tradition as a whole constrained to react.* For it has found itself bound to offer more fertile analogies and conceptualities (and an alternative epistemological basis for them). Hence the ancient notion of *perichoresis*, already referred to, portraying persons in mutually constitutive relationships and offering a creative new basis for defining individuals as persons-in-relation. In this way the Trinity has been conceived more recently through social analogies – though this, naturally, raises the spectre of tritheism and has provoked its own process of careful refinement and qualification.[38]

The point of this brief recapitulation is not to attempt any new insight into it, but simply to recall that the internal dynamics of Christian theology have consistently resisted resolving the doctrine of God into any simple formula of either singularity or plurality. And they have, positively, highlighted relation as a key category. So at the very least this reminds us that if a Christian anthropology is attempting to read off its own shape from the shape of God there will be no mandate either for an abstract and isolated individualism, or for the dissolution of the individual altogether.

But the question still presses. Is it possible to go beyond such a minimal set of parameters? We have already noted that Gunton ventures more, and it is worth recalling the heart of his proposals here. He draws direct lines between doctrinal tendencies (Unitarian and Trinitarian) and consequences for social ethics and policy. Thus the more unitary the conception of God, and especially the more singular the source of power, the more repressive and totalitarian the social order it sanctions or facilitates. Ultimately an individual deity suppresses proper individuality in others. It is in (understandable) reaction against this false doctrine of God, says Gunton, that western modernity displaced deity in the fruitless search for universal patterns of reason, and post-modernity has sunk in a sea of plural and unconnected realities.

Equally, when Father, Son and Holy Spirit are conceived in *perichoresis*, the social consequences change. Once *perichoresis* was characterized in more detail the point became clear. We have to conceive the three persons of the Trinity not merely as 'modes' of the one true and individual God, nor must we think of God as the underlying substance in which they all participate; instead the three actually constitute one another's being by their mutual relatedness.[39] As such this doctrine of God underwrites the meaning and value of particularity without either subsuming it into a whole, or perceiving it as a threat; and by relating particulars to each other it makes community an essential context for individuality to flourish.

As already indicated, I am wary of pressing this too far in practice. There is always a risk of over-simplifying connections between beliefs and social programmes. The causal web includes too many other strands to be sure how far any one theological idea has become embodied in the values of a society, or to be sure how it is applicable to any detail of policy. The distorting reality of sin, evil and countless local contingencies must also be taken into account. Small wonder, then, that history offers plenty of counter examples to Gunton's suggestions. (Who, for instance, would presume to unlock the Balkan conflicts of past and present according to this key? Orthodox Serbs, Catholic Croats and Bosnian Muslims may well represent a spectrum of Trinitarian–Unitarian belief, but that hardly translates slickly into a corresponding spectrum between repression and tolerance.) It has become a familiar point: what may be conceptually valuable is quickly confused or compromised in historical embodiment.

This caveat, along with the need for conceptual clarification about the relative status of relation and being (elaborated above),[40] illustrates well the doctrine's slippery nature mentioned at the outset. The difficulties are both conceptual and practical (moving from ideas to their historical embodiment in realistic social programmes has rarely been surefooted, even with less complex notions than the Trinity). So perhaps after all we cannot go much further than offering the doctrine in very general terms as: (1) the ontological foundation for individuality-in-relationship and (2) a useful overall conceptual pattern for social relationships - but making no hard claims for its historical effective-ness in specific circumstances.

Nonetheless, even this much has elaborated somewhat on the doctrine's relevance - both its limits and possibilities. Furthermore, even such broad parameters can be valuable when they arise out of such a profound vision of God. That is, there is always an important *motivating* force in this Christian ontology. In God, after all, we have an 'ultimate' reason for balance between core ideas of individual value and individualistic (or collectivist) excesses. Here is the ultimate foun-dation for all religious, rational or intuitive attacks on the pernicious notion of the abstract individual: if God himself only exists *qua* God in mutual relation to others, then we, analogously (and made in his image) must accept that we are similarly formed out of others, and the Other.

One further word about the Holy Spirit also deserves some men-tion here - if only to scatter him more widely abroad elsewhere as well. For while the Spirit has been explicitly referred to in this section (to help define the inner life of the Trinity) we should at least note that he could function just as well as the subtitle of every section. That is because the Spirit of the inner life of the Trinity *is* also the Spirit at work in the world, supremely and precisely the work of God in making relationships - in all the ways elaborated under other head-ings. All the theological resources by which we understand and attempt to reintegrate a proper view of personhood could therefore be properly subsumed under the general heading of the Spirit's work. This was the burden of John Taylor's justly celebrated book *The Go-Between God* - a sustained exposition of the work of the Spirit in all relationships within the world.[41] As such it is a salutary reminder of the full implications of a truly perichoretic Trinity, both immanently and transcendentally.

Incarnation

If we now ask similar questions of the doctrine of incarnation then a range of similar issues must be addressed. That is, we must first face the matter of the doctrine's own diversity. For there is, of course, no single concept of incarnation used univocally throughout the history of Christian theology. The language, meaning and concepts employed to convey the significance of Jesus Christ have ebbed, flowed and swirled continuously around the rocks of new knowledge and the changing currents of intellectual fashion. So once again we should not expect its anthropological implications for the nature and significance of individual persons (or its implications for social ethics) to command any easy consensus.

This would become particularly apparent if we were to accept Sarah Coakley's six senses of incarnational meaning in Christian theology. These range from the uncontroversial but trivial generality that God is involved in all human life, to the disputed and highly specific orthodox claims that Christ pre-existed his earthly life as the second person of the Trinity, and became a human individual as Jesus of Nazareth.[42] The former *need* have little direct bearing on the significance of human individuality as such, or social relations, though it certainly need not exclude either. The latter is more obviously fertile ground – but then even at this well-defined end of the spectrum of incarnational meaning, its anthropological implications do not necessarily select themselves solely at one end of *their* spectrum.

So what, if anything, can be said? A strictly orthodox Chalcedonian (or kenotic) doctrine of Christ provides some obvious starting points, and it will serve well as an example of the range of options. To begin with it certainly can be taken as a profound validation of human individuality. Indeed, it can provide the most significant such endorsement strictly conceivable. For if we consider that God himself (that than which nothing greater can be conceived) experienced life as a human individual, then we are faced with a proposition which is virtually impossible to state neutrally (whether or not it is impossible to state *sensibly* is, for the moment, another question).[43] It makes the notion of individuality value-laden to the point of sublimity, as the medieval poet acknowledges picturesquely by locating the wonderment in the womb of Mary: 'In that rose contained was / heaven and earth in littel space: *res miranda*'. 'Littel space' here is, in effect, a testimony to the value of particularity intrinsic in this view of incarnation: it refers to a sense in which God in Christ is here and not there, in this bodily person and not another (or at least not in the same way). Thus incarnation (in this sense) is the most profound demonstration that individuality is divinely endorsed.

But can this be taken further? What particular notion of individuality is being validated?

The answers here will depend partly on wider issues of theological method. Thus if the question rides on the back of a strong natural theology then the fact of incarnation becomes the divine endorsement of those human qualities which are counted to be evident on other grounds. In other words, if core ideas of individualism such as individual responsibility, self-realization, originality, privacy and so on, are deemed to belong essentially to the meaning of individuality, then this doctrine simply validates them further.

But given stronger claims to special revelation in history then more will be entailed. Whatever the difficulties of historical reconstruction and general hermeneutics, the doctrine will require attention to the actual, contingent, empirical characteristics of the individuality of the historical Jesus. So there will be great significance in the nature of the historical portraits which are painted of him. For instance, is he not the one who withdrew to relate individually with God? Perhaps this implies some sense of privacy. Did he not appear (prophetically) to transcend some of the *mores* of his time, as well as being formed by them? If so, perhaps this implies some sense of originality and creativity. To be sure, history is not quite the *terra firma* of dogma on such matters, as we witness 'Jesus the Jew' battling it out with all the other historical reconstructions of the biblical critics. But it will involve precisely this kind of discussion in order to stake out the ground on which the Christian stands in its definitions and valuing of 'true' individuality.

However, all this exemplifies only one aspect of an orthodox reading of Christology. There is another aspect which does not *simply* endorse individuality. For within the same corpus of orthodox tradition the God who was in Christ was also, pre-eminently, a *relational* figure. This too arises from a combination of dogmatic and empirical criteria. He is portrayed as one formed and sustained by his relationship to the Father and the Spirit. He is also quite evidently constituted in some way by his relations with other persons. Thus even when the doctrine of the virgin birth is taken in a literal sense, excluding the genetic involvement of a human father, there is no denying some significant human origin within the womb of Mary. This grounds the origin of his humanity in some fundamental relationship with another human being, as well as in his relationship to the Father. Furthermore, as both Pauline and Johannine theology construes it, he goes on to summon others into a corporate and constitutive relationship. It is a relationship which fulfils both their proper humanity and his own mission: 'I pray ... that they may all be one, even as thou Father art in me, and I in thee, that they also may be in us ... I in them and thou in me, that they may become perfectly one.'[44]

Thus the notion of Christ as a 'corporate' figure emerges as easily from orthodox doctrines of incarnation as does the endorsement of individuality. Indeed, for C. F. D. Moule, it is precisely the corporate nature of Christ which helps define the meaning of his uniqueness as a *divine*-human figure. It is a crucial point which sets the uniqueness of his individuality and particularity within a framework of a unique kind of mutuality and interrelationship. There is no real paradox here, just a rich and complex reading of the full weight of the ortho- dox tradition, which uncovers two distinct but complementary senses of uniqueness. .

All this amply illustrates the fact that a range of anthropological implications could emerge, even from within just one (orthodox) end of the doctrinal spectrum. So again it is a doctrine which offers no pre- cise blueprint for a social ethic. Yet at the same time it also illustrates some general parameters and constraints. For even within this one conception of incarnation the resources both for maintaining *and regulating* core ideas of individualism have become apparent. They have been given profound validation, but they have also been balanced with a thoroughgoing sense of relationality. As such, it is a doctrine which reinforces the general pattern we are beginning to trace through biblical and doctrinal anthropology.

Redemption:

Being in Christ

The notion of the corporate Christ also highlights the integral rela- tionship between Christology and soteriology. In some way or other it is by our incorporation into Christ's person and work that we are saved. This alerts us to the limitations of considering any concept of incarnation in abstraction. It reminds us that it is just as likely to function as a stimulus for anthropological views when it is construed within the wider work of redemption. So this too merits consideration.

As with concepts of incarnation, models of atonement and general doctrines of salvation have been similarly shaped and reshaped with- in the flux of a wider history of ideas and events – and again I cannot rehearse anything like the full text of that story here. But it is still possible to put down some markers where there have been, and remain, significant implications for issues of individuality and individualism. These arise first from this specific notion of a corporate Christ. For this is one aspect of the general struggle to relate the particular achievements of an historically rooted Christ figure with universal or potentially universal effects. It provokes a fertile question with a long history of revealing answers. How may we be related effectively to Christ so that we may be effectively saved?

In one sense the biblical material both raises and answers these questions uncompromisingly, at least in its own categories. It is utterly Christocentric. We are only saved through the particularity of Jesus Christ. This salvation is then appropriated by personal faith and experienced in corporate membership of a body. At the same time it is also potentially universal, for *all* things are reconciled through Christ.[45] All that is stated clearly enough, in its own terms. But of course it gives rise to its own set of paradoxes, and when these are strained through further attempts at human understanding the questions arise again, and the prevailing philosophical climates again produce a variety of solutions.

Thus Irenaeus' doctrine of recapitulation (Pauline in origin), envisaging Christ as a representative of the whole race, depended on a philosophical undergirding in which particulars participated in real universals. Athanasius, Gregory of Nyssa and Gregory Nazianzen all operated in a similar way with a neo-platonic notion of the consubstantiality of all people whereby Christ gains access to our humanity by his own. So the theological issue about the *modus operandi* of redemption must be understood, historically, as an aspect of the general philosophical problem of relating any particular to the universal kind it instantiated.

This became a central issue in medieval philosophy. Indeed, as Hamilton points out, the very meaning of the term 'individual' belonged originally to this debate (that is, it referred primarily to logic and metaphysics, rather than to human relations).[46] And when such discussion was played out specifically in Christian doctrine it yielded (for example) Anselm's atonement theory. Thus for Anselm it was a strong sense of the reality of the universal which led him to construct his doctrine of atonement on the assumption of human solidarity (by which the 'transaction' of the cross affected *all* humankind). But then, as the pendulum swung, and as the debate shifted more into the field of human relations, it also gave birth to Abelard's preference for the primary reality of the individual. Hence:

> For Abelard the individual is of supreme importance; and here he is in accord with the general medieval movement, particularly strong in the eleventh century, towards a more passionate and inward devotion as the individual strove imaginatively to share, for

example, in the sufferings of Christ ... Such an exposition of the atonement marks a transition from the outlook which sees God dealing with humanity as a whole ... to one in which the ethical and psychological qualities of the individual in the community begin to receive fuller recognition.[47]

This is historical testimony to the same sort of interplay between corporate or collectivist and individualist tendencies which we are tracing throughout: that is, a doctrinal debate in which neither tendency entirely overwhelms the other.

But it is not just the pattern of a pendulum swing through time (as Anselm gives way to Abelard). It is also discernible in the constraints and balance that each tendency has been compelled to acknowledge within itself, as the resources of theology resisted the far point to which prevailing philosophy might have lured it. Thus even for Anselm the universal could not be allowed to swallow up individuality and personal moral response: for all his vision of solidarity he also insisted that the pardon effected by the transaction had to be personally *received* (and only some – mostly monks! – would be worthy to receive it). Conversely, Abelard did not find himself able to capitulate to anything like the unfettered fragmentation of modern forms of extreme individualism: that is, he certainly did not deny some sense of universality in which we all participate.

Broadly speaking, the modern cast of mind has continued to oscillate within these same parameters. It has had to struggle with incorporation, to cast around for a new conceptuality with which to understand the notion, and to resist any extreme implications which exclude either proper individuality or real and effective (that is, 'saving') relationship. Thus, on the one hand, our difficulty in making sense of 'real universals' has inclined some modern theology to warm more to Abelard's subjectivism: we are related to Christ only in so far as we individually respond to him (which is the fading force of existentialist theology). Yet this appears to limit the scope of Christ's saving efficacy, and it does little justice to other ways in which we have been driven to conceive human solidarity (that is, the extent to which we are formed by each other out of common genetic, social or environmental inheritance). Hence, on the other hand, the need to revive some crypto-universals under a different guise. We have to acknowledge our participation in *some* way in other universal (or at least trans-individual) realities.

There is no clear consensus of how this might be conceived, particularly in relation to Christ's person and work. We are still searching for categories to describe an intimate interrelationship with an other

who also relates (at least potentially) to all others, and in which relation there is the possibility of our transformation without obliterating
our personal identity. (Baillie's account was one attempt to articulate
such a relation. He summarized the experience in the dictum 'not I but
the grace of God, yet truly I'. But this hardly *explains* the experience,
even though it might aptly describe it.)[48]

All this is further indication of the persistence of the problem of
relating the particular to the universal in Christocentric models of
salvation. The point here, however, is not the usual one: that is, highlighting an enduring conceptual difficulty with traditional claims,
either to debunk, defend or revise the claims themselves (something
I have tried to deal with in another book).[49] Rather, it is simply to
provide further evidence of the way in which Christian theology resists
reduction into any over-simplified anthropological schema: its own
resources simply will not allow it to settle into unfettered individualism or uncritical collectivism, in this matter of redemption as well as
in other matters.

Justification by grace

Another key marker for Christian anthropology, irresistible within any
general history of the doctrine of redemption, has to do with the
notion of justification by grace. Some background to this has already
been referred to. It is partly a matter of Pauline exegesis, which again
has oscillated between various emphases in doctrinal history and
engages ambivalently in the wider history of ideas. It has received
considerable attention recently.

Whether or not Augustine was chiefly responsible (as many seem
to think),[50] a good deal of interpretation of the Pauline material has
assumed that his theology of salvation was built out of his own tor-
mented and introspective conscience: that is, an edifice erected from
'individualistic' foundations of an acute sense of personal moral
responsibility before God, with the corresponding possibility of
individual reconciliation and release. Grace is quite simply a divine
initiative, given in Christ, to liberate individuals from the crippling
burden of guilt and failure. Justified as we are by grace, through faith,
and not through 'works of the law' (religious allegiance or practice),
we no longer stand under the paralysing shadow of personal condem-
nation or alienation from God. This has resonated through much
Reformation theology, and has persisted particularly in Protestant
circles.

At best it has liberated individuals and groups from the oppressive heteronomy of institutional religious corruption and superstition. Individuals need no longer depend on religious authorities to mediate and measure out acceptance by God and a sense of belonging to God. There is immediate access to and acceptance by God without requiring proper standing or right relationship within institutional religion. It has given genuine release for tortured spirits at a personal level. It has given birth to doctrines of atonement which bear the fruit of Wesley's great cry of joy: 'my chains fell off / my heart was free / I rose, went forth, and followed thee'. And we might well note just how existentially pertinent such a belief can be in a fragmented culture of alienated individuals, such as our own. It is precisely this deep metaphysical sense of belonging and acceptance which the isolated post-modern person both lacks and longs for. It can empower the individual spiritually, even when other relationships have failed.

The detailed analysis offered in the first part of the book reinforces the force of this point. We are a people isolated from ourselves (strained by a lack of integrity between private and social roles), and isolated from any wider community of values: so the post-modern psyche is stressed and guilty by a sense of belonging *nowhere*. Furthermore, we have sensed that we cannot adequately reintegrate or 'justify' ourselves by anything else on offer: neither the adoption of managerial values, nor the therapist's attempt to reintegrate us within our private selves, will satisfy. And we certainly cannot wait for the healing of wider society while we live under this acute pressure. Hence the significance of a belief that we belong to God who is the very heart of the universe behind and beyond all present fragmentation; a belief that such belonging comes from God's initiative and does not depend on any impossible 'work' or perfection of our own or in society as a whole. Such a belief should connect powerfully in our current situation. It is, potentially, a doctrine of profound hope and healing.

It is also a doctrine which can set us free to live more effectively. At best it releases us from the existential and ethical paralysis of isolation and fragmentation. Here it illustrates a profound but paradoxical sense of personal freedom in Christian belief and experience (which does not quite fit neatly into Enlightenment notions of autonomy). In so far as an individual's liberation requires the prior declaration and summons of God in Christ he or she is not 'intrinsically' free. Freedom is *given*. Yet the very summons also presupposes some sort of capacity for personal response and responsibility which is recognized in us as individuals, as well as communities of people. So in that sense at least some autonomy is presupposed. And either way this freedom is primarily positive in its orientation. For although freedom is *from* the bondage of sin and its paralysing, fragmenting consequence, the fundamental 'act' of freedom is *for* God and others.[51]

Yet all this expounds only one strand of exegesis. There is another story altogether to be told about this doctrine. This has gained ground considerably in recent years, reinforced by a growing perception that the Augustinian version of grace may also have *contributed* to something of our current malaise. For its reverse side can provide sanction (however spurious) to a 'privatized' notion of faith, and that is a short step to reinforcing the excessive fragmentation of culture in general. As such it has not only produced healthy liberation, it has also borne the rotten fruit of obsessive and isolating guilt. Moreover, the exegetical basis which has given rise to it has itself been challenged significantly. It gives rise to an alternative reading of St Paul, summarized thus by Hamilton:

> The impulse that led Paul to formulate his teaching about justification was not the need to discover a timeless answer to the problem of the Western introspective conscience, but the need to 'justify' the status of Gentile Christians as honorary Jews. His focus is on the unity of mankind and of the whole of creation; it is on love as concern for the community, not on integrity in working out the tensions in each individual soul and conscience.[52]

In short, the idea of justification by grace as a palliative to the individual's conscience is not necessarily the only or 'true' reading of Paul: it may be something projected onto him out of our post-Enlightenment preoccupations with the individual and inwardness (the roots of this are alleged to lie in Augustine's misreading, who in turn led Luther astray). Instead, Paul was chiefly concerned to justify the status of Gentiles as part of the people of God. In other words, the primary meaning of justification by grace is inclusiveness. Grace permits and empowers people of any race, culture (and gender) to belong to the people of God. This again bears on the meaning of freedom. Freedom is given (as before), but here it is even more explicitly given by God *in and for community*, as diverse people accept each other and empower each other to be themselves.

If this alternative is accepted wholesale then this too presents itself as an apposite doctrine in our current social situation – where diversity has become a threat, and fragmentation (rather than freedom) is the result. A belief that the Kingdom of God can and must accommodate diversity as a positive aspect of freedom and fulfilment, while remaining a community, gives theological depth and motivation to precisely the sort of social vision now needed. It echoes similar insights and implications in the social doctrine of the Trinity. (In terms of the internal ordering of Christian doctrine, such a reading of 'justification by grace' would place feminist and liberation theologies as vital subsections of just this doctrine: it is a doctrine to do with the inclusion of the excluded.)

So either way the doctrine is pertinent. But even more so if *both* readings are accepted, and held in mutually regulating tension. For in fact we do not have to choose between Hamilton's stark alternatives. On the one hand it is by no means clear that a so-called 'individualistic' reading of Paul is *wholly* a projection of our post-Enlightenment preoccupations. Equally, I would not wish entirely to relativize the latter 'social' exegesis by dismissing it merely as the function of contemporary concerns. Both strands of exegesis draw out from a rich text insights which, arguably, are both hermeneutically sustainable. They are theologically and logically compatible, both having to do with belonging and acceptance without requiring élitist qualifications or impossible efforts. At least some recent commentators have presented a balance of both readings, rather than a choice between them.[53]

It is precisely when both are allowed full exegetical and expository weight (without undue ideological interference) that the most important point of this discussion emerges. For what it illustrates again is the fact that within the flux of various horizons of interpretation there is an interplay and mutual regulation between positive core ideas of individualism and their development in morally ambivalent and dangerous programmes of thought. When such a doctrine as grace is in danger of being hijacked in the service of excessive privatization, then the 'internal' resources of the doctrine are sufficient to respond and regulate within the hermeneutical process.

Ecclesiology

This debate on Pauline exegesis also raises the matter of ecclesiology. For if we belong to God as individual persons, yet also belong as part of a body of believers, then this immediately begs similar questions of balance and clarification. What kind of endorsement – or critique – of individualistic ideas emerges here in the way the *Church* is conceived? Are there any principles or norms which determine the primary locus of God's dealings with us? For instance, in what form does he most decisively address us within the Church? As individuals, as church communities, or as individuals *through* the authority of the community? In general terms the groundwork for these questions has already been laid in the introductory discussion of 'broad-brush' biblical perspectives. But the more specific question remains about the conception and constitution of church life and authority.

In many respects it is hard to venture much in this context. This is because it is an issue peculiarly resistant to the sort of theological abstraction I am attempting. Here especially the skewing of sin, the pressures of power and the vagaries of cultural relativity, make it particularly hard to disentangle normative theological foundations from actual practice in the institutional Church. It is a difficulty which has been there from earliest times, as C. K. Barrett ruefully laments: 'what stands out when we move from the New Testament to the post-apostolic literature and the post-apostolic church is not so much the addition of something fresh as a deficiency in *theological* criticism' (emphasis mine).[54]

But perhaps this much may at least serve as a signpost. Seminally, there is the Pauline image of the Church as a body and its elaboration in 1 Corinthians.[55] This affirms dignity and worth in *all* its members, established by their differing roles within the Church. Thus particularity and differentiation is valued and constituted within the context of mutual dependence and relationality. It reflects the Trinitarian basis of all right relationship, which must obtain specifically for the Church if it is to be the body *of Christ* (which, in Johannine terms, must relate as the Father loved the Son, 'before the foundation of the world').

This provides at least some sort of a theoretical theological framework for leadership, apostolicity and priesthood. Priesthood should be a corporate notion, exercised collectively by all members through their diverse ministries.[56] Apostolic and prophetic leadership should function as it did at first, in an interdependent relationship with other apostles, wider councils and the 'testing' of the worshipping body.[57] So within the body there is no single overriding locus of divine authority. Neither the representative leaders of the institution nor any individuals have such status. For although notions of leadership and priesthood have subsequently developed hierarchically, there are always traces of this more fundamental pattern of the body reasserting itself, often critically, in relation to current practice.[58] The Reformation has been a key period in that process (but by no means the only one).

One of the most judicious recent surveys of these issues is by Oliver

O'Donovan. Out of his dialogue with this whole process of ecclesio-logical development he offers the following observations. With regard to the *locus* and *form* of the divine dealings with the Church he suggests first, in general terms: 'what we have to discuss, when we touch on the relation between collective and individual, is not a dialectic of individual freedom and collective authority, but a dialectic of two free-doms, in which both community and believer are authorized to be free human agents . . .'.[59] Thus: 'both the church's freedom and the individual's freedom consist in finding fulfilment in each other, and so displaying in outline the lineaments of the Kingdom of God'.[60]

More specifically, this means that God addresses both the individ-ual and community 'directly', but there will be some kinds of address for which the community will be the more appropriate channel, and others for which the individual will be the recipient. In the latter category belong the inner life, thoughts and motives of the individual. So in that area, in so far as God also speaks through the Church, the Church's characteristic form of address to the individual will be counsel rather than command: 'because it [counsel] respects the indi-vidual's status as one whom God also addresses directly, and whose particular decisions are partly hidden from public gaze'.[61] This consti-tutes a distinctively Christian notion of privacy which has less to do with the interference of the state and infringement of property rights, and more to do with the individual's need to internalize and reflect on God's address: an 'internal moment of reflection'.[62] Inwardness *is* sig-nificant. But again, it is not sovereign. For in other areas the collective authority of the Church remains prescriptive (although still provi-sional, this side of the eschaton). These areas are church discipline, to defend its integrity when its members act publicly in breach of its moral teaching.[63]

Such is just the outline of an ecclesiological doctrine that might be abstracted normatively from all the contingencies of historical development and the distorting factors which inevitably drive it. I will press it no further here. But if it does represent a fair attempt, it certainly suggests a theory of the Church to reinforce the general point we are dealing with. In principle the Church should be ordered with-in itself both to value the particularity of individuals and to value the community which helps constitute us persons. Both are subjects of God's concern. Both are counted as agents and spheres of his activ-ity, and are mutually dependent. There is no licence to subordinate either to the other. Notions of privacy and individual autonomy are cherished, but also set in a wider context of responsible belonging.

Resurrection and eschatology

Finally, it is also possible to draw on the history of general eschato-logical concepts, and the resurrection of the body in particular, to illuminate similar themes.

Here, on the one hand, there is a shift which can be traced within Jewish eschatology from the corporate generally, to the small group, then to the individual. In the late apocalyptic literature of the Old Testament, belief in the resurrection of individuals has become a clear and integrated aspect of general notions of judgement and salvation.[64] It derives from the profound sense that human relationship with God is so significant that it would not arbitrarily be ruptured and cast aside at death. This in turn becomes inseparable from the positive power of ideas of personal responsibility, religious self-realization and individual value. There is even (in a tentative pre-modern way) the development of some notion of individual *rights* before the Creator: the seed of this, which never quite took root in Job, flowered in more fertile soil later when the martyrs of the Maccabean period received their reward.

It is a shift which transferred easily to gospel teaching about the Kingdom and the after-life. Although there are corporate aspects of the New Testament images, it is individual aspects which swiftly came to dominate in the exegetes and expositors of the early centuries. In particular, the point of judgement was taken individualistically (in spite of the corporate dimensions in such parables as the sheep and goats). Thus Augustine understands Revelation's 'book to be opened' allegor-ically as the conscience of each individual. The shift ensured that the corporate aspect drifted out of sight, so that 'collective millenarian eschatology waned, and . . . the Kingdom began to be presented (e.g. in Origen) as an event that would take place only in the soul of the individual believer'.[65]

Reformation and Enlightenment-inspired eschatologies, as may be expected, had little incentive to reverse this trend from within their own general theological and philosophical agenda. And by the time we reach the flowering of Liberal Protestantism in the nineteenth century eschatological issues had been largely overtaken by the debate between another kind of balance: the possibilities of this-worldly realization (in an ethical community), as distinct from other-worldly hopes beyond the grave. This means the issue between individual and corporate sal-vation was not resolved at this stage. However, if anything the focus nonetheless remained on the individual. For while there is much talk of realized communities, there is also a strongly individualistic ethic.

Harnack, for example, defines the essence of Christianity and works out his eschatology chiefly in terms of the fatherhood of God and the infinite value of each individual human soul. And the existentialist theologies of the twentieth century, typified by Bultmann, renewed the momentum of an individualizing (as well as realizing) tendency even further.

Yet, equally, there have always been resources in the text and the tradition to regulate such a tendency. Modern studies on the nature of religious language, and especially Jesus' parables, have reinstated readings which allow a *double entendre* between collective as well as individual interpretations. Some images are 'tensive': that is, they bear compound meanings. Thus the Kingdom of God is amongst *us*, individually and corporately, and we would be unwise to choose definitively between the two (any more than we should choose exclusively between its present and future meanings).[66] Nor is this just a conclusion from recent theories of religious language. It is notable, for example, that in both East and West the notion of a communion of saints was a key element in early eschatology. According to Kelly, Ambrose's 'chief thought' is of 'blessed fellowship which the saints have with one another and with God, and of the mutually sympathetic charity which binds them together', and this is an inescapable characteristic of the nature of eternal life as conceived throughout early Christendom.[67] As indicated, later concerns have focused more on the extent to which communion can be realized in this world: but as such it is still precisely a realization of communion. And while Harnack (ambivalently) and Bultmann can be cited for emphasis on the individual, Ritschl and Maurice could equally be selected to illustrate an alternative shift towards the importance of community.

The doctrine of bodily resurrection demonstrates something similar. On the one hand the power of some core ideas of individualism is clearly expressed in the continuity and value of unique personal identity even beyond the grave (taking 'body' here to mean recognizable personal identity). This unique personal identity is transformed, but still known by name and individual relationship, as the stories of the risen Christ are at pains to convey. For these stories easily provide for a legitimate extrapolation about our own expectations, when Christ's resurrection is taken as proto-typical (the 'first-fruits of those who sleep').[68]

As such this doctrine then becomes a concrete, empirical demonstration of a claim about enduring personal identity which was stipulated more speculatively out of the doctrine of creation and our status in *imago dei*. That is, in the risen Christ we actually 'see' that the individual's unique personal identity is secure, stable and continuous when it is rooted in relationship to God. In Christ we see this holds true not only through the changes and chances of this life, but beyond it as well. Personal identity is not doomed to annihilation at death but given back (the 'return' of our identity is perhaps a safer way to speak than its 'continuity', to avoid implying Greek notions of the intrinsic immortality of the soul of which exegetes are so wary: thus 'I' may temporarily cease to be when I die, but 'I' – however changed – am recreated).

Yet, on the other hand, there is another perspective to this story as well. There is also a *corporate* dimension to the notion of a resurrected body which can hardly be avoided both in the history of exegesis and developing doctrines. To begin with, there is that strand of New Testament teaching which suggests that we have to 'wait' at death – both for new bodies and for other persons, before our resurrection is complete.[69] This notion came to be elaborated in medieval theology, which detailed the experiences bodiless spirits must undergo in an interim period (and it takes a tortuous argument to demonstrate how one can experience the sensation of burning without bodies!).[70] It has also given rise to a good deal of philosophical speculation about the nexus of time and eternity, and the sense in which 'waiting' may or may not be conceived temporally.

But although such a notion may have spawned sterile debate and bizarre images, at the heart of it lies this profound but commonsense insight: in one way or another death catches the individual in incompleteness, and 'full' bodily resurrection is only realized and defined by relatedness to others. Thus it is only when we are newly embodied (the body being, amongst other things, a vehicle of recognition and interrelation), and only when we are engaged with the whole company of saints, that salvation is complete for anyone. In this sense *resurrection* has largely been conceived as necessarily corporate, even though *judgement* had tended to be conceived individualistically.

Furthermore, there is another more obvious (if not quite tautological) sense in which 'body' requires to be taken as a corporate image. John Robinson's provocative thesis that the body is simply to be identified with the community of the Church does not have to be accepted exegetically or theologically in that extreme form. But it may still point to a proper extension of the meaning of the body. It is almost certainly a compound and tensive symbol, as much as the Kingdom of God. As such it helps rein in the isolating excesses of an individualism which would have us relate to Christ apart from our relationships to others in Christ.

In short, what Christian eschatology, and the doctrine of resurrection in particular, provides is therefore a finely tuned balance of beliefs to buttress the individual's value, but always within community. In Christ's resurrection the individual person is given the most radical conceivable endorsement: he or she is held by the infinite love of God *into eternity*. Yet at the same time it is not the individual in isolation, but the person-in-relation, who is given such validation. Resurrection is always and only into a new community.

We might also note here that a balance between realized and future eschatology ensures that this sense of value is projected into the foreground of the present world order, not just into the background of eternity. This has logical, not just psychological force: just *because* individuals-in-community are to be 'kept in heaven' their value now is immeasurably enhanced and given an incomparable metaphysical basis. Thus Marx's scepticism and history's ambivalent witness cannot falsify the mature range of Christian belief at this point – only some skewed portion of it. The promise of pie-in-the-sky-when-we-die should increase, not undermine, our determination to share its portions fairly now, so far as we can.

To be sure, this sort of belief has to maintain its credibility over against other kinds of scepticism as well. So we should certainly note the challenge of natural sciences and philosophy, even if it cannot be fully dealt with here. Scientific method, after all, does not find it hard to show that the order of this universe is likely to be temporary, and our own structure of being likewise. It can also demonstrate plausible connections between consciousness and the physico-chemical structure of organisms, which suggest that 'we' cannot outlive our bodies as they exist in this universe. Nor will philosophers of mind necessarily offer much comfort. As we have seen, they are hard-pressed to offer much more than conceptual clarification. Any further ontological basis to personal identity (and its possibilities of survival) is unlikely to command great consensus. Such is the sceptical challenge, at least in embryo.

Yet a rejoinder is not hard either. At the very least it should be pointed out that nothing decisive is being demonstrated in this way. All it shows is that empirical and analytical method cannot think itself out of its own categories. In other words, while the perceived order and configuration of this particular universe suggests little or nothing of life after death within the empirical categories provided by this world's order, that is only to be expected. By contrast, the whole point of a realist Christian ontology rooted in a transcendent God is that it must (by definition) presume possibilities *beyond* such categories. Furthermore, it claims to have revealed those possibilities *within* history, specifically in the resurrection. This is a revelation which reverberates through our intuitions and experiences in all sorts of other ways as well, even though it may be inscrutable to a strictly conceived scientific method.

Incidentally, this does not separate science and theology into entirely unrelated domains. For theology still bears on scientific method, in this matter as in others, by resisting its tendency to epistemological totalitarianism: that is, we do *not* know everything knowable by scientific method alone. And science still bears on theology by purifying its formulations of facile, univocal, uncritical, language in its attempts to speak both of God and eternal life. The task for theology therefore remains clear, particularly in this matter of life after death. It has to speak more radically about God and the nature of his actions, rather than speak naively about the nature of humanity and its possibilities.[71]

Finally it should also be noted how critically this particular belief engages with our present condition. That is, it is not just able to speak credibly about such hopes in terms of the internal coherence of its own beliefs and assumptions. Nor is it just able to fend off the scepticism of other methods of enquiry. It also speaks with existential authenticity. Belief in life after death, no less than the doctrine of justification by faith, is yet another ancient and profound belief which connects with the personal concerns of our age with peculiar urgency.

Its contribution here lies most pertinently in the sense of depth, stability and continuity, that it can legitimately offer to deracinated and fragmented lives. Just because the guarantee of eternal value projects into this life, then this belief can hold a cynical, suffering-saturated society to some semblance of hope and purpose – when it is otherwise tempted to despair. Realized eschatology certainly reinforces this hope, as Moltmann has argued powerfully. But eternity provides its ultimate foundation (a point already made in response to Marx). And this relates specifically to the value we put on individuals. For if every life has, by virtue of its very existence, the possibility of an eternal future, then even a life of unrelieved pain and misery does not live and die pointlessly or valuelessly. What the doctrine of resurrection provides is therefore a kind of logical and psychological 'staying power' in our moral stance, when faced with the huge scale of human suffering and untimely death. It refuses us the refuge of ultimate cynicism.

In short, just as Christian belief has helped put the suffering of ordinary individuals high on the moral agenda, and made us believe that they matter, so it also provides the only ultimately adequate basis for *sustaining* that bewildering belief in such a world as this. These are profound existential implications indeed. Heidegger has not gone far enough: we do not just live unto death; in Christ we live unto life through death.

9

The Logic of Divine Love

A survey of Christian doctrine such as that offered in the previous chapters therefore yields some key categories of individualism. They are inescapable. They belong essentially to Christian faith. Individual personal identity is given value, continuity and security. More specifically, the freedom, autonomy, responsibility, privacy, originality and equality of individuals have all been seen to function in some way in biblical and doctrinal formulations of belief (the notion of self-realization less evidently so: but this will feature soon).

At the same time, and crucially, the survey demonstrates how these categories and core ideas are variously nuanced and contextualized by theological concerns. The nature and value of the individual must always be understood as being-in-relation (to God himself, as well as to others). Christian narratives and doctrines about both creation and redemption establish and secure personal identity within this relational, social context, not in isolated abstraction. The individual self is only truly created and sustained within this wider theological and social narrative. This is the chief controlling context of all the core ideas of individualism. It clothes them in distinctive dress, and does not allow them to develop in abstraction with some dangerous life of their own. This has been seen so far especially in relation to ideas of freedom, responsibility, privacy and rights.

Yet while all this may have been fairly demonstrated, it remains arguable whether a systematic doctrinal survey of this kind is entirely sufficient for its task. The task was both to flush out the fullest possible range of Christian understanding on these issues, and to trace connections with more general moral intuitions. But while much of this may have been achieved, there remains a suspicion that the method of systematics leaves something to be desired – a suspicion that lies within the nature of the language employed.

After all, doctrinal language, especially as it has developed in the western systematic tradition, is largely elaborative and second-order. It attempts to articulate the primary meaning of divine self-revelation under a range of secondary headings. As such it tends to use abstract and technical language, the language with which theologians talk to each other. Ordering the previous chapter under the headings of creation, Trinity, incarnation, redemption, resurrection, and so on exemplifies just this. But can this kind of second-order language adequately convey the full nuances and demands of concrete personal relations? What of the meaning of *love* itself, the defining heart of all relational talk about God and human persons?

In fact there is no reason why second-order language should not be adequate *in principle*, at least within the internal dialogue of the Church as it works out its own structure of belief. For if the primary meaning of divine self-revelation is indeed taken to be love, then creation, incarnation, redemption, resurrection, Trinity, should all help to unfold and specify the full range of that meaning. It is love which motivates creation and, specifically, invests value in people as created beings; the same love drives the deity to incarnation, to the historical act of the stories of redemption, and to the eschatological fulfilment of redemption. Moreover, the movement of giving and receiving within the relational reality of the Trinity *is*, precisely, the movement of love (as we shall see shortly). So when these secondary doctrines are scrutinized specifically for their bearing on individualism this is also, necessarily, an exposition of how divine *love* bears on the matter – and the task should have been achieved after all.

But in practice I suspect the approach still falls short – for two reasons. First, just as the meaning of divine love cannot be fully expressed except through the particular constituent acts of divine revelation (creation, incarnation, and so on), so the converse is also true: the very process of elaborating it in such ways also abstracts from it and risks dissolving it into other categories. It therefore needs stating in its own terms as well. It is much the same with our understanding of human agents in inter-personal relations: I only fully know a person's love towards me by reference to their particular actions; but, equally, I also need some overarching intuition of their love through which to interpret the actions. In other words, actions are constitutive of our understanding of persons, but not wholly self-interpreting as if meaning could be read out of them without some wider frame of reference. (This may sound like a vicious epistemological circle, but it reflects realistically the way we actually come to know people: it straddles both introvert and extrovert traditions in the philosophy of mind and action.)[1]

What it means is this. There is always a risk of the primary and overarching meaning of divine self-revelation (as love) being masked when it is not named and considered in its own right (as well as through its constituent doctrines). And so far as the focus of this book is concerned it means we should subject individualism specifically to this general scrutiny of divine love. 'Love' is a kind of overall safety net through which the issue must be strained. It is a net which has been woven out of all the preceding strands of doctrine but which is still worth trawling with as a whole. It may uncover further perspectives on the issues of individualism which a more systematic approach failed to sift out.

The second reason why love should be considered in its own terms is simply to keep apologetics (and evangelism) on the agenda of *all* theological discourse. As I have said, secondary doctrinal language tends to be abstract, technical, largely for internal consumption within the theological community. Talk of *perichoresis* as a reason for valuing persons is not going to communicate much beyond that community – obviously. But the language of love is a different matter. So we must talk of love – and tell love stories.

This does not for one moment mean that secondary language has no justification. It helps provide a rigorous intellectual mapping of the interior landscape of the faith. This map helps believers maintain intellectual integrity and fulfil the command to love God with their mind. As such it serves (indirectly) to give believers confidence when commending the faith to others. The very existence of such a map marks out the faith as a system of thought which has been internally explored to the full, and may therefore be commended to the full.

But it therefore remains the case that this 'internal' theological language is not entirely *self*-justifying. The theological process and the language which goes with it has to do with sustaining credibility within the Christian community not just for its own sake but for the sake of others too. The Church *believes*, as it exists and acts, not for its own sake but for God's sake and for the sake of God's wider world. Therefore all internal discourse must be capable of being translated into worship and apologetics – and service. Theology is, or ought to be, at least a preamble to mission, even where it cannot sensibly be integral to it. This reiterates the implications of those theological assumptions with which the discussion began: theology always requires this attempt at communication, witness, apologetics. And this simple point therefore follows. Since the language of the love of God (and especially that of love stories) is a much more communicable basis for valuing persons than technical second-order language, then theology needs to speak much of it, *even to itself*: it is a kind of internal memo, a recurring agenda item, to ensure this wider missionary purpose of all theology is never allowed to disappear by default.

So the question presses: what is this primary, concrete, Christian apprehension of the *love* of God? And how does *that* bear specifically on the nature and status of individual persons?

Divine love and the individual

Biblical roots and stories

In its Old Testament background love is first expressed most insistently in terms of God's covenant with the people of Israel (corporately), rather than with individuals. The basis of the covenant is God's election of his people, which is an act of commitment and love (*ahabah*). His faithful care once the covenant is made is a further act of loving-kindness (*chesed*).

However, this corporate relationship is also alluded to metaphorically in the language of love between individuals: as between father and son, man and wife, lover and beloved.[2] As so often, this metaphorical language is providing space to extend the meaning of the divine dealings with humanity. In doing so it clearly allows for that individualizing element which has already been traced as at least part of the Old Testament story.[3]

This was noted generally in relation to individual moral responsibility. But it is also reflected more specifically in the nature of divine love. It is true that the *word* 'love' is only rarely used in relation to particular individuals, and then chiefly to kings who have a representative role. But it is implicit in the covenant nature of the summons to individual prophets, and in the forgiveness of individuals (expressed in some Psalms). It is hard to read God's call to Jeremiah, for example, without feeling the force of a covenant love which is being differentiated in relation to him as an individual, as well as being expressed through him to a people: 'before I formed you in the womb I knew you intimately . . .' (the word 'love' is not used but the verb *yada* conveys 'a strong element of personal commitment').[4]

More generally we may certainly say that the relationship of love is pre-eminently *personal*, and as such necessarily straddles both corporate and individual dimensions. D. D. Williams summarizes thus: 'The place to look for the meaning of love is in the history of a people who have been called into intimate personal relationship with God and who have begun to learn the meaning of responsibility with God, and the consequences of irresponsibility in that relationship.'[5]

The New Testament extends this basis of God's love in covenant election by focusing the fulfilment of it in the election of Jesus Christ. He is *the* beloved and the chosen (*agapetos*). In that sense the individualizing element is exemplified in a more radical way. And this root biblical perception, from which individualizing features of incarnational doctrine have later flowered (as we have already seen), certainly needs to be taken seriously. At the same time he is also that corporate and representative figure which we have already noted: for in and through him the many, the new Israel, are also beloved.

If we then ask whether, or in what sense, the many are loved as individuals, there is a complex set of answers. If we begin with the narrative of the Synoptic Gospels then this does tend to secure the individual at the centre of the divine love. Jesus both summons and receives individuals out of the crowds to be the recipients of his love: people like Zacchaeus, the woman with haemorrhages, the disciples themselves. In fact in the Synoptic Gospels (as in the Old Testament) this love is not much expressed by the use of the word but more by acts of healing, forgiveness or acceptance. These acts, however, are precisely the characteristic outworkings of that covenant love in which Jesus was steeped (and in the Johannine material the meaning of the actions is explicitly and repeatedly identified as love). The same centring on individual needs is also apparent in his teaching. In the cluster of parables about the lost sheep, the lost coin and the lost son, there is the clearest possible focus of concern on the particular and the individual: *He pays attention to people as individuals, and this is part of the essential anatomy of his love.*

However, all that has been said before about the nature of these beloved individuals also remains true. That is, the individuals to whom Jesus pays attention are loved precisely as social beings who must therefore love each other. The summoning, forgiving, healing, accepting acts of love often explicitly include some reference to a wider network of relationships. Thus the healed lepers are encouraged to refer to the priests, the forgiven Zacchaeus voluntarily attempts to put himself right with those he has wronged, and the disciples are formed into a new community. And where the narratives make no specific mention of this, the wider framework of Jesus' teaching makes clear that it must still be understood in this way. We must ask and receive the love of God in forgiveness as we forgive others; it is the love of God's boundless goodness for us which must provoke us to love each other (and to do so beyond a merely contractual arrangement: for we are to love our enemies, not just our neighbours).[6] The Johannine material again reinforces this with more frequent, explicit use of the language of love: 'love one another as I have loved you . . .'.[7] So while we are certainly loved as individual persons, we are always loved as persons-in-relation.

Furthermore, we are also loved as a corporate body. The Johannine corpus, for example, has an individual focus (C. F. D. Moule). Yet it also centres attention on the body of disciples as a corporate recipient of divine love. Love is related to corporateness amongst persons, as well as to individuals as social beings.

In the Pauline material the nature of divine love is then given more discursive exposition. Here its specific character in Christ is portrayed: as gracious and undeserved;[8] as self-giving to suffering and death;[9] as unfathomable in its faithfulness, persistence and capacity to achieve its purposes.[10] This is the primary source for an analytical (as distinct from narrative) understanding of love: a love which was so profoundly 'shed abroad' in experience that it required language itself to be reshaped to express it – hence *agape*. And if we then ask how this is related specifically to issues of individualism we shall find here too a concern about the social nature of the recipients, as well as their individuality. For to receive the love of Christ is *ipso facto* to be committed to building up the body of Christ as well.[11]

But is it possible to be still more specific about the focus of this love, in the Pauline material? Is it singular or plural, individual or corporate?

In the first instance it is notable how much of Paul's exposition uses the first person plural: 'God shows his love for us in that while we were yet sinners Christ died for us'.[12] This properly expresses the collective logic of salvation Paul is working out through the parallelism between Adam and Christ.[13] It culminates with the paeon of praise to the unconquerable love of God in Christ from which nothing in all creation can separate *us*.[14]

Yet there is also an irreducible intrusion of the first person singular (especially in Romans 7). Admittedly its significance is exegetically disputed. Thus Barrett: 'when Paul in this chapter says "I", what does he mean? Mankind? The Jewish people? Himself as a non-Christian

Jew? Himself as a Christian?'[15] And I have already agreed we need to be wary of projecting Enlightenment individualistic and psychological preoccupations onto this sort of text. Equally, I am by no means convinced, even on strictly exegetical grounds, that we are bound to choose between those alternatives to the *exclusion* of Paul's own self-understanding as an individual. That is an exegesis which is just as likely to be operating with a reactionary *post*-Enlightenment prejudice. After all, the use of the first person singular simply to represent generalities more vividly was not particularly common in Greek (and at the very least there may have been a deliberate ambiguity and oscillation of meaning between the individual in himself and as a representative). Furthermore, if we also recall the profound experience Paul claimed to have received *as an individual* on the road to Damascus it seems positively perverse to deny some individual personal experience at the heart of this passage. In short, the individual really cannot be excised. It remains a crucial object of divine love, just as much as the body of people.

Once again all this means that any questions put to the biblical roots of our experiences and doctrines yield no straightforward answer. But we are at least able to affirm this much which has emerged. Negatively, divine love forbids us to dissolve either social reality or the individual person as a centre of the divine attention. Positively, we are attended to as persons-in-relation; and the nature of that attention is *agape*. We are loved, individually and corporately, with this kind of love.

Further exposition

So can we now elaborate the implications of 'this kind of love', which is divine *agape*? What else does it mean specifically for the nature of the individual and the issues of individualism? Here subsequent reflections of Christian tradition extend the story helpfully beyond its biblical roots. Taken overall it is an illuminating narrative, already well charted both historically and conceptually (Vincent Brummer's *The Model of Love* is a particularly valuable recent contribution).[16] All I shall attempt, therefore, is to pull out those elements of the conceptual implications of the story which bear most directly on the issues at stake.

To begin in very general terms: it is, evidently, the very fact that God *loves* which brings us into being and holds us in being, in whatever shape or form of being we may have, individually or socially. This

attribute or attitude of God has been variously conceived as essenti-
alist or voluntarist: that is, he could do no other because it is of his
essential nature to love; or he could (logically) have chosen not to love
because it is of the nature of love that it must be willed not necessitated.

However, this particular debate is less interesting for our present
purposes than the questionable (largely western) assumption which
can lie behind both positions: namely, that God's love is conceived as
an attitude or attribute of God, rather than as a relation. This is an
assumption which Brummer has no hesitation in criticizing:

> If we turn to the Christian tradition . . . we will discover to our sur-
> prise that most of the comprehensive concepts of love developed
> within it have been attitudinal rather than relational. Love has
> generally been taken to be attitude of one person towards another,
> rather than as a relation between persons. This way of thinking can
> probably be explained by the fact that western thought has suffered
> from a systematic blind spot for relations . . .[17]

He then goes on to attribute this blind spot to an Aristotelian
legacy, which sees reality in general only as substance and attribute (so
that relations have been conceived as attributes of one of their terms,
rather than having ontological status in themselves). His preference
is clearly to reinstate the category of relation to proper ontological significance. He therefore conceives the Trinitarian God as being within
himself a relation of love, actually constituting himself as God by being
that relation, as distinct from a God who simply has the attribute of
love. In short, we do not only believe that God loves, we believe that
he *is* love.

This echoes the ontology of the Trinity championed by Zizioulas,
Gunton and others. What it provides, as we saw previously, is an
endorsement of the nature of our being when we are conceived analogously to the Trinitarian divine being: namely, *as particulars constituted
by our relations*. The specific point now that God himself is the relation
of *love* also echoes our previous discussion. That is, by further empha-
sizing that our being derives not only generally from this structure of
ultimate reality, but also that this reality is specifically shaped in the
structure of love, then the *value* of being particulars-in-relation is established beyond all question. The conflation of the meaning of God and
the meaning of love would be decisive, as we have seen, in uniting
fact and value.[18]

Such a conceptuality is not without difficulties, and I have already
suggested some qualifications necessary to safeguard it. If relations are

elevated in themselves to ultimate ontological status, then there is the risk of collapse into a kind of infinite regress in the attempt to maintain sufficiently stable status for the particular and individual. So relation and being must always be defined together. But duly clarified, and now specifically focused through the meaning of love, it stands as a powerful and persuasive world-view within which the significance of the individual and particular person-in-relation can be maintained.

It is also important to note how well this theoretical structure holds up when tested against experience. In particular, it adequately interprets much mystical experience of the love of God. For even the most ecstatic mystics usually acknowledge some sort of relational dimension in the experience, as distinct from merging in complete ontological union with the Godhead. Thus theology and experience witness together in insisting that ultimate personal reality, when it is loving, requires an enduring notion of particularity and individuality for its own self-interpretation. Love entails the otherness of the individual, as well as union.[19] With love, particularity is not subsumed by relation but required by it. This is certainly one significant implication of the logic of love.

Then there are other more specific implications, deriving from the particular characteristics of divine love. To begin with, there is more that follows from its irreducibly *personal* character. For in the anatomy of personal love there are features which compel the lover to regard the individual as well as the group. And this deserves more attention.

Chiefly this derives from the capacity and desire of a personal lover to bestow value on the object of his or her esteem, to 'give it more vigorous existence'.[20] It is a vital aspect of paying attention. It means that love regards its object in sharp relief, differentiated from its surroundings according to its own unique internal lineaments and contours. To love, therefore, is like placing the object of love under centre-stage lighting, in which he or she or the group is gloried in precisely because of its particularity in relation to all else. As such, even if it is a group which stands as the object of love, the true lover will still be paying attention to those individual members which help constitute the particular nature of that 'compound' reality. In other words, within the logic of personal love there is always an intrinsic particularizing tendency.

The particularizing tendency is exemplified especially in romantic love. So much so, it does not stop short at the individual person, taken as a whole. To truly love an embodied person, when love 'gives more vigorous existence', is to love the detail within the person. Thus

Donne: 'And therefore what thou wert, and who / I bid Love aske, and now / That it assume thy body, I allow / *And fixe it selfe in thy lip, eye and brow*'.[21] This is a characteristic trait of the so-called metaphysical poets when they celebrate the anatomy of love. Their profound and often mystical sense of love as a subsisting relation between two lovers was rooted in precise, particular and scrupulously regarded details.

Of course, this attention to detail can occasionally render romantic love susceptible to absurdities. But the chief point remains, that there is a proper particularizing tendency in all true personal love – which does normally settle more sensibly on the individual person as a whole. A particular person may only be fully appreciated with regard to his or her differentiating detail, and that person must include their own differentiating relationships with other persons, but all this still illustrates the way that such love is seeking out its object with a kind of 'centring' instinct for the differentiated particular, whose chief locus remains most obviously the individual person.

Such attention to detail and to the particular is crucial to the logic of love. And when applied specifically to divine love it again helps interpret important dimensions of religious experience. Not least, it illuminates the persistence and propriety of the Christian tradition of belief in personal providence. In the face of (almost) overwhelming experiential and conceptual difficulties with this notion, prayers for the particularities of personal life are still offered, even though they risk the charge of absurdity (as much in the religious domain as in the romantic). *The point is, we can do no other if we have been grasped by a vision of personal divine love which by its very nature must pay attention to detail.* For if we matter to a personal God of love, and if the whole narrative of our lives matters to him, then such prayers are as inescapable as any lover's sublime conviction that their every movement and thought is continually being watched and cherished by their partner.

This attention to the particular also illustrates the extent to which personal love finds – and confers – value specifically in the *irreplaceability*, or uniqueness, of particularity.[22] It is *this* particular, in its distinctness, which commands such attention. This in turn illuminates another implication for individuals arising from the specific nature of *agape*: its unconditionality. For the unmerited and unconditional nature of *agape* love connects with the value of individuality (not least through the doctrine of grace)[23] in this sense: it is precisely the irreplaceability of our particularity which God can value unconditionally. We are valued and loved as unrepeatable particulars, not as instances of some ideal generic notion of humanity. It is as irreplaceable persons that we are loveable, even while we are sinners. God can, and does, value our irreplaceability even 'while we were yet dead in trespasses and sin'.

Again, this resonates with ordinary human experience of love: 'personal value and identity are bestowed on me by the fact that others consider me irreplaceable to them', says Brummer.[24] Roger Scruton offers a similar analysis. He notes that the normal referent for love (and hate) is precisely a particular object, as distinct from some universal idea (which attracts only the language of admiration or contempt). Thus you may have contempt for my weakness, in so far as you see me as an instantiation of some universal moral flaw; but in so far as you are in a personal relationship with me you must still love (or hate) me. *And that is because no one else can take my place* (unlike trees, or blades of grass – however much they are valued in other ways).[25] In this way the phenomenology of human love reflects the structure of divine *agape*, specifically as undeserved grace. Irreplaceability is the crucial gift given to us by God's creative and redeeming love. This is the basis of our secure identity in God and his love, regardless of our shortcomings.

This notion of irreplaceability also illuminates another theological paradox. On the one hand there appears to be a necessary exclusivity in love's regard (whether of the group, or of the individual). We are a *chosen* people, for love attends to me *as distinct from* you when it puts a person centre-stage (thus this woman is healed out of all the crowds, and not another; and John is given a different destiny to Peter, which Peter is not allowed to question).[26] Yet on the other hand there appears also to be a necessary universality, certainly in the creating and redeeming love of God ('for God so loved the *world* . . .'). That is the paradox. However, there is no contradiction precisely when love's regard is ordered and focused according to particularity and irreplaceability. For in so far as we are all differentiated in our particularity, we may *all* be irreplaceable in a different way. In other words, the divine stage manager is operating with a multitude of stage sets, each one giving unique value according to the particularity of each actor. Divine love in this sense is neither forced to order itself hierarchically, nor exclusively, in order to pay proper attention to particularity. Far from having to ration the intensity of its regard and the particular value it bestows, the intensity which derives from each particularity can and must be accorded to every particularity.

Such stamina and scope in the divine love might, I suppose, stretch the imagination to its limits – particularly when the notion is extended on the vast canvas of the whole world's history. The analogy of the stage would certainly crumble quickly under the sheer weight of numbers. But the more obvious and homely analogies of human love will do better. They grant at least a glimpse of love's possibilities. To love one's spouse or partner, *and* children *and* friends, one does not have to do so in any diminished, hierarchical or artificially 'homogenized' way. We must *and can* value each wholly and fully in their different (irreplaceable) realities and relationships with us (and with others). Anything less – or 'more' – would not be proper, particularizing love. (Herein too lies some understanding of the Christian notion that different vocations may all be valued, without needing to grade them hierarchically.)

In short, we are beginning to find in the Christian revelation of *agape* love, as we suspected, an illuminating primary source. It presents itself consistently as a powerful ally to an overall vision of persons-in-relationship. It certainly compels us to pay attention to actual particulars rather than abstract types. In particular, it roots our respect for the uniqueness of individuals in a profound theological vision of grace.

Divine and human loves

One familiar danger still lurks behind the latter part of this analysis, however. It arises from the constant attempt to correlate revelation with experience. The question it raises is this: to what extent are anatomies of human love being *properly* projected into the love of God (that is, to help explicate it) – and to what extent, if any, are they distorting a distinctive revelation from God? After all, we have already drawn on experiences normally associated with *eros* (romantic love) and other ordinary human loves, to explicate the divine *agape*. But Christian theology has not always been at ease with this. *Agape* has sometimes been defined polemically over against *eros*.[27] At the very least *eros* has had to be Christianized and qualified before being deemed suitable for the divine analogy. So this is a debate we cannot entirely avoid.

In fact a key notion in Christian criticism of platonic *eros* has already been incorporated in the previous discussion. It is precisely its tendency to love ideals, and to love persons only for the sake of those ideals or 'types', that has been subject of a Christian critique. And in this sense Augustine's revision of *eros* may be considered as a first step in a properly Christianized version of it. His insistence that we are to love people for the sake of *God* (as distinct from ideals) is more acceptable.

But even this has sounded seriously deficient to more modern sensibilities, which still suspect a de-personalizing and reductionist tendency. It might seem to entail the manipulation of people. It is a conception which might have the effect of treating people as means to serving some other end. As such it may still fail to pay attention to persons in their concrete particularity. Moreover, since God is the source of fulfilment and reward, the offence against true love is compounded. For to love people for the sake of God may appear to use our 'love' for others as a means to the end of our own happiness. Hence the more radical separation of *agape* from *eros*, championed by Nygren. For him only *agape* is sheer gift love, untainted by human need to use others for self-fulfilment. So that alone can properly define the divine love.

Yet this by no means settles the debate. Not surprisingly, Nygren's solution has been deemed to entail too sharp a distinction, failing to do full justice to either Plato or Augustine. And it is within the discussion surrounding their defence that the point of referring to this debate becomes most apparent. This is not just to acknowledge the dangers of anthropomorphism. It is also here, within this debate, that we find another example of how the resources of Christian experience and doctrine interrelate to illuminate and regulate the role and status of the individual. In particular, the debate generates a theologically measured account of notions of self-realization and fulfilment – a core ingredient of modern individualism which has so far eluded much reference from within the Christian perspective.

So more attention needs to be paid to the sympathetic reading of Plato which Augustine's Christianizing perspective begins to provide. And it can be developed as follows. In the first instance, although we may love someone for the sake of an ideal (or God), *this may still be construed in a way which is personal and particular to that person.* This is so when there is a proper attempt to distinguish between the imperfect actuality of the person and their potential perfection. To love that potential perfection is to value the unique 'daimon' which belongs to each individual, that hidden potential to realize the good in his or her own way. At best this love therefore gives persons freedom to move towards a goal, rather than imprisoning them within their actuality. This is part of the empowerment of love. For while love's attention may be paid to individuals unconditionally, its effect is invigorating.

Moreover, if this goal which love draws out of us is an intrinsically relational one, so that the true fulfilment of the individual is always conceived in terms of right relations with other persons and God, then the metamorphosis is complete: that is, the proposition that someone should be loved for the sake of an ideal (God) need be neither de-personalizing, nor self-serving, nor manipulative. On the contrary, it is a dynamic, pro-active, notion of love which seeks to draw the individual potential of persons into a fulfilment which is intrinsically social, though only achieved precisely by valuing particularity. As such it is also a notion of love which allows itself to be reflected in self-love, without collapsing into egoism. For to love oneself for the sake of one's unique potential to contribute to a relational and social goal is quite distinct from the egotism which simply gives value to one's own actuality, in isolation from any wider purpose. There is an obvious difference between caring for one's own mental or physical well-being for the sake of family or career, and doing so *solely* for personal longevity (or vanity). This general point is echoed by McFadyen, stressing the 'social' nature of a proper Christian understanding of self-realization (and associating it with a proper exercise of autonomy as well): 'the "inner nature" which one is trying to realize in autonomous acts of self-realization is constituted through intersubjective processes, and is therefore intimately linked with the reality of others'.[28]

Put like this it is immediately apparent how widely this apprehension of divine love resonates through Christian belief. It is a straightforward exposition of that initiative of redeeming, reconciling and sanctifying love in Christ which is expressed in doctrines of grace, justification and sanctification. It is a love which is able to love the sinner who may be problematic in his or her actuality, but whose potential is actively and dynamically sought and established in and through Christ. It also coheres comfortably with gospel perspectives – where we have full permission to love ourselves and find our own life, but only in the context of loving others and losing our life for another's sake.[29] And as such it is now easy to see how it helps allay those fears of anthropomorphism: it is an analysis of love which is indeed expounding, not distorting, the full revelation of the love of God. Above all, it can also be seen how this meaning of love acknowledges and helps release those creative capacities which were celebrated in the core ideals of self-realization and fulfilment – but which does so by rooting them in a profound 'controlling' context of divine grace and its goal of mutual relatedness.

To be sure, it is arguable whether all this is in fact a proper exegesis of Plato's (and Augustine's) vision. But the wider point remains that the debate itself is revealing for the overall purposes of this chapter, whatever its particular conclusions about Plato or Augustine. It highlights how the primary Christian experience of the love of God in Christ seeks out a variety of philosophical traditions and human experiences with which to articulate itself (it can do no other: revelation must be embodied and made recognizable in some way). But, equally, it shows how the inner dynamic of this divine love remains restless with any one settled position. So it is a process which has engaged Christian belief with ordinary, identifiable, human experiences – with an outcome which both includes and transcends any one form of human love in order to express the divine. As such it provides apologetic credibility in *both* the connectedness and 'transcendence' of the notion that has emerged. More specifically, it is a process which has refocused our attention on particular aspects of the individual and individualism which might otherwise have remained undeveloped – especially the notion of self-realization.

As for this exposition of love as a whole, the substance of what it has revealed in this process may now be summarized like this. In the first instance it undergirds and motivates the creative and redemptive purposes of God in general. It gives us an ultimate reason for being, and specifically for being particular persons-in-relation. It also offers profound and focused attention to particularity and actuality. But because it is dynamic it also pays attention to potentiality as well. It is as such we all *matter*, irreplaceably and irrevocably, in both our present and our future – but always remembering that 'we' include our relations with others, as members of each other.

Love, power and providence

Finally, love provokes one further point. And although this does not relate specifically to the status of individuals, it merits some mention because it bears both on the systematic task and the nature of love in general. It certainly affects the apologetic task of love. It is a question about the power of love, in a guise which has not yet been dealt with. *Can love achieve what it wills?* For while it is one thing to parade the moral power of love's prescriptions, it is quite another to propose its power to perform them. God may will detailed personal providence, but can he in any sense deliver it?

The apologetic point is this. If love does have such power, then the ultimate reassurance of religion is justified. If it does not, then a corrosive acid of ultimate uncertainty seeps into the structure of belief, subtly softening the ground of motivation. For if God's loving will that we should matter cannot be carried through in effective action, then it remains little more than a pious wish. Our being and value remain fundamentally precarious after all. Nietzscherian claims that there is no point in anything apart from the will to power would find all the more space for their mocking last laugh.

The issues here are legion and complex. In the first instance it may be objected that the question must be ruled out of court, almost by definition. Mere reference to Nietzsche, it will be said, betrays a fatal compromise. Love does not have anything to do with power. If it is expressed through power then it is contaminated by it. 'Power to achieve what one wills' cannot belong to the logic of personal love, for love is necessarily, and by definition, vulnerable to rejection and non-coercive. It ceases to be love when it imposes its will.

Second, such an objection of principle is massively bolstered by overwhelming empirical evidence. Our botched and bloody world is the evidence. It is abundantly plain that divine love simply has not succeeded in making every individual matter. At best it appears that God's love struggles through the constraints of natural laws (and contingencies), human freedom (and unfreedom), to achieve some of his regard for some people some of the time.

Most frequently this is expressed in contemporary theology as divine action in and for generalities: that is, overall plans may be fulfilled which encompass the destiny of large groups of people over a period of time, but nothing can be guaranteed for the individual within his or her particular context and time-frame.[30] So while in principle God's love may wish to particularize, in practice the intrinsic risks and resistance of this world always forces the focus of his attention wider. What matters is his suffering struggle and intention to attend to us all, not his success in doing so. That struggle is what we worship him for. And it is the motivating basis for our co-operative action with him.

The rising tide of theological and devotional literature dedicated to this theme is impressive. It receives its most elaborate and thorough treatment in process theology, but ranges more widely.[31] It is also highly persuasive. There is profound truth in love's necessary vulnerability to rejection in personal relationships. Power *is* (potentially) pernicious. And some kind of divine (self-) limitation is always going to have to feature in a religious explanation of this frustrated and frustrating world.

But these themes must not be taken entirely uncritically. My brief synopsis here may have caricatured and packaged them unfairly; but elsewhere, where I have attempted to do them more justice, I have indicated some serious flaws – and some alternatives.[32] Crucially, different kinds of power must be distinguished. Coercive and manipulative power must indeed be rejected. But other kinds of power are not only compatible with love but essential to its meaning. For a start, love must have its own dynamic energy to will and to take initiatives, if it is to be truly relational and other-orientated. A merely passive attitude of 'love' which *only* waits on the other, rather than actively seeking his or her good, is fundamentally self-contained and ultimately self-orientated. So divine love must have a certain 'potency' of personal freedom, whatever constraints there are on its possibilities of action.[33]

Even more important, there is a distinction to be made between two spheres of vulnerability in love. There is that vulnerability which is necessarily open to rejection by the will of the beloved. But there is also that which is frustrated by other factors as well – so that the lover cannot even act effectively within the surrounding circumstances of the beloved. And what I have argued elsewhere is that while divine action must indeed include the former, if it is to be loving, it does not *necessarily* include the latter. The former does indeed belong to the logic of love itself, but the latter derives from the limitations of finite agents, and may not belong necessarily to the creative endeavour of a transcendent God.

In other words, we again need to be sensitive to the danger of *simply* explicating divine love through human experience, without reference to the full revelatory tradition. Too often the analogy of love has been used univocally and uncritically when applied to God. The effect is obvious. Some of the limitations which we have taken to belong to love itself are actually elided with limitations of finitude (which belong to us but not to God, and certainly not to the meaning of love).

To be sure, to go on to assert that divine agency *can* then weave a providential purpose in the circumstances surrounding us all (as actual individuals and not just as contributors to some more general group fulfilment) is a harder task by far. It requires, I believe, a tough-minded eschatological perspective, controversial views of the relationship of God to time and eternity, and a theological epistemology which is resolutely Christocentric. Even then the attempt may not convince everyone.[34] But the chief point here remains: nothing in the logic of love *per se* precludes that possibility, in principle, whatever else may seem to impede it in practice.

Moreover, *unless* love's possibilities are reinstated in some such way (for God), then the empirical evidence of this world counts even more heavily against him. After all, if love by definition must always be actively seeking the best for the other, and if it *cannot*, then it should not create at all. So love itself would veto the creation of a world in which God's capacities are so tragically constrained that individuals simply cannot be effectively attended to. For a love which attempted to justify such a creation in purely general terms, without reference to individuals, would be counted (at best) grossly irresponsible and self-indulgent.

So, either the notion of a personal God is abandoned altogether, or there *must* be more possibilities to the divine agency of love than the empirical data of this world affords. Love itself requires those possibilities. In other words, the 'must' here reflects a moral force in the logic of love. This means that the one option *not* available to illuminate this vale of tears is precisely that persuasive package of ideas which divorces love from power too radically. It is exactly the opposite: divine creative love requires certain kinds of power to count as love at all.

Finally, lest there be any doubt, only such a notion of divine love truly empowers, rather than impedes, the possibilities of human loving as well. For the argument here echoes the final points made about life after death. Like resurrection, only the infinite possibilities of divine love forbid us the refuge of cynicism in such a world as this. Instead they compel us to see everyone, in every kind of situation, with hope. They motivate us to act, with love, on the basis of that faith and hope, even when empirical circumstances demoralize us. In this way we are all invigorated, as we both find and give a more vigorous existence to others.

10

Parameters and Presumptions:
Another Step towards Practice

As an essay in ideas and beliefs this has now drawn to a natural conclusion. It has attempted to trace connections (and collisions) between prevailing ideas of individualism and Christian doctrine. It proposes Christian thought *in principle* as a profound, flexible and still-credible tradition which can secure the value of each individual person within the control of an equally secure relational and social vision. This vision has its origin in the nature of God and his relatedness, within whom we have our particular beings and our relatedness. Substantively, the tradition offers an account of the value of individual persons-in-relation as being both unique and enduring. This is expressed in particular through such doctrines as grace and resurrection, amongst others. It is focused most effectively through the primary revelation and experience of *agape* love. The tradition also provides unique grounds for moral motivation: when ultimate reality is the Trinitarian God revealed in Christ then we are profoundly moved to realize this moral vision. There is no more telling teleology than this kind of theological ontology.

As such it is a tradition of belief which can generate and control moral notions which connect crucially with the wider world of moral discourse which has been outlined. The meaning of moral terms is certainly modified in this theological context. But, equally, the exploration of the tradition has shown no reason to revoke the assumption that some common discourse is possible. This in turn means that the Christian tradition of thought clearly can and must join battle vigorously on various joint fronts. Belief can and must be expressed in action in relation to common concerns, which reiterates ecclesiological assumptions made earlier. It all leaves us at this point of conclusion. To attempt much more about the form this action might take leads us beyond the brief of this book.

Yet to end with such generalities is frustrating. As with the con-
cluding section of the first part of the book, it is tempting at least to
begin testing the shape of ideas in practice, however rudimentarily. So
just these final comments will be ventured. They will take us some
small way, again, into more specific implications for actual practice.
But this time they also claim a more explicit Christian brief to back
them.

Broad parameters

In general terms the battle fronts for Christian action must already be
very clear. To begin with, Christian faith will certainly oppose anything like the unfettered 'bureaucratic' individualism of the kind
characterized by MacIntyre. The abstract notion of the individual this
presupposes, as well as the forms of social life it produces, is wholly
incompatible with a proper relational Christian anthropology. But
equally it will resist any merely reactive movement which launches an
uncritical onslaught on all core ideas of individualism. For these, as we
have seen, belong integrally to Christian doctrine, albeit nuanced in
different ways. And even when they are articulated outside a theological
context their function as vital moral regulators against pernicious
forms of individualism will commend them to Christian moral
thought. Christian belief will also resist any corresponding tendency to
dissolve individual personal identity *simply* into relationality (or mere
illusions of continuity).

More positively it is a tradition which is likely to endorse something
very like the outline of social order which emerged at the end of the
first section. For we have been given a tradition of belief in which
individual persons are essentially and divinely constituted to flourish
by belonging to others in *particular* communities, as well as to God.
We have been presented with a theological and ecclesial claim that
personal security and social integration is established best precisely
through a common structure of particular belief and practice. However, we have also seen it to be a tradition which insists on mutual
responsibilities amongst all people, who must be acknowledged to be
equally created and redeemable. So this permits no ultimate ecclesial
exclusiveness, no entirely isolated communities.

At the same time, the tradition reinforces the value of otherness,
particularity and differentiation within these communities. These are
vital aspects of the anatomy of love. It is a tradition in which the individual person is regarded with such scrupulous divine attention that

the community must also reflect that gaze in its reverence for each member. But equally, the tradition insists that individuals must return that gaze with responsibility and solidarity within their communities. For these are communities to which we all owe an ordered and fulfilled existence. As such, communities belong within the ordinances of God and deserve our allegiance.

Cumulatively, these beliefs evidently cohere with the basic elements of the sketch offered before. That is, they issue naturally in an order in which local subcultures provide a context for belonging and mutual regard, set within a wider framework of mutual responsibility.

But is there anything more specific to be said, to sharpen up the paths we should tread within this very general picture? In particular, what more can be said specifically about our attitudes to individuals, and our status as individuals?

One more step that could be taken, even within the limited remit of this book, is to make explicit some specific principles. These have already emerged implicitly, and may best be described as a set of *presumptions* within which personal and social priorities should be worked out.

Presumptions

I am using 'presumption' here in the following sense. Within the artifice of ethics moral statements can be ranged along a double spectrum.[1] On the one hand they vary according to their authority. On the other hand they vary according to their specificity. On the whole the two scales do not converge (that is, authority is normally gained only at the price of specificity). Thus Joseph Fletcher's one absolute of love is readily accorded the highest authority, but lacks sufficient specific content to be much use; whereas his highly specific rules of thumb are more useful guides to action, but lack sufficient intrinsic authority to carry weight in complex situations.[2] By 'presumptions' I now mean moral axioms which have at least some specificity, but which lie only just short of absolute authority. In this I am not claiming a conceptually new category to solve this ancient problem of ethics, just trying to locate the meaning of what I am doing. (Thus there is at least some similarity in the status of the presumptions, and their implications, with what William Temple called his 'middle axioms': a term intended to indicate an intermediate status between general principles and specific policies and actions.)[3]

Understood in this way, the presumptions themselves, and the way in which they have emerged both in the general discussion and in specific Christian doctrines, may be summarized like this:

1. *All individual persons must be valued (equally) in and through their supporting network of social relations*

The sense of equality here extends to all but does not homogenize all. It includes differentiation and diversity. It is something which *may* be grounded in the expediencies of social organization and survival, or derived from Enlightenment rationalism. But it *certainly* arises from Christian convictions about our common createdness, irreplaceability and redeemability. The specific requirement to attend to each other (equally) *through our social relations* is the crying need unmasked by our current culture of fragmented isolationism. But it is also the ancient, well-grounded wisdom of Christian theology in both the depth and breadth of its historic and systematic thought.

2. *No individual person must ever be valued* only *according to their existing network of social relations*

This has arisen ambivalently in Enlightenment ideals of treating the agent as an autonomous end-in-himself or herself (although core ideas of individualism are corruptible, they remain crucial). It arises more tenuously in some recent analytical treatments of personal identity which allow self-originating potential in the individual person. But it is given much more secure (though controlled) endorsement in a Christian ontology which insists that particular being must never be simply *reduced* to relation.

3. *All individual persons must be valued as continuous selves according to the complete narrative of their lives*

This is required by all attempts to reconstruct some sense of personal unity in the face of current dislocation and alienation. It may be supported in general terms both by neo-Aristotelian notions of narrative unity (MacIntyre) and by at least some analytic and phenomenological accounts of personal identity. But the Christian narrative of God's providential love, grounded in the dynamism of his Trinitarian being, provides *ultimate* grounds for that unity – not only within this life, but also for resurrection life beyond it.

Such are the presumptions which must operate within our social practices and our individual attitudes and behaviour. They should both direct and correct us. We should be subject to their inspiration, and alert to their judgement on us when we fail. They are benchmarks of social and moral health, and safeguards against social and moral dissolution, which cannot be treated as optional. Whatever situation emerges out of our current state of reaction and instability should surely come under their scrutiny as matter of moral necessity, whatever else may be left to the proper choices of pluralism and the uncertainties of relativism.

Some implications: brief snapshots on social priorities, employment, the care of elderly people, marriage

But how may these presumptions operate in practice? So far as the broad shape of social order is concerned, outlines have already been suggested or implied. For example, it is presumptions such as these which rule out any form of utilitarianism which attempts social engineering by manipulating individuals (or groups) as atomized, interchangeable units. Even in extreme circumstances of conflict or economic disaster which might compel (for example) the uprooting of people or closure of industry, the presumptions should still exercise their pressure on policy. They will insist, for instance, that mere financial compensation for redundancy will be entirely inadequate: for they require that social relations and community needs must also be attended to in some way, not simply ignored.

More positive implications of these presumptions have also been implied already. For a start, they simply reinforce the general parameters outlined above. Thus it is these sort of presumptions which commit a society to supporting all local networks of social relations which provide moral support and identity for persons-in-relation. At the same time they would encourage constant communications and mutual responsibility between subcultures to prevent their own fragmentation into unrelated ghettoes – for they do not let us forget that people are attended to properly through the *whole* context of their social relations, not just the closest strands of the web.

Their implications could also be pressed in other more specific issues which have been signalled before. Our attitude to the increasing numbers of very elderly citizens is a case in point, highlighting our attitudes and policies more generally towards people who are socially impaired, incapable or isolated.

To begin with, we are inescapably reminded that the value of such people is entirely equivalent to anyone else's. That is, it must be perceived through their irreplaceability within the immediate web of their personal relations. There is no one else who is this particular person to a son, granddaughter, friend or nurse. So whether or not they are also constituted in wider society within a web of economic relations, as net contributors or beneficiaries, is entirely irrelevant to their primary value (this, I repeat, is the same for every person).

But what happens when the immediate web of personal relations appears to dissolve? This point has to be pressed, of course, since for some long-term elderly people, vagrants, criminals, refugees or other 'outcasts', their circumstances outlast or exhaust these relations. There are always likely to be people who have no such relations and no *evident* capacity to form new relations (for example, when there is serious mental decline). So in purely existential terms they may matter to no one. And it is at this point in particular that a theistic perspective demonstrates a vital and traditional role. Christians have long insisted, rightly and axiomatically, that all persons are still held irreplaceably within the love of God – however isolated they may be from others. So as a matter of fact there is always that relation, whether acknowledged or not (and this in turn, should revitalize our efforts to realize that divine relationship in human terms as well).

This much is familiar. Less obviously, we should also recall the pressure of the second presumption here. This holds us to value people in a different way. It reminds us that no person is to be valued *solely* in terms of their relations in any case. Although we may all have been brought into being by relationality, what we are is a particular being which has value beyond its constituent relations. Our particularity includes relations, past and (usually) present, but it is not reducible to them. This too is a perspective which finds its most secure basis in the theistic ontology of explicit Christian belief.

The third presumption also plays its part. All persons must be valued as continuous selves according to the complete narrative of their lives. This means we cannot abstract the self of a final stage from its previous existence. So to attempt to assess its 'current' value in isolation is to deny that continuity of personal identity which carries value as seamlessly as the taste pervades every layer of a fruit. My frail and fractious grandparent *is* also the toddler who charmed its own parents, the young man or woman who loved and dreamed, the parent of my parents, the worker who struggled with success and failure. He or she is not another or separable person (*pace* Parfit).

To be sure, this does not settle decisions about hard cases at the extreme margins of life. That is because these presumptions do not themselves offer the sort of stipulative definition of personhood which can decide whether, or at what stage, someone actually *is* (or ceases to be) a person (that is, they do not arbitrate on the status of a foetus, or on someone in a persistent vegetative state). That requires another kind of discussion altogether.[4]

What I am concerned with here is rather that vastly bigger arena of life where there is no real doubt that we are in the presence of a person, but where pressure of circumstance tends to devalue that person because of the poverty of their current capacity to relate effectively with wider society or other individuals. In such circumstances all these presumptions reinforce each other with the same effect. They resist absolutely all tendencies to treat *any* category of persons on a diminishing scale of value, simply according to social usefulness, existing relationships, life expectancy or moral standing. At the same time they also compel proper attention to all persons as social beings. That is, they ensure that they are considered in relation to their wider life story and relationships, not just as isolated 'types' (for example, of age, illness, disability or criminal behaviour).

In short, they commit us to an equal full regard for all actual persons in every kind of situation. And while this will not make all our decisions for us in specific situations, it does provide a significant background against which decisions have to be made. The allocation of resources in medical and penal policy is a case in point. Such presumptions simply do not permit these to be short-measured according to some covert notion of a sliding-scale in human value.

As already indicated, this represents a familiar moral stance, not a new one. It is also still fairly general in scope and application. But the point of this essay was not necessarily to offer radical new insights in either moral theory or practice. It was simply to trace how foundations of Christian belief and wider moral instincts outlined before can and do connect with this kind of recognizable moral stance in these sorts of specific issues. *And to have demonstrated that connection is to be held all the more tenaciously to its end results and practical implications, however demanding these may be, or however unfashionable they may become.*

Much the same can be said about other specific issues which are pressing, and where these presumptions might be usefully harnessed. Marriage, for instance, is another clear candidate. In its modern form it is a peculiarly intense form of relatedness in which, experientially, we find we can both define and destroy, illuminate and obfuscate, our identity as persons-in-relation. So if these presumptions can operate constructively here, then they must.

More particularly, they must be related to (and tested in) a situation where the very meaning and possibilities of monogamous marriage and faithfulness are in question. The questioning derives partly from deconstructive critiques of some forms of marriage relationship *in principle*: that is, marriages which have been shaped too much by sexual stereotypes, patriarchy and limitations of the nuclear family. It is also because the wider prevailing social conditions seem so antagonistic in practice. These hardly need reiterating here. They have to do with precisely that unfettered and short-sighted individualism which leads to purely egoistic notions of self-realization. They also have to do with the general fragmentation and isolation of people from themselves, each other and their community, described previously. It is clearly a situation in which long-term loyalties and responsibilities are much harder to sustain – and doubly so under the pressure of a longer life-span for most partners.[5]

There are also specific economic conditions which intensify the difficulties. These centre on those powerful forces in the global economy, already noted, which intensify male unemployment in many of our cities while allowing predominantly female part-time work to flourish. It is this devastating blow to traditional male identity and morale which is one of the most immediate, concrete causes of widespread marital breakdown – and which is likely to remain the case in the foreseeable future, even if there is eventually some widespread change in sexual and gender stereotypes. It is a spiral of fragmentation which is twisted further as the next generation of young males has no male role model within the home at all, and is ejected all the more rapidly onto the streets. All this perpetuates conditions which are, to say the least, hardly promising for developing an integrated, secure, social identity, capable of responding to moral calls for loyalty and responsibility.[6]

So in the light of all this, how should these presumptions operate?

In one sense, clearly, they point powerfully in one direction, at least in their aspirations. They yield what one might expect from principles which have been formed out of an engagement with traditional Christian covenant belief: namely, a strong concern for long-term loyalty. Thus (to begin with the second presumption) it is just because the unique and particular value of a person cannot be reduced solely to their existing relationships that some form of commitment to the person should not cease when the relationship appears to dissolve. The belief that a partner has being and value beyond the existential state of a particular relationship holds us to some form of continuing commitment, even though there may be little (subjective) apprehension of it. Naturally, this does not mean that reciprocal subjective responses are unimportant. Without any prospect of them at all, in any sense, a compelled commitment can become destructive – so the marriage bond is not hereby absolutized, by this or any presumption. The point is rather that this notion of a partner's objective value must still hold us to a profound *attempt* at renewing a viable relationship. To believe in the objective value of someone must entail a serious and sustained effort to rediscover some subjective response to him or her, to match the objective moral truth. It certainly forbids the convenient fiction that our partner no longer *has* any significant being and value, just because we have ceased to experience it.

The third presumption has much the same implication. It forbids us to slide too slickly out of another aspect of promise and commitment. For if we presume a continuous identity within the whole narrative of ourselves, then we cannot easily claim that the partner we married has become 'a totally different person' (a familiar claim). Again, this is not an absolutizing presumption. There are profound tragedies which destroy every recognizable element of a person, and which may compel a separation for the sake of sanity and compassion. Our presumptions *are* only presumptions. But again, this one retains its general force. It forbids us from making such claims about total change too swiftly or glibly. In abstract terms it reminds us of Ricoeur's distinction between a person's sameness and selfhood. More concretely it makes us recall the commonsense logic to which I have already referred, which entitles me to pick up a pension I subscribed to as a fresh-faced (or foolish) adolescent when I am now a battered (or wise) old man of eighty. I do this because I believe myself to be still myself and not another, although much changed. It is precisely the same logic, and the same moral presumption, which requires me to acknowledge that my wife is fundamentally the same person now that I married then. Therefore my promise and commitment must necessarily run through *every* layer of her 'changing' identity, just as she is still herself at every point in that narrative.

To that extent the force and direction of these presumptions, in relation to marriage, is therefore predictable (though none the worse for that). But there is another point here, and one which may take us further. This arises particularly from the first presumption. For this takes us beyond the couple in themselves and reminds us of the futility of considering the marriage commitment in isolation. Indeed, it leads us to consider the futility of considering *any* call to loyalty in isolation from a wider set of relationships. For the presumption requires us to remember that we cannot attend to each other properly just as atomized individuals. And that means we cannot truly commit ourselves to another person without including the wider web of their other social relations, and our own.

At the very least this means that the public dimensions of marriage will be important. These constitute a vital aid both to recognizing and incorporating that wider web of relations within the commitment. Private contracts of commitment may fail significantly to do this. But the point must be taken much further than an affirmation of public ceremony in marriage. If we are acknowledging that a wider network of relationships helps constitute individuals (and a couple) in their identity this implies both an interdependence and a sense of reciprocal responsibility with that wider order at many levels.

The nature of this interdependence is most visible when it is working negatively. It is easy to see how a wider social order undermines an effective sense of identity in individuals and couples if it is itself constantly being disrupted by changed allegiances and broken relationships. This becomes a vicious circle, easy to diagnose. The spreading ripples of broken loyalties eat like an acid into that very network of relations which can help support and sustain the sort of integrated identity which individuals need in order to make successful relationships themselves. In other words, the fewer relationships one can depend on in society *in general*, the more fragmented one's own sense of identity, and the more difficult it is to form stable relationships oneself.

One implication, certainly, is that the importance of long-term loyalty must be reaffirmed in marriage, as one way of breaking into the vicious circle of general instability at some point. This is part of the reciprocal responsibility we have towards the public domain arising out of our interdependence with it. The serious efforts of couples to stay together contribute to a more general climate of stability not just for immediate dependents (for example, children) but more widely still.

But, equally, it would be entirely unrealistic to single out marriage as the only point of re-entry into a more virtuous circle. The very interdependence of our whole web of relationships alerts us to the fact that long-term loyalty is a crucial ingredient in the *whole* moral–social agenda, not just one item of it. So these presumptions lead inexorably to value the notion of loyalty in other contexts as well.

This includes the wider family network. We become bound to value and nourish the extended family of grandparents, aunts, uncles, cousins and so on with the sort of robust commitment which will survive both the structural and existential dislocations of our fast-moving contemporary society. A grandchild's perception of a grandparent and vice versa must be able to transcend both the geographical distance and the cultural incomprehension which may have cut them off from each other (gaps which may be due to such disparate causes as unemployment, credit facilities, drugs or computer literacy).

Notions of loyalty will also need to extend generally to the local community and its institutions, to its own narrative traditions, and even beyond that to the nation and its own international allegiances. More specifically, they must also be allowed to exert pressure within the culture of employment. It will be vital to create a climate of employment which values persons concretely, according to the wider and longer-term narrative of their lives and relationships within a company or institution (rather than abstractly as mere units of work or expertise). This kind of climate needs to be reclaimed from the current culture of extreme mobility, insecurity and short-term consultancy which deprives both employee and employer of the benefits of personal loyalty.

To be sure, this last example immediately reminds us of the point made previously in relation to marriage: creating some such climate simply is not as easy as that in the face of wider economic forces. There are social and economic counter-pressures for growth, flexibility, innovation or fresh enterprise which often pull powerfully in the opposite direction, splintering the very loyalties which are so desirable in other respects. (Thus the prospect of jobs for life may not be realistic in present conditions, and notions of personal loyalty will *have* to be worked out in other terms than this, at least in the immediate future: 'loyalty' itself, as we have seen, is not a self-interpreting notion; it requires a wider context of meaning.)

All this means that the mere assertion of moral presumptions is not likely to reverse trends of instability either in marriage or in any other sphere of life. Strident moralism alone, whether from Church or state, will not suffice. Its effectiveness will always be severely limited unless it operates in conjunction with changed social, political and economic priorities and policies. It simply may not be heard clearly unless and until such change occurs. The need for detailed discussion about particular economic and social policies, in the light of these presumptions, therefore becomes paramount (highlighting again the strict limitations of this essay, which stops short of that much harder enterprise).

Moreover, moral assertions also need to operate out of a strong narrative tradition and community of values. 'Disembodied' or abstracted moral beliefs may have their use as unifying factors and rallying points in a pluralist situation, but they cannot free-float effectively for ever. This has been a critical point of much of our previous discussion.

Yet none of this renders these moral presumptions redundant. Even if they can only be heard effectively through changed economic and social conditions, then they must still operate precisely at that level (that is, they must be allowed to exert pressure on political and economic ideology, on practical policy, and they must motivate greater allegiance to particular communities). Furthermore, we still should not abandon straightforward moral exhortation even in 'disembodied' form. For unless we have become complete structural determinists about moral behaviour we shall believe that some moral imagination *can* still be kindled and inspired by individuals within even the most unfavourable social conditions – by words, deeds and especially by personal example. Where such moral heroism does exist it should not be deprived of the support of explicit moral teaching, just because we are also waiting and working for wider social change to make it more realistic elsewhere. This would be to deny the possibilities of a prophetic voice and way of life which can rise above its situation and which can sometimes be heard, against all odds: a phenomenon whose vitality and independence is precisely one of those better flowers of individualism we have wished to flourish. In short, these sorts of presumptions must be allowed to shape individual attitude and social reality *in whatever way they can*.

So these are the presumptions – and just a taste of their significance in practice. They lay no particular claim to originality. On the contrary, it has been a chief aim of the essay to demonstrate how such basic moral ideas and presumptions are rooted in a coherent and credible *tradition* of Christian belief. The aim has also been to show the extent to which they can express consensus from a much wider spectrum of non-religious moral belief. In one way or another they actually *need* to connect with existing intuitions, and to demonstrate that they have a history.

Nonetheless, although they draw strength from their traditions, they still have the potential to be creative, radical and critical. They may still shape new practices when they are applied to new social situations. They could certainly prove uncomfortable in the loyalties and commitments they require. Above all they are offered as aids in the overall artifice of ethics which are particularly pertinent in our current situation. A situation of extreme individualism which is unstable and reactive, and a (possible) emerging movement of communitarianism which is already provoking its own counter-reaction, needs some such firm prescriptions and parameters. With these presumptions we may be able to shape at least some answers to commend to a confused culture.

Paying Attention to People

We therefore end where we began. Attention must be paid to individual people. This axiom must hold in our own age, as in any age. People *mattering* is an inescapable moral foundation of all healthy social order, and written in to the very essentials of Christian faith and practice. In particular, the 'ordinary' salesman matters as much as anyone. He matters according to his individuality, and within the whole web of his social relationships, and within the whole narrative of his life. As such he is irreplaceable. We should pay scrupulous attention to him, as to every individual person. He should be loved.

Why? We have found reason for this beyond the bounds of conscious Christian faith. Basic intuitions about the value of persons operate widely, without the explicit metaphysic of faith. They have received impetus in western culture from a long and complex history of ideas incorporating a huge variety of sources. They also connect widely across different traditions of thought and belief within that history. And if the argument of this essay fails adequately to demonstrate this then some of the finest literary symbols can surely do so. One has only to think of the atheist doctor and the believing priest attending together to the dying victims of the plague in Albert Camus's celebrated novel. They are demonstrating just this power of some core moral intuitions to transcend any particular tradition.[1] It is but one example out of a multitude of narratives, in fiction and life, and it is all evidence for the value of persons and a reason for attending to them. There are *transcendent* moral intuitions which deserve respect, and some of the core ideas of individualism (duly qualified and controlled) are amongst them.

As I hope to have made clear, such transcendence is the last thing Christians can or should deny. It belongs to the logic of Christian theology itself. Christians should rejoice and co-operate in it, contributing wherever they can to such moral intuitions, and without requiring

agreement on their ultimate origin. For in one sense it does not mat
ter whether the moral claim grasps a doctor entirely independently of
faith, or whether it only found him out because of the influences of a
Christian past (or some other religion). If a doctor of the plague really
is motivated by 'faithless', freestanding moral intuitions, then so be it.
Indeed, in Kantian terms this might even seem to be a safer, starker,
vision of their moral grandeur '. . . as if, the metaphysical crust having
been eroded by the wind and rains of critical analysis, the moral strata
were laid bare and stood out in lonely eminence'.[2] Hence all the efforts
of this essay to offer moral presumptions which can connect widely,
with or without faith. Hence, too, its concern to defend the role of
core ideas of individualism (suitably qualified) as central to maintaining
these transcendent moral intuitions. They are vital points of connection in a fluid, fragmented world.

Yet there is also no doubt that faith provides its own distinctive
reasons as well. There are reasons for this moral demand which *can*
clearly be located in a specific tradition of faith and belief. Judaeo-
Christian belief in particular *has* contributed profoundly to this basic
moral intuition, both historically and conceptually. In principle, whatever its practice, it offers uniquely coherent and compelling reason for
paying attention to people.

It is a tradition of belief which begins and ends with the fact that
God himself is love. This is expressed variously both through Christianity's own persuasive narrative and through its cluster of interrelated
doctrines, themselves well tried and tested through time and change.
As love God values us all as individual and irreplaceable persons-in-
relationship, giving us complete security in that manner of being – for
eternity. As persons-in-relationship we are made *for* love, to enjoy it
and multiply it. This love is given unconditionally, but it also confers
something. It 'gives more vigorous existence'. And so it brings returns
of vitality, fulfilment, creativity. Ultimately it must therefore bring
mutual well-being, personal and social.

It will always be vital to press these distinctive Christian claims, as
well as appealing to more general moral instincts. It will be particularly
important in this disorientated, sceptical, pluralist, post-modern
world, when the *grounding* of moral intuitions is so problematic,
however persistent and widespread they may still be.

To be sure, there will also be powerful voices suggesting that further grounding is not necessary. Hence Iris Murdoch, writing about
an existentialist position: 'it is as if only one certainty remained; that
human beings are irreducibly valuable, *without any notion why or how*

they are valuable or how the value can be defended' (emphasis mine).[3] But when the further turn of the post-modern screw shatters the very notion of a self at all, can even this last moral certainty really remain intact *'without any notion why or how* ... '? It is unlikely. The analysis of social fragmentation offered in this essay surely suggests that we need *some* more reason for our values, some better foundations for our intuitions. It means we shall need a sense of community, bearing some sort of narrative tradition, to provide such foundations. Crucially, it means we shall need the reasons of a mature faith and tradition which will not tip our proper regard for the individual into unfettered individualism.

Hence the sustained and unashamed effort of this essay consistently to commend explicit Christian belief, to provide such a faith and such a foundation. It is commended as a continuing bulwark against moral disintegration. It offers a profound and responsible reason for paying attention to individual people. Its tradition of belief incorporates, inspires and controls values and attitudes which are recognizably related to the core values of individualism, but always in a corporate context.

Finally, and by virtue of all this, it is a tradition which can also be seen to offer reassurance to the more pressing existential questions as well. It can convey credible security to those who are losing their grip on personal identity and value; those who now wonder if their identity was ever anything more than a transient creation of their culture – or their imagination. The Christian tradition of belief resists all such reductionism. Our personal identity is no mask, no flickering shadow of a changing role, strutting and fretting briefly on the stage, and then no more. It is an infinitely precious and enduring gift of God, formed and constantly refashioned out of all the relationships he has granted us, but always uniquely and enduringly *you* and *me*.

Notes

INTRODUCTION

1. For a balanced survey and assessment of developing trends in this area see Shlomer Aviner and Avner de-Shalit (eds), *Communitarianism and Individualism* (Oxford, Oxford University Press, 1992); also Daniel Bell, *Communitarianism and its Critics* (Oxford, Clarendon Press, 1993). For signs of the emergence of a counter offensive to this communitarian reaction see, for example, the more populist tract: Alan Duncan and Dominic Hobson, *Saturn's Children* (London, Sinclair-Stevenson, 1995).
2. cf. Charles Taylor's comments in his monumental but careful attempt at a history of ideas: *Sources of the Self* (Cambridge, Cambridge University Press, 1989), espec. chs 4 & 12.
3. See Robert Hamilton, 'The Monodic Quest', in *Theological Studies* 38.1 (1987).
4. See Bibliography for some indication of the range of recent writing.
5. cf. T. B. Strong, *God and the Individual* (London, Longman, Green & Co., 1903). The starting point of his discussion was, precisely, a situation in which he perceived reaction and dialectic between apparent opposites:

   The question is, what is the relation between God and the individual according to Christianity? Some Christians in modern times will answer that the relation is so immediate that all sacraments, and even the organization of the Christian Society, are impediments rather than help . . . A study [of the Bible] will, I feel sure, lead to a serious modification of the individualism, which underlies so much of our current theology, without landing us in the unmodified ecclesiasticism which we identify with Rome (Introduction).

6. See, for instance, Colin Gunton, *The Promise of Trinitarian Theology* (Edinburgh, T. & T. Clark, 1991); *The One, The Three, and The Many* (Cambridge, Cambridge University Press, 1993); Christoph Schwöbel and Colin Gunton (eds), *Persons, Divine and Human* (Edinburgh, T. & T. Clark, 1991); John Zizioulas, *Being as Communion* (London, Darton, Longman & Todd, 1985); Alistair McFadyen, *The Call to Personhood. A Christian Theory of the Individual in Social Relationships* (Cambridge, Cambridge University Press, 1990).
7. See pp. 88–91.
8. See, for example, Iris Young's discussion in *Justice and the Politics of Difference* (New Jersey, Princeton University Press, 1990).

175

9. cf. Marilyn Friedman, 'Feminism and Modern Friendship: Dislocating the Community', *Ethics* 99 (1989).
10. See p. 47.

CHAPTER ONE

1. Alasdair MacIntyre, *After Virtue* (London, Duckworth, 2nd edn 1990), p. 35.
2. MacIntyre, *After Virtue*, p. 68.
3. Charles Taylor, *Sources of the Self* (Cambridge, Cambridge University Press, 1989); cf. also *The Ethics of Authenticity* (Cambridge, Mass., Harvard University Press, 1991).
4. Carver T. Yu, *Being and Relation. A Theological Critique of Western Dualism and Individualism* (Edinburgh, Scottish Academic Press, 1987) p. 25.
5. Yu, *Being and Relation*, ch. 4.
6. What follows owes a considerable debt to Steven Lukes, *Individualism* (Oxford, Basil Blackwell, 1973).
7. Edmund Burke, 'Speech on Economic Reform' 1780, in *Works* (London, The World's Classics Vol. 2, 1906), p. 357; cited by Lukes, *Individualism*, p. 3. See also *Reflections on the Revolution in France* 1790 (London, Everyman's Library, 1910).
8. See Lukes, *Individualism*, chs 1–5, for detailed discussion.
9. Robert Hamilton, 'The Monodic Quest', in *Theological Studies* 38.1 (1987).
10. See A. D. Lindsay, 'Individualism', in *Encyclopaedia of the Social Sciences* (New York, Macmillan, 1930–35), Vol. 7; cited by Lukes, *Individualism*, p. 40.
11. See E. Troeltsch, *The Social Teaching of the Christian Churches* 1912 (Engl. transl. London, George Allen & Unwin, 1931).
12. See Max Weber, *The Protestant Ethic and the Spirit of Capitalism* 1904 (Engl. transl. London, George Allen & Unwin, 1985).
13. See Lukes, *Individualism*, p. 41.
14. John Milbank, *Theology and Social Theory* (Oxford, Basil Blackwell, 1990), chs 11 & 12.
15. cf. Taylor, *Sources of the Self*, ch. 7. See also p. 28.
16. For this analysis see especially MacIntyre's account in *After Virtue*. One of his most severe critics in this respect is Robert Wokler. See 'Projecting the Enlightenment', in John Horton and Susan Mendus (eds), *After MacIntyre* (Oxford, Polity Press, 1994), ch. 6. His complaint is that MacIntyre spuriously projects the Enlightenment as a unified whole, by selectivity. MacIntyre makes some response in 'A Partial Response to my Critics', *After MacIntyre*, ch. 15.
17. MacIntyre, *After Virtue*, p. 38.
18. Taylor, *Sources of the Self*, p. 313.
19. Taylor, *Sources of the Self*, p. 313.
20. MacIntyre, *After Virtue*, p. 61.
21. See Sir Ernest Barker (ed.), *Social Contract* (Oxford, Oxford University Press, 1960), p. viii.
22. Barker, *Social Contract*, p. xi.
23. John Locke, 'An Essay Concerning the True Original. Extent and End of Civil Government' II:14, 1690, in Barker, *Social Contract*.

24. cf. Alasdair MacIntyre, *A Short History of Ethics* (London, Routledge & Kegan Paul, 1967), p. 158.
25. Locke, 'Essay', 11:13.
26. Taylor, *Source of the Self*, p. 194.
27. Richard Hooker, *Treatise on the Laws of Ecclesiastical Polity* 1594, Book I. sect. 10.
28. Locke, 'Essay', 11:6. But note Stephen Clark, *Civil Peace and Sacred Order* (Oxford, Clarendon Press, 1989), p. 17, who warns against an over-individualistic misinterpretation of Locke.

CHAPTER TWO

1. Steven Lukes, *Individualism* (Oxford, Basil Blackwell, 1973), p. 52.
2. cf. Oliver O'Donovan, *Resurrection and Moral Order* (Leicester, IVP, 2nd edn 1994), p. 107.
3. See Max Weber, *The Protestant Ethic and the Spirit of Capitalism* 1904, (Engl. transl. London, George Allen & Unwin, 1985) pp. 104-7.
4. W. Stark, *The Sociology of Religion: A Study of Christendom* Vol. 3 (London, Routledge & Kegan Paul, 1967); cited by Lukes, *Individualism*, p. 95.
5. In moral theology especially. See, for example, James Gustafson, *Protestant and Roman Catholic Ethics* (London, SCM, 1979).
6. cf. Robert Roberts, 'Kierkegaard on Becoming an Individual', in *Scottish Journal of Theology* 31.2 (1978).
7. See Basil Mitchell, *Morality: Religious and Secular* (Oxford, Clarendon Press, 1980), p. 11.
8. C. Taylor, *Sources of the Self* (Cambridge, Cambridge University Press, 1989), p. 489.
9. See, for example, R. M. Hare, *Freedom and Reason* (Oxford, Clarendon Press, 1963); cf. John Rawls, *A Theory of Justice* (Oxford, Oxford University Press, 1973).
10. Lukes, *Individualism*, p. 86.
11. Taylor, *Sources of the Self*, p. 12
12. J. S. Mill, *On Liberty*, cited by Lukes, *Individualism*, pp. 63-4.
13. Ancient Civilization saw it this way, according to Hannah Arendt: cf. *The Human Condition* (Garden City, Doubleday, 1959). See Lukes, *Individualism*, p. 60.
14. Isaiah Berlin, 'Two Concepts of Liberty', in *Four Essays on Liberty* (Oxford, Oxford University Press, 1969).
15. Reinhold Niebuhr, *Moral Man and Immoral Society* (New York, Scribners, 1942).
16. See Basil Mitchell, *Law, Morality and Religion in a Secular Society* (Oxford, Oxford University Press, 1970).
17. Mitchell, *Morality: Religious and Secular*.
18. Taylor, *Sources of the Self*, p. 185: cf. also Herbert N. Schneidau, 'Biblical Narrative and Modern Consciousness', in Frank McConnell (ed.), *The Bible and the Narrative Tradition* (Oxford, Oxford University Press, 1986), p. 140, citing origins of inwardness in the Hebrew prophetic tradition.
19. See Lukes, *Individualism*, pp. 59-62.
20. Berlin, 'Two Concepts of Liberty'.

21. Taylor, *Sources of the Self*, p. 376.
22. See Lukes, *Individualism*, pp. 19–21.
23. See Lukes, *Individualism*, p. 71.
24. For more on this see pp. 153–4.
25. Cited in Lukes, *Individualism*, p. 67.
26. See pp. 58–71 for fuller discussion.
27. cf. Helen Oppenheimer's helpful discussion in *The Hope of Happiness* (London, SCM, 1983), ch. 11.
28. cf. Helen Oppenheimer, 'Mattering', in *Studies in Christian Ethics* 8:1 (1995).
29. Karl Popper, *The Open Society and its Enemies* Vol. 2 (London, Routledge & Kegan Paul, 1945), p. 245.
30. Immanuel Kant, *Groundwork of the Metaphysic of Morals* 1785 (Engl. transl. New York, Harper & Row, 1964), pp. 95–6.
31. See pp. 144–7 for further discussion.
32. See Lukes, *Individualism*, p. 46.
33. See G. E. M. Anscombe, 'Modern Moral Philosophy', in *Philosophy* 33 (1958); cf. discussion in W. D. Hudson, *Modern Moral Philosophy* (London, Macmillan, 2nd edn 1983), p. 384.
34. See p. 12.
35. A. N. Wilson, *Against Religion* (London, Chatto & Windus, 1991), pp. 28–9.
36. J. Locke, 'An Essay . . . of Civil Government', V.
37. Ronald Dworkin, 'Rights as Trumps', in J. Waldron (ed.), *Theories of Rights* (Oxford, Oxford University Press, 1984), p. 153; cited in Kieran Cronin, *Rights and Christian Ethics* (Cambridge, Cambridge University Press, 1992).
38. cf. Margaret MacDonald, 'Natural Rights' in Waldron (ed.), *Theories of Rights*; cited by Cronin, *Rights and Christian Ethics*.
39. cf. Kai Nielsen, 'Scepticism and Human Rights', in *The Monist* 52 (1968); cited by Cronin, *Rights and Christian Ethics*.
40. cf. R. Frey, *Rights, Killing, Suffering* (Oxford, Basil Blackwell, 1983); cited by Cronin, *Rights and Christian Ethics*.
41. Richard Wasserstrom, 'Rights, Human Rights, and Racial Discrimination', in James Rachels (ed.), *Moral Problems* (New York, Harper & Row, 3rd edn 1979).
42. See Cronin, *Rights and Christian Ethics*, ch. 3.
43. Stanley Hauerwas, *Suffering Presence: Theological Reflections on Medicine, the Mentally Handicapped and the Church* (Edinburgh, T. & T. Clark, 1986).
44. Cronin, *Rights and Christian Ethics*, ch. 4.

CHAPTER THREE

1. Steven Lukes, *Individualism* (Oxford, Basil Blackwell, 1973), p. 125.
2. Lukes, *Individualism*, p. 51.
3. Lukes, *Individualism*, p. 58.
4. Lukes, *Individualism*, p. 72.
5. E. Barker, *Social Contract* (Oxford, Oxford University Press, 1960), pp. vii–viii.
6. cf. Charles Taylor, *Sources of the Self* (Cambridge, Cambridge University Press, 1989), pp. 215f.
7. Taylor, *Sources of the Self*, pp. 12ff.

8. cf. Vernon White, *Atonement and Incarnation* (Cambridge, Cambridge University Press, 1991), pp. 91ff., on the concept of retribution.
9. Taylor, *Sources of the Self*, p. 13.
10. Taylor, *Sources of the Self*, p. 14.
11. cf. Kieran Cronin, *Rights and Christian Ethics* (Cambridge, Cambridge University Press, 1992), pp. 99ff.
12. Dostoevsky, *The Brothers Karamazov* (Engl. transl. Harmondsworth, Penguin, 1958); cf. Jonathan Sutton's illuminating discussion of the creative balance within Russian thought between the individual and the community: 'On Russian Philosophy: The Individual and the Community as Central Categories of Religious Discourse' (unpublished paper).
13. Arthur Koestler, *Darkness at Noon* (London, Jonathan Cape, 1940).
14. Charles Taylor, *The Ethics of Authenticity* (Cambridge, Mass., Harvard University Press, 1991). See pp. 53–4.
15. See, for example, Peter Singer, *Practical Ethics* (Cambridge, Cambridge University Press, 1979).
16. It is one of Rawls' concerns to respond to these obvious criticisms of Mill's Utilitarian theory: cf. John Rawls, *A Theory of Justice* (Oxford, Oxford University Press, 1973).
17. Susan Parsons, 'Feminist Ethics after Modernity: Towards an Appropriate Universalism', in *Studies in Christian Ethics* 8.1 (1995).
18. Parsons, 'Feminist Ethics after Modernity'.
19. F. de Lamennais, 'Des Progrès de la revolution et de la guerre contre l'église', in *Oeuvres Complètes* (Paris, 1836–7), Vol. IX, ch. 1, pp. 17–18; cited in Lukes, *Individualism*, pp. 5–6.
20. This is analogous, though not identical, to MacIntyre's much wider discussion about rationality in general, and rational justification in particular. In *After Virtue* the historical and social context of all values seems almost wholly determinative of their meaning, and the possibility of rational justification for comparison of one tradition over against another seems remote, if not impossible. In his later book, *Whose Justice? Which Rationality?* (London, Duckworth, 1988), that possibility is opened up a little further: 'standards of rational justification themselves emerge from and are part of a history in which they are vindicated by the way in which they transcend the limitations of and provide remedies for the defects of their predecessors within the history of that same tradition' (p. 7).
21. MacIntyre, *After Virtue*, ch. 3.
22. MacIntyre, *After Virtue*, p. 33.
23. MacIntyre, *After Virtue*, p. 172.
24. W. K. Frankena in *Ethics* 93 (1983), p. 500. See also John Milbank, *Theology and Social Theory* (Oxford, Basil Blackwell, 1990), John Horton and Susan Mendus (eds), *After MacIntyre* (Oxford, Polity Press, 1994).
25. cf. John Boyd, 'What Are the Clergy For?', *Theology* XCVIII (1995).
26. See, for example, Fay Weldon's *Affliction* (London, HarperCollins, 1994): a savage critique of therapy, arising from a very personal agenda.
27. cf. Anthony C. Thiselton, *Interpreting God and the Postmodern Self. On Meaning, Manipulation and Promise* (Edinburgh, T. & T. Clark, 1995), pp. 131–4.
28. Taylor, *The Ethics of Authenticity*, p. 3.
29. Taylor, *The Ethics of Authenticity*, p. 4.
30. Taylor, *The Ethics of Authenticity*, p. 5.

31. Taylor, *The Ethics of Authenticity*, p. 29.
32. Taylor, *The Ethics of Authenticity*, ch. 4.
33. Carver T. Yu, *Being and Relation. A Theological Critique of Western Dualism and Individualism* (Edinburgh, Scottish Academic Press, 1987).
34. Yu, *Being and Relation*, ch. 4.

CHAPTER FOUR

1. For example see John Gray, *Beyond the New Right* (London, Routledge, 1993).
2. cf. John Horton and Susan Mendus, *After MacIntyre*: '. . . one of the deepest difficulties with the argument of *After Virtue* is that the very extent of its critique of the modern world would seem to cast doubt on the possibility of any realistic revival under the conditions of modernity of Aristotelianism which MacIntyre advocates' (p. 3).
3. Stephen Clark, *Civil Peace and Sacred Order* (Oxford, Clarendon Press, 1989), p. 36.
4. See p. 46.
5. Carver T. Yu, *Being and Relation. A Theological Critique of Western Dualism and Individualism* (Edinburgh, Scottish Academic Press, 1987), p. 141.
6. Colin E. Gunton, *The One, The Three and The Many* (Cambridge, Cambridge University Press, 1993), ch. 2.
7. e.g. Steven Lukes, *Individualism* (Oxford, Basil Blackwell, 1973), ch.11; also D. Bell, *Communitarianism and its Critics* (Oxford, Clarendon Press, 1993).
8. Karl Marx, *A Contribution to the Critique of Political Economy* 1857 (Engl. transl. Chicago, 1913); cited in Lukes, *Individualism*, p. 76.
9. Stephen Clark, *A Parliament of Souls* (Oxford, Clarendon Press, 1990), p. 2.
10. Clark, *A Parliament of Souls*, p. 6.
11. Gray, *Beyond the New Right*, p. viii.
12. Gray, *Beyond the New Right*, p. 52.
13. Gray, *Beyond the New Right*, pp. 136-7.
14. cf. Rom Harré, 'Persons and Selves', in Arthur Peacocke and Grant Gillett (eds), *Persons and Personality* (Oxford, Basil Blackwell, 1987); also *Personal Being* (Cambridge, Mass., Harvard University Press, 1984).
15. Alasdair MacIntyre, *After Virtue* (London, Duckworth, 2nd edn 1990), p. 86.
16. See Peter Singer, *Practical Ethics* (Cambridge, Cambridge University Press, 1979), p. 230.
17. Hence Rawls' liberal critique of Utilitarianism. See n. 16 p. 44.
18. See especially Richard Swinburne's contributions in, for example, Sydney Shoemaker and Richard Swinburne, *Personal Identity* (Oxford, Basil Blackwell, 1984); cf. also John Foster, *The Immaterial Self: A Defence of the Cartesian Dualist Conception of the Mind* (London, Routledge, 1991).
19. J. R. Searle, *The Rediscovery of the Mind* (Cambridge, Mass., Harvard University Press, 1992).
20. Harold Noonan, *Personal Identity* (London, Routledge, 1989), pp. 12-13.
21. See especially Derek Parfit, *Reasons and Persons* (Oxford, Oxford University Press, 1984); cf. also discussion in Peacocke and Gillett, *Persons and Personality*, ch. 5.

22. Paul Ricoeur, *Oneself as Another* (Engl. transl. Chicago, Chicago University Press, 1992).
23. Ricoeur, *Oneself as Another*, p. 196.
24. Ricoeur, *Oneself as Another*, pp. 297ff.; cf. A. C. Thiselton's comment, *Interpreting God and the Postmodern Self. On Meaning, Manipulation and Promise* (Edinburgh, T. & T. Clark, 1995), pp. 77–8: 'Ricoeur's profound achievement is to undermine equally the autonomous self which commands the centre of the stage in high modernity and the reduced, de-centred self of postmodernity'. He then adds, significantly: 'This comes closest to the self of scripture'.
25. This is the question which helped to provoke the sequel to *After Virtue: Whose Justice? Which Rationality?* Here the choice itself, of an Aristotelian ethic of virtue, has hardened: but the criteria for that choice are still not settled so clearly.
26. cf. Yu, *Being and Relation*.
27. See E. Levinas, *Autrement qu'etre ou au-dela de l'essence* (La Haye, 1974); cf. Michael Moxter, '(Human) Subjectivity and Metaphysics', paper given at the European Society for the Philosophy of Religion: 11th Conference 1994.
28. See further, Chapter 7.
29. See p. 53.
30. The moral case against a Parfitean position can also appeal to another basic intuition. To adapt the golden rule: we should treat others, in general, as they would like to be treated themselves. *Therefore we should respect persons as they normally perceive themselves to be persons.* And in western culture at least that normally does include some profound principle of continuity, certainly for the vast majority. Thus it would be a gross and irresponsible act of intellectual totalitarianism to impose a general theory which deconstructed the value of people's lives as a whole, when it flatly contradicts the way most people perceive their own value. The testimony – or ideology – of some particular individuals that their own personal identity does not matter may be noted, but the burden of proof lies squarely with them: they cannot project this onto others without consent.
31. cf. A. I. McFadyen, *The Call to Personhood: A Christian Theory of the Individual in Social Relationships* (Cambridge, Cambridge University Press, 1990). Although he does not set out to isolate core ideas in the way I have done they occur and re-occur in precisely this 'redeemed' sense. See especially pp. 224ff., where freedom, autonomy, self-realization, privacy, rights, are all employed in a relational sense – and applied in a public domain.

CHAPTER FIVE

1. Alasdair MacIntyre, *After Virtue* (London, Duckworth, 2nd edn 1990), p. 263.
2. John Gray, *Beyond the New Right* (London, Routledge, 1993), p. 52.
3. Stephen Clark, *Civil Peace and Sacred Order* (Oxford, Clarendon Press, 1989), p. 67. (In context the chief point of this quotation has to do with the importance of women and children in the structures of society.)
4. cf. Shlomer Aviner and Avner de-Shalit, *Communitarianism and Individualism* (Oxford, Oxford University Press, 1992), p. 9.

5. It also highlights a contradiction in MacIntyre's position. See n. 2, Chapter 4.
6. Carver T. Yu, *Being and Relation. A Theological Critique of Western Dualism and Individualism* (Edinburgh, Scottish Academic Press, 1987), p. 45.
7. See pp. 51–2.

CHAPTER SIX

1. Justin Martyr's designation: cf. John 1.4, 9.
2. Acts 17.16ff.
3. See p. 18.
4. See Jürgen Habermas, 'Transcendence from Within, Transcendence in this World', in D. S. Browning and F. Schüssler Fiorenza (eds), *Modernity and Public Theology* (New York, Crossroad, 1993), ch. 9.
5. Stanley Hauerwas, *A Community of Character* (Notre Dame, University of Notre Dame Press, 1981), p. 105.
6. Literature about this is legion. But because this book refers to the Greek background of some Christian origins, Ancient Greek culture makes a particularly interesting point of comparison. See, for instance, Kenneth Dover, *Greek Popular Morality in the Time of Plato and Aristotle* (Oxford, Basil Blackwell, 1974). Here he points out the *distinctions* between Ancient Greek and Christian valuations of the individual person, in particularly stark terms. The more general question of whether (in a pluralist situation) it is now *legitimate* for theology to consider any religious tradition in isolation has been raised in a recent book by Keith Ward, *Religion and Revelation. A Theology of Revelation in the World's Religions* (Oxford, Clarendon Press, 1994). He has a point. However, no particular theology or theologian can realistically be required to have exhaustive knowledge of *all* religious, philosophical and cultural traditions, as Ward himself concedes. And once more limited terms of reference are permitted in principle then the restricted discussion of this essay must also be allowed. It does at least engage with some wider cultural and philosophical contexts, though not with other religions.
7. *Pace* MacIntyre, in *Whose Justice? Which Rationality?*, where he depends heavily on the Aristotelian–Augustinian–Thomist tradition of Christian theology.

CHAPTER SEVEN

1. Keith Ward, *The Battle for the Soul. An Affirmation of Human Dignity and Value* (London, Hodder & Stoughton, 1985), p. 162.
2. Stephen Clark, *Civil Peace and Sacred Order* (Oxford, Clarendon Press, 1989), p. 37.
3. Anthony Thiselton demonstrates incisively how Don Cupitt has fallen victim to this process, and exposes the incoherence of it. See A. C. Thiselton, *Interpreting God and the Postmodern Self* (Edinburgh, T. & T. Clark, 1995), especially chs 13 & 17.
4. John Milbank, *Theology and Social Theory* (Oxford, Basil Blackwell, 1990), pp. 294–5.
5. See for instance David A. Hart, *Faith in Doubt* (London, Mowbray, 1993); cf. Thiselton, *Interpreting God and the Postmodern Self,* loc. cit., for critique.

6. Vernon White, *The Fall of a Sparrow: A Concept of Special Divine Action* (Exeter, Paternoster, 1985), espec. pp. 72–80.
7. Milbank, *Theology and Social Theory*, p. 295.
8. Milbank, *Theology and Social Theory*, p. 423.
9. Milbank, *Theology and Social Theory*, pp. 424, 426.
10. Milbank, *Theology and Social Theory*, p. 295.
11. Karl Barth, *Church Dogmatics* (Engl. transl. Edinburgh, T. & T. Clark, 1956–77), 111/4, p. 373.
12. Barth, *Church Dogmatics* 1/1, pp. 369ff.; cf. Eberhard Jüngel, *The Doctrine of the Trinity. God's Being is in Becoming* (Engl. transl. Edinburgh, Scottish Academic Press, 1976).
13. cf. Ingolf Dalferth, 'Karl Barth's Eschatological Realism', in S. W. Sykes (ed.), *Karl Barth: Centenary Essays* (Cambridge, Cambridge University Press, 1989).
14. cf. Gary Deddo, 'The Grammar of Barth's Theology of Personal Relations', *Scottish Journal of Theology* 47 (1994).
15. John D. Zizioulas, *Being as Communion. Studies in Personhood and the Church* (London, Darton, Longman & Todd, 1985).
16. Colin E. Gunton, *The One, The Three and The Many* (Cambridge, Cambridge University Press, 1993).
17. cf. Gunton, *The One, The Three and the Many*, pp. 188ff. He admits the difficulty of using the language of substance, not least because of its associations with traditional views about *underlying* being (which can have the effect of weakening the particularity of persons and things because it finds their 'real' being in something behind or beyond them). Although generally sympathetic to Barth he finds that he too replicates this problem when he uses the term 'mode of being' to describe the persons of the Trinity (Gunton, *The One, The Three and The Many*, p. 191 n. 11). However, when suitably defined in the way indicated, substance (or 'substantiality') does help to give proper ontological weight to particularity.
18. cf. Gunton, *The One, The Three and The Many*, ch. 2 (he traces the tendency to Plato in particular).
19. Gunton, *The One, The Three and The Many*, p. 195.
20. Gunton, *The One, The Three and The Many*, p. 196.
21. Gunton, *The One, The Three and The Many*, p. 226.
22. Gunton, *The One, The Three and The Many*, p. 214.
23. A. I. McFadyen, *The Call to Personhood. A Christian Theory of the Individual in Social Relationships* (Cambridge, Cambridge University Press, 1990).
24. McFadyen, *The Call to Personhood*, espec. ch. 3.
25. McFadyen, *The Call to Personhood*, p. 313.
26. McFadyen, *The Call to Personhood*, p. 285 n. 3.
27. McFadyen, *The Call to Personhood*, p. 285 n. 3.
28. There is here more than a faint echo of the vulnerability of process conceptions of God to a similar infinite regress. There it is a regress of passivity: that is, out of what resources does one pole of the divine being actively organize incoming reality when it is itself constituted by nothing except 'passive' experiences? I have discussed this more fully in *The Fall of a Sparrow*, pp. 72–80.
29. See pp. 163–9.
30. Gunton, *The One, The Three and The Many*, p. 26.
31. Gunton, *The One, The Three and The Many*, p. 39.

32. cf. Gunton, *The One, The Three and The Many*, pp. 64–5.
33. cf. Gunton, *The One, The Three and The Many*, p. 26. n. 1, citing David Nicholls, *Deity and Domination. Images of God and the State in the Nineteenth and Twentieth Centuries* (London, Routledge, 1989).
34. See pp. 115f..
35. See p. 36.
36. McFadyen, *The Call to Personhood*, p. 229.

CHAPTER EIGHT

1. cf. Helen Oppenheimer, 'Mattering', in *Studies in Christian Ethics* 8.1 (1995).
2. Bruce Malina, *The New Testament World. Insights from Cultural Anthropology* (London, SCM, 1981).
3. For instance, Malina rightly draws attention to the fact that in the New Testament world honour and shame (that is, assessment by others) is more important than guilt (understood as internalized self-assessment). But when he goes on to assert that the New Testament personality is one whose self-image is *indistinguishable* from the image presented to him by family, village, city or nation, he surely overstates his case. Is this really true of Jesus, for example? And how could this view adequately accommodate the prophetic tradition? More generally, how could we *know* this to be the case? (cf. Malina, *The New Testament World*, ch. 3). For another, more balanced, assessment of cultural differences and continuities see H. N. Schneidau, 'Biblical Narrative and Modern Consciousness', in F. McConnell (ed.), *The Bible and the Narrative Tradition* (Oxford: Oxford University Press, 1986).
4. H. Wheeler-Robinson, *The Religious Ideas of the Old Testament* (London, Duckworth, 1913).
5. Claus Westermann, *Creation* (Engl. transl. London, SPCK, 1974).
6. Ezek. 18.20; cf. Jer. 31.29.
7. Wolfhart Pannenberg, *Anthropology in Theological Perspective* (Engl. transl. Edinburgh, T. & T. Clark, 1985).
8. J. R. Porter, 'The Legal Aspects of the Concept of "Corporate Responsibility" in the Old Testament', in *Vetus Testamentum* 15 (1965).
9. John Rogerson, 'The Hebrew Conception of Corporate Personality: A Re-examination', in *Issues in Religion and Theology 8: Anthropological Approaches to the Old Testament* (London, SPCK, 1985).
10. J. A. T. Robinson, 'The Body. A Study in Pauline Theology', in *Studies in Biblical Theology* No. 5 (London, SCM, 1952).
11. cf. especially E. P. Sanders, *Paul and Palestinian Judaism* (London, SCM, 1977), and *Paul, the Law and the Jewish People* (Philadelphia, Fortress Press, 1983).
12. C. F. D. Moule, 'The Individualism of the Fourth Gospel', in *Essays in New Testament Interpretation* (Cambridge, Cambridge University Press, 1982).
13. Walter Eichrodt, *Theology of the Old Testament* Vol. 2 (Engl. transl. London, SCM, 1967), pp. 245–6.
14. Eichrodt, *Theology of the Old Testament*, Vol. 2, pp. 245–6.
15. Eichrodt, *Theology of the Old Testament*, Vol. 2, pp. 249–50.
16. Paul Hanson, *The People Called. The Growth of Community in the Bible* (San Francisco, Harper & Row, 1986).
17. Hanson, *The People Called*, p. 223.

18. Hanson, *The People Called*, p. 208.
19. Hanson, *The People Called*, p. 211 (citing Prov. 11.11).
20. D. E. H. Whiteley, *The Theology of St Paul* (Oxford, Oxford University Press, 1964), p. 45.
21. Whiteley, *The Theology of St Paul*, p. 191.
22. Whiteley, *The Theology of St Paul*, p. 198.
23. Hanson, *The People Called*, p. 501.
24. Hanson, *The People Called*, p. 501.
25. Hanson, *The People Called*, p. 501.
26. Westermann, *Creation*.
27. Gen. 1.27. Barth's contentious exegesis of the image of God as male-female relationality (*Church Dogmatics* III/I pp. 181ff.) is only part of a more sustainable general exposition of the relationality of the image; cf. J. Barr's criticism of Barth here in *Biblical Faith and Natural Theology* (Oxford, Clarendon Press, 1993), p. 160; also A. C. Thiselton's response in 'Barr on Barth and Natural Theology', *Scottish Journal of Theology* 47 (1994), p. 527.
28. cf. Christoph Schwöbel and Colin Gunton (eds), *Persons, Divine and Human* (Edinburgh, T. & T. Clark, 1991), espec. chs 1 & 2.
29. Colin Gunton, 'Trinity, Ontology and Anthropology: Towards a Renewal of the Doctrine of the Imago Dei', in Schwöbel and Gunton, *Persons, Divine and Human*, p. 59.
30. See pp. 102–5.
31. This may be compared with a related, but not identical, basis for equality in individual value proposed by David Brown. Following Levinas, Brown sees the irreducible *otherness* implied in a relationship with God (and others) as the sign that we are truly *noted*. It is in the 'resistance' we encounter in otherness that we know we have value. See David Brown, *Continental Philosophy and Modern Theology. An Engagement* (Oxford, Basil Blackwell, 1987), p. 86: 'In the face of every "other" we encounter a resistance to our own wills that is indicative of an independent, irreducible moral value. Experiencing the other as other is enough. It is clearly so basic to all our experience of humanity as not to raise the question of degrees of worth.'
32. These categories of the human condition (freedom and finitude) have been explicitly used to help explain the 'occasion' of sin by a number of writers, not least Reinhold Niebuhr (though see also Judith Plaskow's critique in *Sex, Sin and Grace: Women's Experience and the Theologies of Reinhold Niebuhr and Paul Tillich* (Lanham, University Press of America, 1980).
33. cf. Bruce Vawter, *On Genesis. A New Reading* (New York, Doubleday, 1970), pp. 152ff.
34. cf. James Gustafson, *Protestant and Roman Catholic Ethics* (London, SCM, 1979), espec. ch. 1.
35. For example, Plaskow, *Sex, Sin and Grace*.
36. See pp. 152–5.
37. See, for instance, Jürgen Moltmann, *The Trinity and the Kingdom of God* (Engl. transl. London, SCM, 1981). Moltmann is anxious to include the notion of substantial individuals within the category of relation lest the Holy Spirit be denied full subjectivity and personhood within the Trinity.
38. cf. Colin Gunton, *The Promise of Trinitarian Theology* (Edinburgh, T. & T. Clark, 1991).
39. Gunton, *The Promise of Trinitarian Theology*; also *The One, The Three and The Many* (Cambridge, Cambridge University Press, 1993), pp. 163ff.

186 Notes

40. See pp. 102–5.
41. John V. Taylor, *The Go-Between God. The Holy Spirit and The Christian Mission* (London, SCM, 1972).
42. Sarah Coakley, *Christ Without Absolutes* (Oxford, Clarendon Press, 1988).
43. cf. my discussion in V. P. White, *Atonement and Incarnation. An Essay in Universalism and Particularity* (Cambridge, Cambridge University Press, 1991).
44. cf. John 17.20ff.
45. cf. Col. 1.20.
46. R. Hamilton, 'The Monodic Quest', in *Theological Studies* 38.1 (1987), p. 78.
47. Hamilton, 'The Monodic Quest', p. 79.
48. D. M. Baillie, *God Was in Christ* (London, Faber & Faber, 1961).
49. White, *Atonement and Incarnation*.
50. cf. Hamilton's account of Augustine, 'The Monodic Quest', pp. 84ff.
51. This fundamentally Pauline notion is given extended application in A. I. McFadyen's social analysis: *The Call to Personhood. A Christian Theory of the Individual in Social Relationships* (Cambridge, Cambridge University Press, 1990), espec. pp. 224ff.
52. Hamilton, 'The Monodic Quest', p. 82.
53. A more measured and balanced assessment is suggested in, for example, A. E. McGrath, *Christian Theology, An Introduction* (Oxford, Basil Blackwell, 1994), pp. 392ff.; cf. also an interesting discussion by Francis Watson, 'Christ, Law and Freedom: A Study in Theological Hermeneutics', in Colin E. Gunton (ed.), *God and Freedom* (Edinburgh, T. & T. Clark, 1995). See further in this essay, p. 147.
54. C. K. Barrett, *Church, Ministry, and Sacraments in the New Testament* (Exeter, Paternoster, 1985), p. 100. But cf. also Denis Edwards, 'The Church as Sacrament of Relationships', in *Pacifica* 8.2 (1995) for a recent attempt to provide a properly theological basis for specific forms of church order.
55. 1 Cor. 12.12ff.
56. cf. 1 Pet. 2.9; Rev. 1.6; taken in conjunction with 1 Cor. 12.
57. cf. Acts 15.
58. cf. Edwards, 'The Church as Sacrament of Relationships', p. 198, on different senses of hierarchy in a 'relational' ecclesiology.
59. O. M. T. O'Donovan, *Resurrection and Moral Order* (Leicester, IVP, 2nd edn 1994), p. 164.
60. O'Donovan, *Resurrection and Moral Order*, p. 170.
61. O'Donovan, *Resurrection and Moral Order*, p. 171.
62. cf. McFadyen, *The Call to Personhood*, p. 229. He rightly goes on to extend this need for 'internal reflection' on God's address to the address of others as well; he also develops some social and material implications of this sort of notion of privacy.
63. O'Donovan, *Resurrection and Moral Order*, pp. 173ff.
64. For example in the 'Isaiah Apocalypse' (Isa. 26) and Daniel (Dan. 12); cf. Brian Hebblethwaite's comments in *The Christian Hope* (Basingstoke, Marshall, Morgan & Scott, 1984).
65. Hamilton, 'The Monodic Quest', p. 80.
66. Hamilton draws on this in 'The Monodic Quest'. He cites Philip Wheelwright, *Metaphor and Reality* (Bloomington, Indiana University Press, 1962) to establish the category of 'tensive' symbol: that is, a symbol whose meaning cannot be exhausted by any one referent. See also N. Perrin, *Jesus*

and the Language of the Kingdom: Symbol and Metaphor in New Testament Interpretation (London, SCM, 1976). More generally, cf. E. P. Sanders' useful summary of the balance of emphasis between corporate and individual, present and future, in Jesus' teaching on the Kingdom of God: E. P. Sanders, *The Historical Figure of Jesus* (Harmondsworth, Penguin, 1995), ch. 12. He stresses the corporate dimensions of God's choice of Israel, and the inclusion of the Gentiles, but never to the exclusion of individuals, for the present or future. See especially pp. 193f.:

> One of the most striking things about Jesus is that, despite the fact that he thought about the coming kingdom on a large scale, he nevertheless left behind a rich body of teaching that stresses the relationship between individuals and God in the here and now. The future orientation might have led him to be indifferent to individuals: eschatologists often thought of whole blocks of people who would be saved or destroyed at the end . . . but this is not what dominates Jesus' message.

67. J. N. D. Kelly, *Early Christian Doctrines* (London, A. & C. Black, 4th edn 1968), p. 488.
68. 1 Cor. 15.20.
69. For example, 1 Thess. 4.13ff.
70. cf. Hebblethwaite, *The Christian Hope*, p. 63.
71. Hebblethwaite, *The Christian Hope*, pp. 175–6.

CHAPTER NINE

1. cf. my discussion on this in Vernon White, *The Fall of a Sparrow. A Concept of Special Divine Action* (Exeter, Paternoster, 1985), pp. 98ff.
2. For example, Ps. 103.13; Jer. 2.2; Hos. 1–3.
3. See pp. 109–14.
4. Jer. 1.5; cf. commentary by J. A. Thompson, *Jeremiah: The New International Commentary on the Old Testament* (Grand Rapids, Michigan, Eerdmans, 1980).
5. D. D. Williams, *The Spirit and the Forms of Love* (Welwyn, Nisbet, 1968), p. 22.
6. cf. Matt. 5.23ff.
7. John 13.34; 17.21ff.
8. Rom. 5–8.
9. Rom. 8.31–9.
10. Eph. 3.18–21.
11. 1 Cor. 13ff.
12. Rom. 5.8.
13. Rom. 5.12ff.
14. Rom. 8.38–9.
15. C. K. Barrett, *A Commentary on the Epistle to the Romans* (London, A. & C. Black, 2nd edn 1962), 7:7.
16. Vincent Brummer, *The Model of Love* (Cambridge, Cambridge University Press, 1993).
17. Brummer, *The Model of Love*, p. 33.
18. See p. 108.
19. cf. Brummer, *The Model of Love*, pp. 67ff.

20. Brummer's phrase, *The Model of Love*.
21. John Donne, 'Aire and Angels'.
22. On the importance of the notion of irreplaceability see especially Helen Oppenheimer, *The Hope of Happiness* (London, SCM, 1983).
23. See pp. 129–30.
24. Brummer, *The Model of Love*, p. 166.
25. cf. Roger Scruton, 'Emotion, Practical Knowledge, and Common Culture', in A. O. Rorty (ed.), *Explaining Emotions* (Berkeley, University of California Press, 1980); cited by Brummer, *The Model of Love*.
26. John 21.23.
27. See especially Anders Nygren, *Agape and Eros* (Engl. transl. London, SPCK, 1932).
28. A. I. McFadyen, *The Call to Personhood. A Christian Theory of the Individual in Social Relationships* (Cambridge, Cambridge University Press, 1990), p. 228.
29. cf. Matt. 16.25.
30. cf. my discussion of these positions in *The Fall of a Sparrow*.
31. An enormously influential popularization of process views has been W. H. Vanstone, *Love's Endeavour Love's Expense* (London, Darton, Longman & Todd, 1977).
32. White, *The Fall of a Sparrow*.
33. cf. O. M. T. O'Donovan, *Resurrection and Moral Order* (Leicester, IVP, 2nd edn 1994), p. 107.
34. The attempt is made in *The Fall of a Sparrow*. Keith Ward, *Divine Action* (London, Collins, 1990), pp. 143–4, and David Brown, 'God and Symbolic Action', in B. L. Hebblethwaite and E. Henderson (eds), *Divine Action. Studies Inspired by the Philosophical Theology of Austin Farrer* (Edinburgh, T. & T. Clark, 1990), take issue with it in some respects. But other recent literature has been concerned to reinstate a strong view of divine sovereignty and providence more in line with the overall position taken in *The Fall of a Sparrow*. See, for example, Gijsbert Van Den Brink, *Almighty God. A Study of the Doctrine of Divine Omnipotence* (Kampen, Pharos, 1993); cf. also Paul Helm, *The Providence of God* (Leicester, IVP, 1993).

CHAPTER TEN

1. The 'artifice' of ethics is a phrase coined (I think) by Gordon Dunstan, *The Artifice of Ethics* (London, SCM, 1974).
2. cf. Joseph Fletcher, *Situation Ethics* (London, SCM, 1966).
3. cf. William Temple, *Christianity and Social Order* (Harmondsworth, Penguin, 1942), p. 73. Temple's approach in general offers a useful point of comparison, in terms of the overall presuppositions, possibilities and priorities of a Christian social perspective implied by this essay. While the discussion of this essay is not so tied to Temple's underlying Hegelian optimism about the capacities of human rationality (that is, the view that we can, in principle, comprehend *everything* in a shared intellectual and moral scheme of reality), nonetheless some communicative basis *has* been argued. This essay also falls short of Temple's much more detailed treatment of the role of the state and practical social policy. Nonetheless, it does cohere with his three principles about the positive freedom and dignity of each

individual, the social nature of persons, and our function to serve the needs of others. And of course it also follows Temple's general project of grounding these principles in Christian doctrine. See Alan M. Suggate, 'New Occasions teach New Duties? 8. The Church, the Person, and the State', in *Expository Times* 105.11 (1994).

4. A full bibliography on this goes beyond the scope of this essay. But see, for example, J. Mahoney, *Bioethics and Belief* (London, Sheed & Ward, 1980); O. M. T. O'Donovan, *Begotten or Made?* (Oxford, Oxford University Press, 1984).

5. These issues have been widely analysed. The Church of England report, *Something to Celebrate* (London, Church House Publishing, 1995) provides a useful summary and bibliography of the issues as they relate to marriage in particular.

6. This is an instance of the more general analysis of our contemporary situation offered on p. 80.

CONCLUSION

1. Albert Camus, *The Plague*.
2. cf. Basil Mitchell, *Morality: Religious and Secular* (Oxford, Clarendon Press, 1980), p. 124.
3. Iris Murdoch, *Sartre, Romantic Rationalist* (Cambridge, Cambridge University Press, 1953), p. 81: cited by Mitchell in *Morality: Religious and Secular*, p. 124.

Bibliography

Includes all published works referred to, excluding literary and fictional works, and secondary references to ancient texts.

Anscombe, G. E. M., 'Modern Moral Philosophy', in *Philosophy* 33 (1958).

Arendt, H., *The Human Condition* (Garden City, Doubleday, 1959).

Aviner, S. and de-Shalit, A. (eds), *Communitarianism and Individualism* (Oxford, Oxford University Press, 1992).

Baillie, D. M., *God Was in Christ* (London, Faber & Faber, 1961).

Barrett, C. K., *A Commentary on the Epistle to the Romans* (London, A. & C. Black, 2nd edn 1962).

Church, Ministry, and Sacraments in the New Testament (Exeter, Paternoster, 1985).

Barker, E. (ed), *Social Contract* (Oxford, Oxford University Press, 1960).

Barr, J., *Biblical Faith and Natural Theology* (Oxford, Clarendon Press, 1993).

Barth, K., *Church Dogmatics* (Engl. transl. Edinburgh, T. & T. Clark, 1956-77).

Bell, D., *Communitarianism and its Critics* (Oxford, Clarendon Press, 1993).

Berlin, I., *Four Essays on Liberty* (Oxford, Oxford University Press, 1969).

Boyd, J., 'What are the Clergy For?', in *Theology* XCVIII (1995).

Brown, D., *Continental Philosophy and Modern Theology: An Engagement* (Oxford, Basil Blackwell, 1987).

'God and Symbolic Action', in Hebblethwaite and Henderson (eds), *Divine Action*.

Browning, D. S., and Schüssler Fiorenza, E. (eds), *Modernity and Public Theology* (New York, Crossroad, 1993).

Brummer, V., *The Model of Love* (Cambridge, Cambridge University Press, 1993).

Burke, E., 'Speech on Economic Reform' 1780, in *Works* (London, The World's Classics, Vol. 2, 1906).

Reflections on the Revolution in France 1790 (London, Everyman's Library, 1910).

Clark, S. R. L., *Civil Peace and Sacred Order* (Oxford, Clarendon Press, 1989).

A Parliament of Souls (Oxford, Clarendon Press, 1990).

Coakley, S., *Christ Without Absolutes* (Oxford, Clarendon Press, 1988).

Cronin, K., *Rights and Christian Ethics* (Cambridge, Cambridge University Press, 1992).

Dalferth, I., 'Karl Barth's Eschatological Realism', in Sykes (ed.), *Karl Barth: Centenary Essays*.

Deddo, G., 'The Grammar of Barth's Theology of Personal Relations', in *Scottish Journal of Theology* 47 (1994).

Dover, K., *Greek Popular Morality in the Time of Plato and Aristotle* (Oxford, Basil Blackwell, 1974).

Dworkin, R., 'Rights as Trumps', in Waldron (ed.), *Theories of Rights*.

Duncan, A. and Hobson, D., *Saturn's Children* (London, Sinclair Stevenson, 1995).

Dunstan, G. R., *The Artifice of Ethics* (London, SCM, 1974).

Eichrodt, W., *Theology of the Old Testament* Vol. 2 (Engl. transl. London, SCM, 1967).

Edwards, D., 'The Church as Sacrament of Relationships', in *Pacifica* 8.2 (1995).

Fletcher, J., *Situation Ethics* (London, SCM, 1966).

Foster, J., *The Immaterial Self: A Defence of the Cartesian Dualist Conception of the Mind* (London, Routledge, 1991).

Frankena, W. K., 'MacIntyre and Modern Morality', in *Ethics* 93 (1983).

Frey, R., *Rights, Killing, Suffering* (Oxford, Basil Blackwell, 1983).

Friedman, M., 'Feminism and Modern Friendship: Dislocating the Community', in *Ethics* 99 (1989).

Gray, J., *Beyond the New Right* (London, Routledge, 1993).

Gunton, C. E., *The Promise of Trinitarian Theology* (Edinburgh, T. & T, Clark, 1991).
'Trinity, Ontology and Anthropology: Towards a Renewal of the Doctrine of the Imago Dei', in Schwöbel and Gunton (eds), *Persons, Divine and Human*.
The One, The Three and The Many (Cambridge, Cambridge University Press, 1993).
(ed.) *God and Freedom. Essays in Historical and Systematic Theology* (Edinburgh, T. & T. Clark, 1995).

Gustafson, J. M., *Protestant and Roman Catholic Ethics* (London, SCM, 1979).

Habermas, J., 'Transcendence from Within, Transcendence in this World', in Browning and Schüssler Fiorenza (eds), *Modernity and Public Theology*.

Hamilton, R., 'The Monodic Quest', in *Theological Studies* 38.1 (1987).

Hanson, P. D., *The People Called. The Growth of Community in the Bible* (San Francisco, Harper & Row, 1986).

Hare, R. M., *Freedom and Reason* (Oxford, Clarendon Press, 1963).

Harré, R., *Personal Being* (Cambridge, Mass., Harvard University Press, 1984).
'Persons and Selves', in Peacocke and Gillett (eds), *Persons and Personality*.

Hart, D. A., *Faith in Doubt* (London, Mowbray, 1993).

Hauerwas, S., *A Community of Character* (Notre Dame, University of Notre Dame, 1981).
Suffering Presence: Theological Reflections on Medicine, the Mentally Handicapped and the Church (Edinburgh, T. & T. Clark, 1986).

Hebblethwaite, B. L., *The Christian Hope* (Basingstoke, Marshall, Morgan & Scott, 1984).
With Henderson, E. (eds), *Divine Action. Studies Inspired by the Philosophical Theology of Austin Farrer* (Edinburgh, T. & T. Clark, 1990).

Helm, P., *The Providence of God* (Leicester, IVP, 1993).

Horton, J. and Mendus, S. (eds), *After MacIntyre* (Oxford, Polity Press, 1994).

Hudson, W. D., *Modern Moral Philosophy* (London, Macmillan, 2nd edn 1983).

Jüngel, E., *The Doctrine of the Trinity. God's Being is in Becoming* (Engl. transl. Edinburgh, Scottish Academic Press, 1976).

Kant, I., *Groundwork of the Metaphysic of Morals* 1785 (Engl. transl. New York, Harper & Row, 1964).

Kelly, J. N. D., *Early Christian Doctrines* (London, A. & C. Black, 4th edn 1968).

Lamennais, F. de, 'Des Progrès de la revolution et de la guerre contre l'église', in *Oeuvres Complètes* (Paris, 1836-7).

Levinas, E., *Autrement qu'etre ou au-dela de l'essence* (La Haye, 1974).

Lindsay, A. D., 'Individualism', in *Encyclopaedia of the Social Sciences* (New York, Macmillan, 1930-35).

Locke, J., 'An Essay Concerning the True Original, Extent and End of Civil Government' 11:14 1690 in Barker (ed.), *Social Contract*.

Lukes, S., *Individualism* (Oxford, Basil Blackwell, 1973).

Mahoney, J., *Bioethics and Belief* (London, Sheed & Ward, 1980).

Malina, B. J., *The New Testament World. Insights from Cultural Anthropology* (London, SCM, 1981).

Marx, K., *A Contribution to the Critique of Political Economy* 1857 (Engl. transl. London, Lawrence & Wishart, 1971).

MacDonald, M., 'Natural Rights' in Waldron (ed.), *Theories of Rights*.

MacIntyre, A., *A Short History of Ethics* (London, Routledge & Kegan Paul, 1967).
   After Virtue (London, Duckworth, 2nd edn 1990).
   Whose Justice? Which Rationality? (London, Duckworth, 1988).
   'A Partial Response to my Critics', in Horton and Mendus (eds), *After MacIntyre*.

McConnell, F. (ed.), *The Bible and the Narrative Tradition* (Oxford, Oxford University Press, 1986).

McFadyen, A. I., *The Call to Personhood. A Christian Theory of the Individual in Social Relationships* (Cambridge, Cambridge University Press, 1990).

McGrath, A. E., *Christian Theology. An Introduction* (Oxford, Basil Blackwell, 1994).

Milbank, J., *Theology and Social Theory* (Oxford, Basil Blackwell, 1990).

Mill, J. S., *Utilitarianism, On Liberty and Considerations on Representative Government* (London, Everyman, J. M. Dent., 1910).

Mitchell, B. G., *Law, Morality and Religion in a Secular Society* (Oxford, Oxford University Press, 1970).
   Morality: Religious and Secular (Oxford, Clarendon Press, 1980).

Moltmann, J., *The Trinity and the Kingdom of God* (Engl. transl. London, SCM, 1981).

Moule, C. F. D., 'The Individualism of the Fourth Gospel', in *Essays in New Testament Interpretation* (Cambridge, Cambridge University Press, 1982).

Murdoch, I., *Sartre, Romantic Rationalist* (Cambridge, Cambridge University Press, 1953).

Nicholls, D., *Deity and Domination. Images of God and the State in the Nineteenth and Twentieth Centuries* (London, Routledge, 1989).

Niebuhr, Reinhold, *Moral Man and Immoral Society* (New York, Scribners, 1942).

Nielsen, K., 'Scepticism and Human Rights', in *The Monist* 52 (1968).

Noonan, H. W., *Personal Identity* (London, Routledge, 1989).

Nygren, A., *Agape and Eros* (Engl. transl. London, SPCK, 1932).

O'Donovan, O. M. T., *Begotten or Made?* (Oxford, Oxford University Press, 1984).
   Resurrection and Moral Order (Leicester, IVP, 2nd edn 1994).

Oppenheimer, H., *The Hope of Happiness* (London, SCM, 1983).
'Mattering', in *Studies in Christian Ethics* 8.1 (1995).
Pannenberg, W., *Anthropology in Theological Perspective* (Engl. transl. Edinburgh, T. & T. Clark, 1985).
Parfit, D., *Reasons and Persons* (Oxford, Oxford University Press, 1984).
Parsons, S., 'Feminist Ethics after Modernity: Towards an Appropriate Universalism', in *Studies in Christian Ethics* 8.1 (1995).
Peacocke, A. R. and Gillett, G. (eds), *Persons and Personality* (Oxford, Basil Blackwell, 1987).
Perrin, N., *Jesus and the Language of the Kingdom: Symbol and Metaphor in New Testament Interpretation* (London, SCM, 1976).
Plaskow, J., *Sex, Sin and Grace: Women's Experience and the Theologies of Reinhold Niebuhr and Paul Tillich* (Lanham, University Press of America, 1980).
Popper, K. R., *The Open Society and its Enemies* Vol. 2 (London, Routledge & Kegan Paul, 1945).
Porter, J. R., 'The Legal Aspects of the Concept of "Corporate Responsibility" in the Old Testament', in *Vetus Testamentum* 15 (1965).
Rachels, J. (ed.), *Moral Problems* (New York, Harper & Row, 3rd edn 1979).
Rawls, J. *A Theory of Justice* (Oxford, Oxford University Press, 1973).
Ricoeur, P., *Oneself as Another* (Engl. transl. Chicago, Chicago University Press, (1992).
Roberts, R., 'Kierkegaard on Becoming an Individual', in *Scottish Journal of Theology* 31.2 (1978).
Robinson, J. A. T., 'The Body. A Study in Pauline Theology', in *Studies in Biblical Theology No. 5* (London, SCM, 1952).
Rogerson, J., 'The Hebrew Conception of Corporate Personality: A Re-examination', in *Issues in Religion and Theology 8: Anthropological Approaches to the Old Testament* (London, SPCK, 1985).
Rorty, A. O. (ed.), *Explaining Emotions* (Berkeley, University of California Press, 1980).
Sanders, E. P., *Paul and Palestinian Judaism* (London, SCM, 1977).
Paul, the Law and the Jewish People (Philadelphia, Fortress Press, 1983).
The Historical Figure of Jesus (Harmondsworth, Penguin, 1995).
Searle, J. R., *The Rediscovery of the Mind* (Cambridge, Mass., Harvard University Press, 1992).
Schwöbel, C. and Gunton, C. E. (eds) *Persons, Divine and Human* (Edinburgh, T. & T. Clark, 1991).
Schneidau, H. N., 'Biblical Narrative and Modern Consciousness', in McConnell (ed.), *The Bible and the Narrative Tradition*.
Scruton, R., 'Emotion, Practical Knowledge, and Common Sense', in Rorty (ed.), *Explaining Emotions*.
Singer, P., *Practical Ethics* (Cambridge, Cambridge University Press, 1979).
Stark, W., *The Sociology of Religion: A Study of Christendom* Vol. 3 (London, Routledge & Kegan Paul, 1967).
Strong, T. B., *God and the Individual* (London, Longman, Green & Co., 1903).
Suggate, A. M., 'New Occasions Teach New Duties? 8. The Church, the Person, and the State', in *Expository Times* 105.11 (1994).
Swinburne, R. and Shoemaker, S., *Personal Identity* (Oxford, Basil Blackwell, 1984).
Sykes, S. W. (ed.), *Karl Barth: Centenary Essays* (Cambridge, Cambridge University Press, 1989).

Taylor, C., *Sources of the Self* (Cambridge, Cambridge University Press, 1989).
　The Ethics of Authenticity (Cambridge, Mass., Harvard University Press, 1991).
Taylor, J. V., *The Go-Between God. The Holy Spirit and The Christian Mission* (London, SCM, 1972).
Temple, W., *Christianity and Social Order* (Harmondsworth, Penguin, 1942).
Thiselton, A. C., *Interpreting God and the Postmodern Self. On Meaning, Manipulation and Promise* (Edinburgh, T. & T. Clark, 1995).
　'Barr on Barth and Natural Theology', in *Scottish Journal of Theology* 48 (1995).
Thompson, J. A., *Jeremiah: The New International Commentary on the Old Testament* (Grand Rapids, Michigan, Eerdmans, 1980).
Troeltsch, E., *The Social Teaching of the Christian Churches* 1912 (Engl. transl. London, George Allen & Unwin, 1931).
Van Den Brink, G., *Almighty God. A Study of the Doctrine of Divine Omnipotence* (Kampen, Pharos, 1993).
Vanstone, W. H., *Love's Endeavour Love's Expense* (London, Darton, Longman & Todd, 1977).
Vawter, B., *On Genesis. A New Reading* (New York, Doubleday, 1970).
Waldron J. (ed.), *Theories of Rights* (Oxford, Oxford University Press, 1984).
Ward, K., *The Battle for the Soul. An Affirmation of Human Dignity and Value* (London, Hodder & Stoughton, 1985).
　Divine Action (London, Collins, 1990).
　Religion and Revelation. A Theology of Revelation in the World's Religions (Oxford, Clarendon Press, 1994).
Wasserstrom, R., 'Rights, Human Rights, and Racial Discrimination', in Rachels (ed.), *Moral Problems.*
Watson, F., 'Christ, Law and Freedom: A Study in Theological Hermeneutics', in Gunton (ed.), *God and Freedom.*
Weber, M. *The Protestant Ethic and the Spirit of Capitalism* 1904 (Engl. transl. London, Allen & Unwin, 1985).
Westermann, C., *Creation* (Engl. transl. London, SPCK, 1974).
Wheeler-Robinson, H., *The Religious Ideas of the Old Testament* (London, Duckworth, 1913).
Wheelwright, P., *Metaphor and Reality* (Bloomington, Indiana University Press, 1962).
White, V. P., *The Fall of a Sparrow. A Concept of Special Divine Action* (Exeter, Paternoster, 1985).
　Atonement and Incarnation. An Essay in Universalism and Particularity (Cambridge, Cambridge University Press, 1991).
Whiteley, D. E. H., *The Theology of St Paul* (Oxford, Oxford University Press, 1964).
Williams, D. D., *The Spirit and the Forms of Love* (Welwyn, Nisbet, 1968).
Wilson, A. N., *Against Religion* (London, Chatto & Windus, 1991).
Wokler, R., 'Projecting the Enlightenment', in Horton and Mendus (eds), *After MacIntyre.*
Young, I., *Justice and the Politics of Difference* (New Jersey, Princeton University Press, 1990).
Yu, C. T., *Being and Relation. A Theological Critique of Western Dualism and Individualism* (Edinburgh, Scottish Academic Press, 1987).
Zizioulas, J. D., *Being as Communion. Studies in Personhood and The Church* (London, Darton, Longman & Todd, 1985).

Index

195